D0211033

Manager Redefined

The Competitive Advantage in the Middle of Your Organization

Thomas O. Davenport
Stephen D. Harding

JOSSEY-BASS
A Wiley Imprint
www.josseybass.com

Copyright © 2010 by Towers Watson. All rights reserved.

Published by Jossey-Bass
A Wiley Imprint
989 Market Street, San Francisco, CA 94103-1741—www.josseybass.com

No part of this publication may be reproduced, stored in a retrieval system, or transmitted in any form or by any means, electronic, mechanical, photocopying, recording, scanning, or otherwise, except as permitted under Section 107 or 108 of the 1976 United States Copyright Act, without either the prior written permission of the publisher, or authorization through payment of the appropriate per-copy fee to the Copyright Clearance Center, Inc., 222 Rosewood Drive, Danvers, MA 01923, 978-750-8400, fax 978-646-8600, or on the Web at www.copyright.com. Requests to the publisher for permission should be addressed to the Permissions Department, John Wiley & Sons, Inc., 111 River Street, Hoboken, NJ 07030, 201-748-6011, fax 201-748-6008, or online at www.wiley.com/go/permissions.

Readers should be aware that Internet Web sites offered as citations and/or sources for further information may have changed or disappeared between the time this was written and when it is read.

Limit of Liability/Disclaimer of Warranty: While the publisher and author have used their best efforts in preparing this book, they make no representations or warranties with respect to the accuracy or completeness of the contents of this book and specifically disclaim any implied warranties of merchantability or fitness for a particular purpose. No warranty may be created or extended by sales representatives or written sales materials. The advice and strategies contained herein may not be suitable for your situation. You should consult with a professional where appropriate. Neither the publisher nor author shall be liable for any loss of profit or any other commercial damages, including but not limited to special, incidental, consequential, or other damages.

Jossey-Bass books and products are available through most bookstores. To contact Jossey-Bass directly call our Customer Care Department within the U.S. at 800-956-7739, outside the U.S. at 317-572-3986, or fax 317-572-4002.

Jossey-Bass also publishes its books in a variety of electronic formats. Some content that appears in print may not be available in electronic books.

Library of Congress Cataloging-in-Publication Data

Davenport, Thomas O., 1952–
Manager redefined : The Competitive Advantage in the Middle of Your Organization / Thomas O. Davenport, Stephen D. Harding.
    p. cm.
    Includes bibliographical references and index.
ISBN 978-0-470-62772-3 (hardback); 9780470884911 (ebk); 9780470884942 (ebk); 9780470884966 (ebk)
1. Management. 2. Performance–Management. 3. Supervision of employees.
I. Harding, Stephen D. II. Title.
HD31.D243 2010
658.3′14–dc22

                                                                                        2010028492

Printed in the United States of America
FIRST EDITION
HB Printing   10 9 8 7 6 5 4 3 2 1

CONTENTS

Part II: Implementation 103

PREFACE

Observers of the business environment often refer to the workplace as an ecosystem. This metaphor seems apt. Our working habitats have climates (from warm and embracing to frigid and formal), contain an abundance of species (ranging from the ruby-throated sales rep to the saber-toothed CFO), and respond to climatic change (such as rapid warming of the competitive landscape).

If we accept that most of us inhabit some kind of workplace ecology, then supervisors and first-line managers occupy what scientists call an ecotone. An ecotone is an area of transition between two communities, a boundary space that separates one environment from another.[1] The manager ecotone lies between the world of employees and the territory occupied by senior leaders.

Ecotones are not tranquil places. They experience constant instability caused by interaction between the boundary environments. In the manager ecotone, inhabitants face continuous pressure to mediate between the needs of employees and the demands of company executives. The flora and fauna in an ecotone may differ from what lives on either side, because properties of this intermediate zone are unique. Likewise, managers often find their interests dissimilar to those of the employee population from which they came, but not fully aligned with the perspectives of the executive population into which they are expected to evolve. Ecologists say ecotones are centers of evolutionary novelty, spaces where change is perpetual and sometimes dramatic.

Many managers we know would say they could stand a little less novelty. The pressures of living in an in-between world bring constant stress. On one side, the managers get criticism from employees for being inattentive, unresponsive, and distant. In our worldwide analysis of employee attitudes, less than half of the respondents said their managers:

- Have enough time to handle the people-related aspects of their jobs

- Effectively handle poor performers

- Help people get access to learning opportunities outside the organization

- Do a good job of explaining changes that happen inside the company

The prospect of moving to the adjacent organizational ecosystem—the higher-altitude one occupied by senior executives—engenders little inspiration among managers. Among the respondents to Towers Watson's 2010 global workforce study, less than 40 percent of managers define their career advancement as achieving a senior leadership position; 61 percent think of advancement simply as making a lot more money (but only 37 percent think that's achievable). A little more than half of the manager respondents say delivering results on the job is the most important determinant of advancement, but a cynical 29 percent say that whom you know in the organization is the most important factor in getting ahead. Almost 60 percent think executives are paid too much for the work they do. Only half of the managers in our global survey agree that senior leadership has a personal commitment to developing the talent most critical to the organization's future success.[2]

These data paint a picture of a corporate species under pressure, underinspired, and underappreciated. Too many executives see supervisors and managers as targets for downsizing or as acceptable casualties in the quest to flatten the organization. The Human Resources department (HR) often views them with skepticism, as an impediment to communication or a population of policy transgressors who need policing. We look at the picture differently, however. We view supervisors and managers as a center of power and influence, more latent than actual in many companies, but real nonetheless. We think organizations have simply lost sight of this potential. Managers know what it's like to be a worker and to do the work, because they all were once in those roles themselves. They know how things function around the company, because they often operated those systems in a prior life. They've probably spent enough time with and around executives to know where the enterprise is headed and what that means for people in the department. Think of the power they could unleash if they brought this accumulated knowledge and experience to bear for the benefit of employees and the organization.

Unleashing that power is our aim with this book.

We propose to do that by energizing organizations to rethink their perspectives on the manager's potential contribution to organizational success. We challenge executives and Human Resources to see managers in a different light, as more than just message amplifiers, system executors, future executives, or (heaven forbid) a necessary evil required mainly to keep employees in line. We urge companies to think of their managers instead as a potential source of competitive advantage, a marketplace edge that competitors can't easily replicate.

For many organizations, shifting the perspective from manager-as-inert-organization-layer to manager-as-competitive-advantage will require a philosophical leap. To help with that effort, we have provided a blueprint for the new manager role and a detailed performance model that complements it. To construct our model, we've selected from the best building material available. Some elements are novel (for example, the manager's influence on employee well-being), whereas others are classic (the emphasis on employee autonomy, for instance). We believe we have created a sound and practical structure that reflects both current workplace reality and archetypal human traits. We also believe we've described an important step forward, a way of thinking that is challenging but within the reach of most managers and most organizations.

Embedded in the architecture we have laid out is an important point: to perform successfully as a supervisor or manager in the twenty-first century means to create an environment that fosters employee success and then gives people all the freedom they need to make the most of their work. You might call it, as Stanford professor Robert Sutton does, "management by getting out of the way."[3] We take our inspiration from a quotation by Lao-tzu, Chinese philosopher and central figure in the development of Taoism. His description of an effective leader captures the concept we have in mind: "As for the best leaders, the people do not notice their existence. The next best the people honor and praise. The next, the people fear, and the next the people hate. When the best leader's work is done, the people say, 'We did it ourselves.'" Consistent with this notion, we will make the case that line managers and supervisors are critical to organizational success, but their influence is often indirect, nuanced, and light-handed. We will refer to this as "offstage management." We will define what we mean by the term, why we think it's important, and how to make it successful.

We certainly don't mean to suggest that strong executive leadership isn't critical to organizational success. But we also know that, from day to day, executive influence is often remote and dispersed, an undeniable force but one with only intermittent presence in the work lives of employees. Supervisors and managers, in contrast, are around workers all the time, a constant and present factor. We agree with Jack Unroe, former chief executive of Accountants International (and one-time boss of one of the authors), who says, "At the extremes—really bad and really good—executive leadership probably makes some difference in the lives of individual employees. But for everything in between, the first-line manager has much more influence over whether people feel inspired or demoralized on the job."

We vote for inspired.

A Few Words about Our Information Sources

We are fortunate to be part of a large consulting firm with extensive employee attitude databases and substantial analytical know-how. Our access to both information and number crunching horsepower increased on January 1, 2010, when Towers Perrin and Watson Wyatt merged to form Towers Watson. We attribute source material that existed prior to the merger to the appropriate legacy firm. Material produced after the merger carries the Towers Watson reference.

We have drawn liberally on our firm's data and analysis capabilities. In particular, we have used our global database of employee survey responses to test and prove the manager performance model we propose. That analysis is supported throughout our discussion by reference to the many special reports produced by our Talent and Rewards group. But data take the discussion only so far, so we have supplemented our core analysis with case examples. Many of these come from our client experiences; others are taken from secondary research on companies we know to have a relevant story to tell about the meaning and the evolution of manager capability.

Acknowledgments

Authors are expected to share credit for their final product with many other contributors. Sharing credit is especially appropriate in our case. A work that attempts to present a coherent narrative crafted from a wide variety of quantitative and qualitative information cannot succeed without plenty of support. We needed people who could manipulate data, find information, provide access to companies, contribute domain-specific expertise, and generally keep us from straying too far from the main point. Fortunately, we had ample access to such people. Patrick Kulesa and his team of research colleagues (including Catharina Anandikar, Jurate Cingiene, Amy Johnson, Angela Paul, Kayla Schnacky, and Nathan Schneeberger) gave us all the numerical support we needed, often under tight deadlines. Krisztina Csedo, Vlad Geister, Gloria Gowens, Tom Keebler, Irina Konstantinovsky, Evan Metter, Brian Reidy, and Angela Stefatos provided expertise in their areas of specialty, which covered workforce patterns, call center operations, performance management systems, social media, and airline management. Suzanne Stoller and Masha Day spent more time than they would probably like to recall digging for answers to obscure questions about quirky topics.

In a sense, books are nothing more than words on a page. For the words ever to make it to the page requires people who can transform incomplete and error-ridden raw material into something a reader can actually follow. We thank Deborah Ellis, Diane Marie, Suzanne Ng, and Caryl Yule for their work in helping us turn our thoughts into language. Deborah also did double duty as an Internet researcher, demonstrating admirable tenacity in tracking down hard-to-find source material. Once the words were on paper, four of our colleagues read the manuscript from cover to cover. The final product owes much to their suggestions for improvement. For this effort we thank Max Caldwell, Adam Hall, Tim Houk, Harriet Sebald, and Sharon Wunderlich. Marie Andel of AAA, Brian Cloughley of Autodesk, Peter Navin of Shutterfly, Cynthia Starz of United Airlines, and Geraldine Coy and Dale Nissen of WorkSafe Victoria each gave us a window into their companies and generously allowed us to use their organizations as case examples. Cameron Anderson from the Haas School of Business at the University of California, Berkeley; Denise Rousseau of Carnegie Mellon University; and Paul Zak of the Claremont Graduate University provided the academic perspective on many key topics. We are grateful to all for their willingness to share.

Our editors at Jossey-Bass deserve much credit for the way they managed us and our deadlines. Given the latitude, we might have taken forever to pull the book together. That we did it in less time speaks to the deftness with which they combined patience and firm insistence. It's a rare balance, and we needed it.

Finally, and doubtless most important, we thank our wives, Sue Davenport and Diana Harding, for their many contributions. Sue read and edited the entire manuscript and improved it immeasurably. Her effort is a tribute not only to her skill as an editor and grammarian, but also to her stamina. Diana Harding showed her usual good humor, perceptive insights, and superlative tea-making skills during weekends and holidays when book writing dominated the family scene.

All of these have added to whatever is insightful, useful, and entertaining about this book, and we acknowledge them with thanks. For whatever is mundane, impractical, and boring, we take full responsibility.

Part I
Context

CHAPTER OUTLINE

A Brief History of Management

Defining Management and Leadership

The Definition, and the Power, of Engagement

1

Do Managers Matter?

One author (Tom) was fortunate enough to spend part of the summer of 2009 in France observing 65th-anniversary commemorations of the 1944 Allied liberation. Story after story of the D-Day invasion recounted the bravery, resourcefulness, and foresight displayed by Army leaders—not generals, colonels, or majors, but corporals and sergeants.

They performed well in part because they adhered to Army values (including loyalty, honor, and personal courage). But their success also came from following the requirements of what the Army leadership manual calls "direct" leadership: As the manual expresses it, "Direct leaders develop their subordinates one-on-one.... They are close enough to the action to determine or address problems. Examples of direct leadership tasks are monitoring and coordinating team efforts, providing clear and concise mission intent, and setting expectations for performance."[1] The D-Day mission was victorious in large part because noncoms consistently demonstrated the attributes expected of them: character (integrity and devotion to duty); presence (which calls for composure, confidence, and resilience); and intellectual strength (mental agility and sound judgment). It all sounds fairly ordinary until you remember that wavering in any of these means battles are lost and soldiers are wounded or killed.

Like sergeants, a company's first-line managers are the pivot point for strategic success. They too lead one person at a time, developing each subordinate and making sure everyone is capable of executing the organization's mission. They too must show empathy, build resilience, and be creative. Tom's nephew (who is a master sergeant with the New Mexico National Guard) puts it this way: "My boss is a captain. He tells me generally what he needs to get done, and I get it done." He adds, with no small amount of pride, "Sergeants make everything happen." So, we would argue, do first-line managers.

A Brief History of Management

The Italian word *maneggiare* began to appear in the late Middle Ages in connection with governance of property and business. However, the functions of management as we think of them today didn't emerge with full force until the industrial era. It was then that mass production reduced the importance of the individual worker and increased the emphasis on organizational productivity.

The years following World War II brought prosperity that strengthened, and was strengthened by, the success of commercial enterprises, especially large ones. Writer Robert Samuelson describes post-war America's faith in large commercial, cultural, and political institutions: "Americans increasingly defined their well-being in terms of how well large institutions were performing and how well such institutions were delivering on their explicit or implicit promises. Individual effort and responsibility were diminished and, to some extent, devalued. Institutions were expected to deliver."[2] But even in the early days following World War II, when management became formalized as a craft, confusion existed about what "management" really meant. In his 1954 classic *The Practice of Management*, Peter Drucker offered his definition of a manager's tasks. Managers, he wrote, are "specifically charged with making resources productive, that is, with the responsibility for organized economic advance."[3] But Drucker also pointed out the confusion that continued to surround the definition of the manager and his job. Except for the gender assumption and the salary figure, he might have been describing the post-millennium world of work when he said, in 1954: "In American business at least [the supervisor's job] is a hodgepodge—the end product of decades of inconsistency. Everybody knows, or says he knows, what the supervisor should be doing. He is expected to be a clerk shuffling papers and filling out forms. He is to be the master technician or the master craftsman of his group. He is to be an expert on tools and equipment. He is to be a leader of people. Every one of these jobs he is expected to perform to perfection—at four thousand dollars a year."[4]

Fast-forward to the 1990s, when large organizations found themselves under increasing economic pressure. They had become victims of their own success: too rigid, too unwieldy, and too inflexible to respond to new challenges from an array of sources, including more nimble foreign rivals, accelerating domestic deregulation, and new technologies. At the same time, a kind of hubris had spread through the ranks of American enterprise. It was the legacy of Frederick W. Taylor and Max Weber: the notion that strong executive managers could manage anything. Steadily declining financial performance suggested otherwise. Total pretax profits for all American businesses were about 59 percent higher in the decade of the 1960s than they had been in the 1950s. Economy-wide profits in the 1970s increased even more dramatically, totaling 123 percent of the 1960s total. But the slide began in the 1980s. That decade's total corporate profits were only 72 percent greater than the total for the prior decade.[5] As profit growth slowed, profit margins declined, slipping from 10.7 percent in the 1970s to 8.7 percent in the 1980s.[6] The management philosophies and techniques that had made companies prosperous after World War II had ultimately failed them. Organizations had to do something as declining profits and increasing corporate debt threatened to erode shareholder value.

And so, in the early 1990s came the era of downsizing. Staffing cost reductions from organizational downsizing hit a peak in 1990–1991.

Some 56 percent of the firms responding to an American Management Association survey said that they had cut their workforces during that period.[7] Although job cuts slowed, the percentage of companies making significant reductions remained in the mid-40s over the next several years. Unskilled or hourly workers felt the brunt of the layoffs, accounting for 45 percent of job losses in 1994.[8]

The experiences of the early and mid-1990s represented a watershed in management thinking. As companies began to recover from the trauma of major staff reductions (unemployment had dropped to 5.6 percent by June 1995, compared with 7.8 percent in the same month of 1992),[9] a new phrase echoed through the halls of corporate America. "Employees are our most important assets" became the sound bite of the day, de rigueur for inclusion in annual reports and press releases. On the one hand, some companies tried to live up to the spirit of the phrase. They genuinely challenged traditional ways of building organizational structures, managing work, and fostering learning. Rigid departmental boundaries became permeable as organizations instituted cross-functional teams to get work done. Many tried to increase their focus on quality, realizing that it was possible to produce a high-quality product at a low cost. Japanese companies did it routinely, to the chagrin of manufacturers in Detroit. Self-managed teams were turned loose to find ways to improve product and service quality. In some organizations, it had indeed become the era of the empowered employee-asset.

On the other hand, the phrase often had a hollow ring. In Towers Perrin's 1995 People Strategy Benchmark Awareness and Attitude Study, the consultants said, "Although 90 percent of the 300 executives interviewed said their employees are the most important variable in their company's success, they ranked specific people-related issues far below other business priorities."[10]

As the hierarchical pyramids that had defined organization structure began to break down, many companies took steps to link twin concepts separated at birth: downsizing and delayering. The logic was seductive. It flowed something like this:

- We've downsized to cut costs, but we can reduce our workforce only so far.

- Plus, we need to increase quality at the same time—otherwise the Japanese will kill us.

- So, let's declare that employees aren't really just costs—they're assets that we can empower to find ways of improving quality and reducing expenses.

- And—here's the beauty part—if we have empowered employees (and, of course, inspiring executive leadership), we won't need all those expensive supervisors and managers. We pay them more than we do rank-and-file workers, so laying off a few managers saves as much money as firing lots of employees.

For many organizations, this thinking represented the first bright line between the roles of leaders, who could move the company forward and energize employees, and managers, who were expendable.

The next step was inevitable: take out as many first-line and middle managers as possible. Where feasible, slice whole layers out of the organization. In 1994, cuts in the supervisory ranks of organizations accounted for about 18 percent of total reductions. Middle managers represented 15 percent of the layoffs, despite making up only about 8 percent of the workforce.[11] Into the years beyond 2000, when companies laid off employees, they continued to let go a higher proportion of managers. From 2002 to 2003, as the U.S. economy emerged from recession, total employment rose by a bit less than one percent. Employment in management occupations fell by 0.2 percent during that period.[12]

Defining Management and Leadership

The reasoning that underlies many downsizing and delayering strategies relies on often unspoken definitions of leadership and management—definitions that are at best imprecise and at worst largely wrong. In particular, the distinction between *manager*[13] and *leader*, though hardly a new topic among consultants, academics, and business practitioners, has taken on increasing importance. Table 1.1 captures some of the ways organizations have differentiated the two groups, in practice if not in theory.

This comparison suggests why the practice of management has lost cachet and the calling of leadership has gained momentum. One source describes middle management as "a layer of management in an organization whose primary job responsibility is to monitor activities of subordinates while reporting to upper management."[14] The definition adds this chilling afterthought: "In pre-computer times, middle management would collect information from junior management and reassemble it for senior management. With the advent of inexpensive PCs this function has been taken over by e-business systems. During the 1980s and 1990s thousands of middle managers were laid off for this reason." How well we remember.

In fact, the content of Table 1.1 barely begins to capture the denigration and disrespect heaped on the manager's role over the last fifteen years. Organizations (along with academics, consultants, and gurus) have relentlessly elevated leadership at the expense of management. "Decades ago," says one company culture expert, "a major disservice was done to business when the idea that … leaders were 'better' than managers was introduced. Sadly, that attitude is still in force today."[15] Leadership, the conventional thinking goes, is more enlightened and nobler—and it pays a lot better too. In the words of one team of experts in leadership competency and development, "There is a romantic attachment to, and a cult of personality about, leaders in Western thought … the focus on how individual leaders are perceived as opposed to how well their teams perform is consistent with the prevailing individualistic orientation of American psychology."[16] In a *Harvard Business Review* article in 2003, Jonathan Gosling and Henry Mintzberg wrote, "Nobody aspires to being a good manager anymore; everybody wants to be a great leader." And then they added a warning note: "But the separation of

Table 1.1: Differences Between Manager and Leader

Element	Manager	Leader
Organizational nomenclature	Frequently a title, usually denoting positions at or below the middle of the organizational ladder	Rarely a title—more a reflection of expected motivational technique, often associated with executive positions
Action focus	Directs action by deploying assets, overseeing processes, and running systems. Often described as task-focused. Concentrates on: • Planning and budgeting • Organizing and staffing • Coordinating and controlling • Monitoring and problem solving	Concentrates on giving people a reason to move along a path toward a destination by showing the way and appealing to their personal motives Builds energy toward accomplishment of the goal and removes obstacles to its achievement
Relationship to the enterprise	Works within the existing organizational systems Seeks and then follows direction Executes plans	Defines the organization's high-level systems Provides direction by defining and communicating vision and strategy Devises the plans that get executed
Image within the enterprise	Mundane, pedestrian, necessary, but should be limited	Lofty, important—can't get enough of it

management from leadership is dangerous. Just as management without leadership encourages an uninspired style, which deadens activities, leadership without management encourages a disconnected style, which promotes hubris."[17] "You don't manage people, you manage things. You lead people," said the late Admiral Grace Hopper.[18] Jack Welch, alpha dog in the CEO ranks, barks it out in this way: "Managers slow things down. Leaders spark the business to run smoothly, quickly. Managers talk to one another, write memos to one another. Leaders talk to their employees, talk *with* their employees, filling them with vision"[19] (emphasis in original).

When Jack Welch says that people like you slow things down and waste time, your self-esteem might well take a hit. On the one hand, Welch is simply encouraging everyone who oversees a team to think and act like a leader and not (merely) like a manager. On the other hand, if your title has "manager" in it, and your job is so overloaded that you spend most of your time reading and writing memos, does that automatically make you ineffective and incompetent? What if you would like to follow Jack's advice to talk with employees and be visionary, but you're too busy going to meetings, filling in budget templates, and producing…whatever? And, moreover, what if it's executives at or near Jack's level who have allowed—or required—your job to become almost unmanageably complex?

But let's pause for a moment and examine our terminology more closely. What do "leader" and "manager" really mean to the functioning of an organization? Table 1.1 makes clear that the terms denote different actions and different outcomes—but what actions and what outcomes? If we extrapolate a bit from what Admiral Hopper said—that managers focus principally on assets, and leaders concentrate on people—we can clarify both definitions. Leadership, we submit, entails:

- Envisioning an improved situation (for instance, achieving an organizational goal, changing strategic direction, emerging from a crisis)

- Determining the best path for reaching that desirable end

- Inspiring in others the self-motivation to reach the appealing state (that is, creating the conditions under which people feel the intrinsic motivation to move ahead)

- Boosting energy (by recognizing success, for example), removing obstacles that impede progress (political constraints, for instance), and demonstrating resilience (remaining steadfast in spite of failures), so that people can make speedy and efficient strides toward the goal

A leader is like the captain of a fifteenth-century Portuguese ship sailing out of sight of land for the first time in search of gold, silver, and spices. The captain envisions the destination, plots the course (with the help of a skilled navigator, of course), and engenders courage among the sailors ("Don't worry men, I'm pretty sure we won't sail off the edge of the earth"). Of course, the mission will fail if the boat springs a leak, the sails become shredded, or the food goes rotten. Seeing to the soundness of those assets is the responsibility of a manager. With all this in mind, we suggest that managing consists of:

- Acquiring, deploying, building, preserving, and exploiting assets (tangible ones like forklifts, financial ones like investment dollars, and intangible ones like brand equity)

- Overseeing processes and implementing systems for putting those assets to use

- Monitoring results and making adjustments

Without leadership, people lack the vision and courage to set sail and discover the New World. Without management, the boat sinks before it gets there.

Leadership and management do not lie on the same definitional spectrum. In particular, it is wrong to imply that management sits at the mundane, quotidian end of a continuum on which leadership, elevated and inspiring, occupies the other end. They represent two different disciplines, each critical for business success. They do not compete with each other, nor are they in opposition. In the quest for clear nomenclature, it doesn't help that most people called "manager" are expected both to lead and to manage (hence the hodgepodge job to which Drucker refers, and that still exists). We occasionally see the phrase "managerial leadership," a term meant to connote an executive style that concentrates on maintaining stability, preserving the existing order, and taking care of short-term business. Some business philosophers contrast managerial leadership with loftier forms like visionary or strategic leadership.[20] By our definition, "managerial leadership" is a contradiction, like "doggish cats." The terms refer to different species.

We can further clarify our terms by considering leadership along the same two dimensions: organizational scale and quality of performance. Exhibit 1.1 illustrates the two dimensions and provides examples.

It is dangerous to set up any single executive as a paradigm of enterprise-level leadership, given the frequency with which so many have been disgraced and replaced. As with any complex human behavior, the performance of executives, including CEOs, tends to vary. Nevertheless, we can identify a set of attributes that consistently characterize successful

Exhibit 1.1: Dimensions of Leadership

	Low	High
Large (Enterprise)	Celebrity CEO who drives only for shareholder value and won't listen to bad news	Publicity-shunning CEO who encourages dissent, learns from mistakes, and knows that employee performance and customer satisfaction create shareholder wealth
Small (Unit)	Accounts receivable manager who focuses only on the numbers and not on the people	Accounts receivable manager who engages each individual to help achieve the unit's goals for reducing problem accounts

Scale of Leadership

Quality of Leadership Performance

leaders of large-scale organizations. They inspire goal-oriented action among followers by virtue of their focus on, and dedication to, organizational success, though not necessarily through personal charisma. For example, former Colgate-Palmolive CEO Reuben Mark was known for his down-to-earth approach to leadership. He traveled coach class on overseas flights, disdained the common executive obsession with golf, and avoided publicity. As one acquaintance said, he wanted the company, not himself, to be the superstar.[21]

In searching for the best way to achieve organizational goals, the most effective top-level leaders tolerate, indeed encourage, healthy dissent. They don't limit the information they receive to good news only. Roger Enrico instilled this kind of free information flow down the line at PepsiCo, observers say. They foster meritocracy within their organizations, in service of a commitment to organizational achievement. They are also aware of their own limitations and therefore ensure that others around them have compensating strengths. Cisco's John Chambers is known for this sort of intellectual honesty. Faced with obstacles, high-performing executive leaders bolster judgment with analysis and balance deliberation with action. They also learn from their mistakes, as Yum! Brands CEO David Novak did from a marketing debacle that occurred when he was marketing chief at PepsiCo. Pepsi introduced Crystal Pepsi, a drink that looked like rival 7UP but failed dramatically. Novak later said that he had learned to weigh the testimony of naysayers (the Pepsi bottlers who had told him the new drink tasted nothing like Pepsi) despite a natural inclination to ignore them.[22]

We would add that the best executive leaders make shareholder value a derivative priority, one that follows a focus on employees and customers. Roger Martin, dean of the Rotman School of Management at the University of Toronto, says that concentrating primarily on creating shareholder wealth is ultimately a loser's game. The reason: the only sure way to increase shareholder value is to raise the markets' expectations about the organization's future results. "Unfortunately," Martin says, "executives simply can't do that indefinitely. ... Talented executives can grow market share and sales, increase margins, and use capital more efficiently, but no matter how good they are, they can't increase shareholder value if expectations get out of line with reality."[23]

We advocate that, instead of training her gaze directly on shareholder returns, a high-performing executive leader should pay attention to the performance of employees and the linkage of employee performance with customer satisfaction and purchase behavior. Companies like Marriott, Southwest Airlines, and Starbucks all follow this creed. "Take great care of your employees and they will take great care of your customers," says Marriott executive vice president Mike Jannini.[24] In the prologue to his book *Pour Your Heart into It*, Starbucks chairman and CEO Howard Schultz says, "A company that is managed only for the benefit of shareholders treats its employees as a line item, a cost to be contained. Executives who cut jobs aggressively are often rewarded with a temporary run-up in their stock price. But in the long run, they are not only undermining morale but sacrificing the innovation, the entrepreneurial spirit, and the heartfelt commitment of the very people who could elevate the company to greater heights."[25] In describing how the company created its brand, Schultz says, "We built the Starbucks brand first with our people, not with consumers—the opposite approach from that of the crackers-and-cereal companies. Because we believed the best way to meet and exceed the expectations of customers was to hire and train great people, we invested in employees who were zealous about good coffee.... That's the secret of the power of the Starbucks brand: the personal attachment our partners feel and the connection they make with our customers."[26]

Leadership enacted on a smaller scale—in an individual unit or department—both resembles and differs from executive leadership. On the one hand, first-line leaders should display the same humility, tolerance for contradictory information, and focus on employee contribution displayed by competent executives. On the other hand, clearly, they perform their roles on a smaller stage. In the words of management expert Marcus Buckingham, great senior executives (that is, leaders who do their jobs at the business or enterprise level) "discover what is universal and capitalize on it. Their job is to rally people toward a better future. Leaders can succeed in this only when they can...tap into those very few needs we all share." He contrasts this with the form of leadership exercised by someone who probably has the word "manager" in her title but who has a more circumscribed span of responsibility. This leader's challenge, he says, is to "turn one person's particular talent into performance. Managers will succeed only when they can identify and deploy the differences among people, challenging each employee to excel in his or her own way."[27]

In other words, leadership at the unit head level comprises the same components as leadership at the top of the corporation: envisioning a goal, plotting a path to achieve it, engendering motivation to get there, clearing obstacles, and providing boosts along the way. But unit-level leadership simply focuses on a few people, one person at a time, rather than on many people who share a few common aspirations. A skilled leader who is also the head of accounts receivable will, for example, help each employee find a reason and a way to contribute to the department's goal (reducing problem accounts, perhaps). For each person, the stimulus may be different. It's the leader's job to discover those individual motivations and activate them.

Clear enough, but a gray area remains. It involves the human asset, something that is intangible and highly personalized. Assets are inert elements of the production equation, valuable only when someone manipulates (or manages) them. Employees aren't assets the way forklifts, land, and bond holdings are. Organizations do not own people (not legally, anyway), do not control them, and do not directly reflect their value on the balance sheet. Management professor Henry Mintzberg has strong opinions on the degradation implied by putting employees into the same classification as an organization's tangible and financial resources: "Viewing them as resources is deadly. It turns them into robots. And you can't possibly get them enthusiastic about their jobs when you're treating them that way. It's not coincidental that the rise of the term *human resources* coincided with a wave of downsizing"[28] (italics in original).

So if employees aren't assets, what are they? Our answer: they are the *owners* of an asset, the asset that economists call human capital.[29] Human capital comprises the knowledge, skills, talents, and behaviors of workers. It catalyzes all other assets. A fundamental goal of managers, therefore, is to help employees build it and to evoke its investment, in support of a big-picture strategy or a specific tactic. A rational employee will make this investment only if it yields a payoff—in effect, a return on human capital investment. As capitalists of the true human asset, workers decide when they will invest, how they will invest, and how much they will invest. The desired return on investment takes a variety of forms, both financial (pay, benefits, stock options) and nonfinancial (intrinsically fulfilling work, learning and advancement opportunities, recognition for contribution). Organizations have many ways to generate ROI on human capital contributed. The manager plays a critical part in the creation and delivery of many of those elements. A leader-*cum*-manager must show each individual how his or her contribution of human capital will not only help to achieve an organizational goal but also to produce a personal ROI.

The Definition, and the Power, of Engagement

The degree to which managers matter depends, in part, on how effectively they contribute to employee engagement. We believe that, of all the attitudes and behaviors of employees in companies across the world, engagement best captures the energy and dedication that underlie human capital investment. We will refer to the power of engagement frequently throughout the book. Research performed by our colleagues at Towers Watson shows that engagement comprises the three distinct dimensions: rational, emotional, and motivational. The thinking (rational) component of engagement refers to how strongly employees understand and support the goals and values of the organization for which they work. The feeling (emotional) component of engagement describes the affective attachment that individuals feel toward their organizations. The behavioral (motivational) element encompasses employees' willingness to engage voluntarily in discretionary efforts for the good of the company—that is, to invest more of their human capital than is required just to keep their jobs.[30]

When organizations succeed at generating engagement among their employees, those employees not only score high on the three engagement dimensions, but also channel their human capital investment into areas the company cares about. Figure 1.1 shows the relationship between

Figure 1.1: The Engagement Gap—and What Happens When Companies Close It

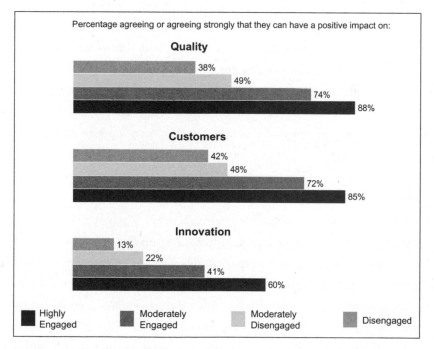

Source: *Closing the Engagement Gap: A Roadmap for Driving Superior Business Performance,* Towers Perrin, 2007.

engagement and employees' belief in their ability to contribute to quality, customer behavior, and innovation.

But how much does employee engagement really matter to firm performance? Our research says that it matters a lot. We confirmed this conclusion by following 40 global companies over a three-year period. At the beginning of the study, we separated the 40 companies into high-engagement and low-engagement categories according to their employee engagement scores. We found that, over a period of 36 months, companies with a highly engaged employee population turned in significantly better financial performance (a 5.75 percent difference in operating margins and a 3.44 percent difference in net profit margins) than did low-engagement workplaces. Those are the kinds of returns that accrue for organizations that have a competitive advantage.[31]

Using the worldwide respondent base from our 2010 global workforce study, we examined the drivers of employee engagement and employees' intent to stay with their current organizations. We found that the number one engagement driver is the perceived strength and performance of senior leaders. The behavior and effectiveness of direct supervisors falls well down the engagement driver list, at number 21. But a closer look shows that the direct manager's influence is woven throughout the list of employee engagement factors. For example, the number 3 engagement driver is career development opportunity. As we will see in Chapter Six, managers pay a crucial role in employee learning and development. The fourth most important engagement driver is empowerment; we will talk about the manager's role in empowerment (and, more important, in fostering autonomy) when we discuss task execution and development in Chapters Five and Six. Establishing clear and energizing goals, an activity that clearly requires manager involvement, came in at number 5 on the engagement list.[32] Our conclusion: manager performance matters to employee engagement, often indirectly and through a number of interrelated channels.

When we've looked at the manager population on a broad, multi-organization scale, we've seen another facet of this story. Our analysis indicates that improvements in manager performance are associated with disproportionately strong gains in employee engagement. The curve in Figure 1.2 tells the story.

The horizontal axis reflects performance on an index of items derived from the manager effectiveness model we will set out in Chapter Three. The vertical axis refers to employee engagement as we've defined it. When manager effectiveness declines from point A (the arithmetic mean performance score) to point C, employee engagement goes down by the amount shown as Y. Conversely, an equal increase in manager proficiency (from point A to point B) is correlated with a 25 percent *larger* gain in engagement. These findings tell us, in other words, that the improvement associated with good manager performance outweighs the loss linked with poor performance by a small but important margin. We believe that the relationship between manager performance and engagement reflects the multitude of factors influenced, directly and indirectly, by managers. Their actions alone do not drive engagement, but they

Figure 1.2: Manager Performance—More Upside Than Downside

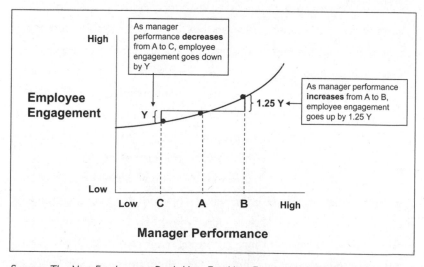

Source: The New Employment Deal: How Far, How Fast and How Enduring, Towers Watson, 2010.

touch and influence many factors that push employee engagement up and down. This analysis also underscores just how much organizations have to gain from increasing the effectiveness of their supervisors. Curves like these, showing increasing returns to incremental improvements, rarely appear in business. Companies should therefore seize the opportunity to make improved manager effectiveness a cornerstone of their efforts to enhance employee engagement.

ENGAGEMENT, MANAGERS, AND FINANCIAL RESULTS—ONE COMPANY'S EXPERIENCE

We got a close look at the relationship between manager performance and employee engagement when we did a research project for the AAA of Northern California, Nevada, and Utah. AAA is a service-oriented company that provides an array of automotive, insurance, travel, and financial offerings. We used employee engagement survey data and insurance industry financial data to assess the correlation between employee engagement and financial performance in the property casualty insurance industry in which AAA competes. The survey team analyzed the relationship between employee engagement and financial results for a population of sixteen insurance companies. We developed a statistical model using insurance industry engagement and financial data and applied it to AAA. The model indicated that a 5 percent increase in employee engagement at AAA is associated with $47 million in financial gains in the insurance, membership, and travel businesses.

We also looked at the data to determine whether a relationship exists between manager effectiveness and employee engagement. Our team worked with AAA to identify fourteen engagement survey items and compile them into a manager performance index. The index contained such elements as "My manager works with me to align my goals with the goals of the department," or "My manager regularly coaches me and provides feedback on my performance," and "My manager encourages me to come up with new and better ways of doing things." We correlated the engagement and performance indices across nine major units within AAA, including the company overall. Our analysis showed that there is a 0.63 correlation between manager performance and engagement at AAA, where 1.0 would indicate a perfect linear relationship and zero would mean no relationship. Although there are too few data points for the correlation to have strong statistical significance, it nevertheless suggests a connection between the manager performance and employee engagement measures.

Reflecting on this analysis, Marie Andel, senior vice president of People & Performance for AAA, said, "We continue to have relatively high engagement scores. And we know you can't focus on everything at once. In the six years we have been measuring engagement, we have had positive results in identifying an area of focus and applying actions, and we have seen the benefit in the scores. An organization focus on diversity and inclusion, the role of supervisors, and brand pride are all areas where we have made a commitment and seen the results. We have focused a good deal of attention on our supervisor group—reinforcing their role in performance management discussions, providing organizational context regarding strategy, having better career development discussions—and the result has been very positive. The formula almost seems too simple— select an area of focus, commit to addressing it, be explicit about why you are making the changes, and the results follow."[33]

Throughout our discussion, we will refer to employee engagement as a powerful force in energizing successful business strategy. And we won't hesitate to suggest that manager performance energizes employee engagement through an array of important factors.

(Continued)

It's true, of course, that managers don't work alone in their quest to increase engagement and build human capital. Our analysis shows that organization-wide elements like executive performance, company image, and corporate values are also important engagement drivers. Nevertheless, efforts to improve employee engagement must go beyond enterprise programs. Theresa Welbourne, a professor at the University of Michigan and an expert in executive and manager behavior, puts it this way: "Engagement cannot be a corporate initiative.... Corporate initiatives live out their life and then go away. The people who deliver the corporate initiatives have to make engagement happen, and those people *must be your managers*"[34] (emphasis added).

SUMMARY: THE MEANING OF THE MANAGER

Management and leadership have been with us since humans invented work. For most of the last two decades, however, the manager position has been under direct assault. It's become a ragged conglomeration of pieces and parts, designed to do too many things and engineered to do few of them well. People both higher and lower on the organizational hierarchy question its value, resent the power it confers, and criticize the competence of the people who do it. We see evidence in complaints about ubiquitous micromanagement, and in the prevalence of Web sites with bad boss stories, jokes, quotes, and tips for handling your abusive, ignorant, or just plain incompetent manager. Browse Amazon.com or your corner bookstore and you can pick up titles like *Brutal Bosses and Their Prey* and *Does Someone at Work Treat You Badly?*

Differentiating leadership from management, we believe, helps clarify some of the confusion that surrounds the manager role. This isn't to say that the two kinds of activities don't often blend, however. A manager who engages the people in a unit in devising a new work process could be said to be practicing both leadership (by involving employees) and management (by focusing on a process). But the blending doesn't mean it's not important to keep the elements separate in our minds. A chef mixes eggs and milk to make a soufflé, but that doesn't mean that eggs and milk are the same thing (at least not to the chicken and the cow). Keeping the ingredients separate allows focused development of the different management and leadership elements (that is, improve the soufflé by working with the chicken to upgrade the eggs and separately with the cow to perfect the milk).

So, do managers matter? We answer the question with an unambiguous "yes." As we expand the scope of managerial meaning beyond employee engagement to encompass competitive advantage for an organization, we will argue for the adoption of a specific model of managerial performance. Using company examples and research data, we will describe the components of the model and recommend ways of constructing the manager role to engineer it for success. The second part of the book will expand on each element of the performance model. We will end by suggesting how an organization can build and support a population of supervisors and managers who contribute to competitive success and enterprise prosperity.

CHAPTER OUTLINE

Employees Are Smart and Demanding

We Have Ambivalent Feelings about Leadership and Followership

We Really Don't Like Being Told What to Do

Managers Behave Badly

2

Why Managers Have a Tough Job

Lion tamer, U.S. president, inner-city high school teacher, air traffic controller. To this list of the most stressful jobs, add one more: manager. The headline on a tech industry blog suggests, "First, Kill All the Managers."[1] Another blog, entitled "I Don't Want to Be a Manager," says, "Middle management has become a euphemism for meddling, ineffectual supervision and frustrating career coma."[2] It's surprising that more people don't hide under their desks when the boss comes around to tell them they've been promoted.

In fact, it appears that many people do hide when faced with the prospect of a promotion into management. A 2009 study by Randstad, the global temporary staffing company, found that more than half of employees say they don't want to move into management roles.[3] A consultant reports that, in one of his client organizations, more than one-third of engineers promoted to management jobs went back to their old roles in less than six months. Why? "Because [software] code does what you tell it to do the first time and you don't have to ask how the kids are."[4]

What makes being a manager so unattractive? On one level, the answer is obvious—just look around today's workplace. As downsizing lengthens everyone's to-do list, expanding workloads add new burdens to the manager's job. With many organizations expecting managers to act as player-coaches, both performing and overseeing work, their roles often become complex and unwieldy. Organizational flattening and widening of managers' spans of control stretch their ability to spend time coaching, or even to become acquainted with, any individual employee. It's hardly surprising that respondents to the Randstad study cited increased stress as the number-one reason for avoiding management responsibility. They also said they hated the idea of handling disgruntled employees (like themselves, perhaps), dealing with loads of administrative paperwork, and having to terminate people, many of whom were peers not long before.[5] Given the disinclination of people to take on manager jobs, Randstad predicts what it calls a "looming manager shortage."[6] They recommend that, to deal with the shortfall of managers, organizations need to reconsider how they define managerial roles. We would agree—and we have tried to do so in Chapters Five through Nine.

When you consider the full array of leadership and management responsibilities that fall to people with supervisor and manager titles, one thing becomes clear—managers have difficult jobs. Workload pressure from downsizing, unworkable ranges of responsibility, and wide spans of control all burden managers' jobs, increase their stress levels, and reduce their effectiveness. Little wonder employees are skeptical about the competence of the people to whom they report.

Familiar as these factors are, however, they don't fully explain why managers so often find their jobs frustrating and unfulfilling. To understand that story, we must look beneath the superficial effects of workday realities. We must go to a deeper stratum of mental and emotional elements that affect how people experience their work and their relationships with peers and managers. Thanks to our psychological infrastructure, we workplace inhabitants have many attitudes, behaviors, and characteristics that can make life miserable for managers.

Employees Are Smart and Demanding

What about the workforce itself—how has it evolved, and what does that evolution mean for the challenges managers face? A few data points describe salient traits of the current workforce:

- *More human capital to invest.* About 30 percent of the U.S. civilian labor force now has at least a bachelor's degree, compared with about one-quarter in 1998. Between 1992 and 2010, employment grew by about 21 percent, while the proportion of participants with degrees grew by 63 percent.[7]

- *Confident in their ability to direct their own work.* In Towers Watson's 2010 global workforce study, 78 percent of the respondents said they feel comfortable managing their work on their own, with little direct oversight from managers.[8]

- *Willing to stay put, if it pays off.* Average tenure with their current employers stayed relatively stable from 1996 (at 5.0 years) to 2008 (5.1 years) for all workers 25 years and older.[9] That stability stretches back to 1983, when the average tenure for this worker group was also 5.0 years. More than 80 percent of respondents to our 2010 global workforce study said they either had no plans to leave their current employers or were not actively looking to move but would consider another offer if presented. About two-thirds defined their preferred career model as working for no more than three organizations over the course of their professional lives.[10]

- *Willing to move if staying put doesn't pay off.* Average tenure for workers in the prime earning ages of 45 to 54 dropped from 8.3 years to 7.6 years between 1996 and 2008. For workers in the 55–64 age group, average tenure fell from 10.2 years to 9.9 years. Social strictures against changing jobs have decreased for all age groups. Seasoned workers with plenty of knowledge and experience (that's right, human capital) are ready to change companies if they think it will pay off, in financial and other ways. This behavior seems particularly characteristic of the male working population. Average tenure for men in the 45–54 age group fell from 10.1 years in 1996 to 8.2 in 2008.[11]

- *Highly connected to information sources.* Some 63 percent of adult Americans now have broadband Internet connections at home, compared with about 42 percent in 2006. More than 80 percent of homes with educational attainment at the college level have home broadband.[12]

- *Highly connected to each other.* The average corporate user of e-mail can expect to send and receive more than 150 messages per day. That number is projected to grow to more than 230 by 2012. Business users report that they currently spend about one-fifth of the workday on e-mail.[13]

- *Connected in evolving new ways.* Social media play a growing, though still modest, role in the workplace. On the one hand, more than half of office workers with Web access have at least one social networking account (Facebook, MySpace, LinkedIn, Plaxo, Twitter, YouTube, Flickr, and the like).[14] The social networking site Facebook claims to have more than 400 million active users.[15] And it's not just teenagers who are friending each other; the fastest-growing Facebook demographic group is women above the age of 55. Almost half of Facebook's U.S. audience is now 26 years of age or older.[16] Meanwhile, Twitter has put together a community of millions of users in little more time than it takes to tweet your BFF. By one report, total tweet volume exceeded one billion messages a month as of the beginning of 2010, more than double the volume four months earlier.[17] On the other hand, only about a one-fifth of computer-enabled workers say they access their social media sites during work hours.[18] In-person contact remains the number one channel of conversation about work-related news and events (49 percent of global workforce study respondents choosing it most often) compared with various forms of online connection (37 percent selecting these as most frequent).[19]

- *Well-informed about employers.* Google lists hundreds of job search Web sites. These include megasites like Monster.com and Careerbuilder.com that offer about a million current job listings. Web sites like Salary.com and Vault.com provide detailed reward and culture information on almost any large company.

- *Hardened by ups and downs in the labor market.*[20] People who have been in the labor force since 1992 have witnessed cycles of unemployment that graph like an Alpine postcard. Unemployment went from 7.8 percent in June of that year down to 3.8 percent in April of 2000, back up to 6.3 percent in the middle of 2003, down to 4.4 percent in March of 2007, and up again to 10 percent in December of 2009.[21] Periodic mass layoffs have weakened the bonds between individual and organization. From 1998 through 2010, annual mass layoffs (defined as single-establishment separations that lead to 50 or more individual filings for unemployment insurance) ranged from a low of about 900,000 in 1999 to highs of more than 1.5 million in 2001 and 2.1 million in 2010.[22]

- *Ready to look out for themselves.* About three-quarters of the participants in our 2010 worldwide survey said they carry the primary responsibility for managing their careers, ensuring their financial futures, and seeing to their personal health and well-being. Far lower percentages said they felt confident in their ability to execute these responsibilities.[23]

These trends have produced a smart, savvy, self-sufficient, and wary workforce. In the words of one observer, "Today's workplace requires an enlightened, demanding, and independent workforce that has no problem voting with its feet when unhappy."[24] These workers want a manager who recognizes their abilities, meets their need for information, tells them the truth, respects their freedom, and rewards their success. The manager who fails finds himself with an investor who withholds his human capital, or who takes his investable portfolio to a job that offers a higher return.

We Have Ambivalent Feelings about Leadership and Followership

In his movie *History of the World, Part 1*, Mel Brooks (as King Louis XVI of France) explains why people—some of us anyway—strive to achieve leadership positions. As he skeet-shoots catapulted peasants, the Brooks character faces the camera and says, "It's good to be the king." Any evolutionary psychologist worthy of his autographed photo of Charles Darwin can tell you why it's good to be the one on top. The answer is simple—because being higher on the organizational ladder brings more of the goodies that everyone values. In one laboratory experiment, high-powered individuals more often helped themselves to extra food, chewed with their mouths open, and got crumbs on their faces and on the table.[25] And high-level people feel better too—on surveys, those with greater power more frequently express and experience positive moods and emotional states.

Some form of leadership emerges any time groups coalesce. Even in laboratory settings, leader-follower structures quickly appear. Despite many organizations' new-age efforts to create leaderless teams, there really is no such thing. Leaders arise spontaneously, even when groups set out to be leaderless.[26]

It's easy to see why leadership behaviors would tend to evolve among humans—their survival and reproductive advantages are obvious. But what is the one thing absolutely required to be a leader? Followers, of course. And why would a followership psychology exist? After all, followership benefits are much less obvious than the gains from being top dog. Indeed, at the individual level, we can expect that followers will generally do worse than leaders in terms of resource accumulation, survival, and reproductive success. Who will most likely obtain more wives and girlfriends (let alone more financial and other resources), Donald Trump or a janitor in one of his buildings? Because of the wealth and status that have accompanied Trump's elevated position, his fitness advantages (that is, factors that help people find mates, survive to reproduce, and thereby pass their genes on to future generations) are staggering.

Yet followership has its benefits too. Corporations headed by successful leaders tend to do better than corporations with mediocre leadership. At the micro level, consider a military unit led by an effective noncommissioned officer. Good sergeants train their troops well, build teamwork and camaraderie, help motivate soldiers to take the hill, and do all they can to keep them alive and safe. In the words of one senior Air Force officer, "The First Sergeant is the heart and soul of a healthy organization and is absolutely critical to a unit's ability to achieve mission success... not only do they professionally know their Airmen, and therefore the climate of the unit, they're also uniquely gifted at reading the indicators of a potential problem well in advance, and act quickly to mitigate....I contend they're some of the most powerful leaders... you'll find in any unit."[27] Because followership has its rewards, many of us are content to fall in behind a successful leader. Indeed, the human mind has an evolved facility for evaluating one's relative status in a hierarchy and assessing the costs and benefits of competing for a higher position.[28] In choosing to follow, we avoid potentially dangerous status battles required of those who aspire to leadership dominance. Those battles range from physical conflicts to political contests to proxy fights.

Nevertheless, in forgoing the battle for status, we inevitably give something up. Hence, the decision to follow rather than lead is bound to engender resentment. So followers end up with a deep ambivalence. As one anthropologist sums it up, "This would have produced in each individual a complex set of competing motivations—including tendencies both to dominate and not to dominate, both to defer and to resist domination, both to share and to be opportunistically selfish, all according to circumstance."[29] When modern organizations foster hierarchies that frustrate our counterdominant tendencies, stress builds. And we direct our frustration at those who benefit from their higher positions in the hierarchy. We have to wonder how much of the resentment about micromanagement has a genuine cause (an overattentive, controlling supervisor) and how much of it stems from internal conflict that leads us to label any manager actions as micromanagerial. Perhaps the fault, dear employees, lies not (entirely) in our managers, but (partly) in ourselves.

We Really Don't Like Being Told What to Do

Our inherent internal conflict about leadership has an important corollary: we really don't want to follow orders. Being directed reminds us that someone else gets to call the shots. Still, if we must give up authority, we want those who have it to exercise it appropriately. As a result, we place a heavy burden on managers to hit a small target between being too assertive and not assertive enough. A research study conducted by Daniel Ames and Francis Flynn at Columbia University concluded that there are two ways to get assertiveness wrong: by falling short when it's time to take charge ("Why won't she deal with the lazy sales reps who are dragging down the team's performance?") or by acting too aggressively ("Being hard-driving is fine, but this guy just won't listen to anyone else's opinion").[30]

The happy medium is happy indeed—it constitutes the most effective behavior in the eyes of employees. The research showed that managers who manifest moderate levels of assertiveness accomplished just as much as the most assertive, but with far lower social costs (in the form of disgruntled employees). This doesn't mean, however, that effective leaders are always moderately assertive. Rather, they display a range of situation-specific behavior. They take firm control of the reins when necessary and let the horses run free when they're headed in the right direction. The researchers concluded that, in the optimum range, "assertiveness may fade into the background, allowing other attributes with positive, linear relations with leadership to become more salient.... Like salt in a sauce, too much overwhelms the dish; too little is similarly distracting; but just the right amount allows the other flavors to dominate our experience. Just as food is rarely praised for being perfectly salted, leaders may somewhat infrequently be praised for being perfectly assertive."[31]

Every time a manager makes the wrong choice, he creates discontent. Of the two possible transgressions, of course, too much assertiveness engenders greater resentment. Hunter-gatherer groups that survive today try to force the right balance by maintaining highly egalitarian structures. They deal with their assertiveness aversion by insisting that their leaders circumscribe their roles and submit to the will of the groups they lead. Attempts by individuals to assert dominance can lead to disobedience or ostracism of the leader. In extreme cases (as among the San bushmen of Africa, Eskimos of North America, and Yaruro of South America), the band may execute the offending leader.[32]

In corporate organizations, bad boss behavior rarely leads to violence, but it can lead to lawsuits. In 2007, legislation was pending in New Jersey and at least three other states to give employees the right to seek damages if a manager created an abusive environment. In New Jersey, the bill specified that an individual who felt he or she had been wrongfully treated could sue for as much as $25,000.[33]

Managers Behave Badly

Our data suggest that the behavior of supervisors and managers explains some of the resentment that people experience. If we define a manager's job in ways consistent with our definitions of leading and managing, a summary position description would contain elements like these:

- Defines what the group needs to accomplish and suggests performance goals that are strategically relevant and challenging but achievable

- Communicates strategic requirements clearly and openly and obtains the resources necessary to achieve success

- Understands what motivates each person and creates opportunities to get people to invest their human capital toward achievement of the collective goal

- Uses an egalitarian process to determine what actions the team should take and consults employees before making decisions that affect the jobs they do

- Coaches and builds people's strengths (that is, enhances their human capital) so that they become increasingly skilled at executing the tasks required for individual and group success

- Builds teamwork and a sense of togetherness among group members

- Monitors group and individual performance and ensures that results are recognized and that rewards are fairly distributed

- Holds people accountable for their performance and their contribution to achieving group objectives

- Encourages new ideas and novel ways of doing things, to improve the group's arsenal of processes and techniques

Table 2.1 shows ratings of managers from Towers Perrin's 2007 worldwide study of ninety thousand employees. The right-hand column indicates percentage of employees who agreed or agreed strongly that their managers effectively perform the job sketched out above.

In four of the nine areas—providing reasonable performance goals, understanding individual motivation, consulting employees, and coaching to build skills—managers fail to exceed the 50 percent favorable mark. In every area, managers fall short of 60 percent favorable, a modest enough goal.

Little wonder employees are irritable—the downside of manager performance takes a high emotional toll. A study of workplace emotion by a team of researchers from the University of Minnesota led to this conclusion: "Our results revealed that employees experience less optimism, happiness, and enthusiasm when they interact with supervisors than when they interact with customers, clients, and coworkers."[34] In another study, researchers tracked the emotional states of employees in a light manufacturing company. Using palmtop devices, the employees received periodic signals during the workday; the signals prompted them to record what they had been doing and what emotions they were feeling. Over the course of several weeks, people said that about 80 percent of the interactions they recorded with supervisors were positive.

Table 2.1: Managers Behaving Badly—Employees Give Managers Low Performance Scores

Survey Item	Percent Agree/ Strongly Agree
My immediate manager:	
Provides performance goals that are challenging but achievable	50
Communicates clearly and openly	51
Understands what motivates me	43
Consults employees before making decisions that affect them	44
Effectively coaches and builds the strengths of employees	43
Supports and promotes teamwork	57
Recognizes and appreciates good work	59
Holds people accountable for performance goals	57
Encourages new ideas and new ways of doing things	51

Source: *Closing the Engagement Gap: A Roadmap for Driving Superior Business Performance*, Towers Perrin, 2007.

By comparison, the participants scored about 70 percent of coworker interactions in the positive category.[35] But the real story emerged when the researchers calculated the power (rather than just the prevalence) of positive and negative interactions. Whereas negative coworker experiences produced a depressing effect about 3.6 times as great as the positive emotional effect of positive peer interactions, negative experiences with supervisors were more than ten times as powerful as positive ones.[36] Clearly, when it comes to interactions with managers, a win some/lose some approach doesn't produce a balanced emotional state over time. Little wonder employees find that overassertiveness and other manager transgressions reduce the engagement, enthusiasm, and optimism they feel at work. And little surprise that managers, faced with the emotional outcomes of this asymmetrical effect, so often find their jobs stressful and unfulfilling.

SUMMARY: THE MANAGER PARADOX

The next chapters will challenge common assumptions about managers' roles and the means by which they contribute to organizational success. As we explore the meaning of the job, we will remain mindful of the human desire for autonomy and self-determination. These needs are deeply programmed into our psychology. The implication: the best manager does his work with the lightest touch. As one team of sociologists has written, "Leadership may be unnecessary and even resented when people face relatively simple or routine coordination problems. ... Here lies an important leadership lesson: except for certain well-defined situations, people will perform better if they are left alone."[37]

This admonition will guide us in developing a new model of manager performance, a model that makes managers central to an organization's quest for competitive advantage, but paradoxically out of the limelight. We will suggest that the best line supervisors influence the work environment directly, defining tasks, developing employees' human capital, and planning for the future. They focus unerringly on creating the context for individual success, but they deal with employees in subtle, nuanced, and effective ways. We saw an example of this notion with supervisor assertiveness. Managers who exercise the right level of assertiveness produce strong results with low levels of social strain, but draw less attention to themselves than either their too-quiet or too-intense counterparts. This paradox (manage better by managing less) will serve as our compass as we navigate the manager's job beyond its currently charted boundaries.

Some of what we will build into the manager's job will make it seem easier than its current form ("Great, I can waste less energy trying to design circuits with one hand and write performance reviews with the other"). In fact, the recommended role will actually prove both more challenging and more fulfilling, just as creating an impressionist work is harder but ultimately more rewarding than painting by the numbers. We may not transform managing into an art, but we hope to upgrade it to a valuable, and fully appreciated, craft.

CHAPTER OUTLINE

Managers and Competitive Advantage
>A Semiconductor Example
>An Airline Example
>A Software Example

The Manager Performance Model
>Executing Tasks
>Developing People
>Delivering the Deal
>Energizing Change
>The Foundation–Authenticity and Trust

3

A New Model of Manager Performance

We usually think of innovation and the economic benefits of rapid learning as modern phenomena, or at least human phenomena. As it turns out, however, even monkeys have learning curves. A psychologist observing a group of vervet monkeys saw an older female monkey dip an acacia pod into a pool of liquid in the cavity of a tree trunk. She soaked the pod for a few minutes and then ate it. No one, human or monkey, had ever seen this behavior before, even though people had observed this group regularly for many years. Within nine days, four other members of the old female monkey's family had begun dipping their pods as well. Eventually, seven of the ten troop members adopted this behavior. Having learned from the initial innovator, they moved quickly along the learning curve and improved their feeding experience.[1]

Any group, whether a troop of monkeys or a team of employees, can enhance its chances for success by innovating and passing on successful methods the way the vervet monkeys did. The goal, in primate or human terms, is an edge over the competition—other bands of monkeys or other companies. Corporations that achieve and sustain competitive advantage consistently deliver superior financial results. Sources of competitive advantage take three basic forms:

- *Product and service differentiation.* Producing an offering with features that stand out from the competitors' offerings in some important way, enabling a company to charge a higher price and enjoy a larger profit margin. Developing product features others can't duplicate (through meaningful innovation, for example) and achieving quality levels others can't match are two ways a company's products can yield a differentiation advantage.

- *Operating efficiency.* Producing goods and services at a lower cost than competitors can manage, permitting the firm to price below the competition and still make a profit. Cost advantages can come from many sources: less expensive raw materials, greater production efficiencies, and less waste in manufacturing and distribution, to name a few.

- *Customer focus.* Designing and delivering an offering that so accurately matches their needs that customers buy higher volumes and purchase more often than they do from other competitors. Successful customer-focus strategies thereby generate a revenue boost. In some cases, a firm may enjoy a cost advantage as well, as customer loyalty and word-of-mouth praise can reduce the need for investments in promotion.[2]

Organizations do best when they focus relentlessly on one source of competitive advantage. By the same token, all competitors must meet at least threshold levels for product features, cost, and customer attentiveness. They can't afford to fall behind a reasonable market standard in any area. In our experience, many organizations choose a major and a minor—a primary strategy supported by a secondary focus. We will see examples of that in the case discussions that follow.

Organizations devote significant time and energy to defining and implementing a strategy that executives believe will yield a competitive advantage in one of the three target areas. In this chapter, we will focus specifically on one element that can contribute to success in any of the three competitive advantage areas. We will look in detail at how the performance of first-line managers can help an organization achieve and maintain a competitive edge. By assessing specific company experiences and using our employee survey database, we will develop a model that we believe defines strong manager performance and addresses the performance and leadership concerns we raised in Chapters One and Two.

Managers and Competitive Advantage

Management guru Peter Senge has famously said that the only sustainable competitive advantage is the ability to learn faster than your competition. Although learning is certainly necessary (just ask any well-fed vervet monkey), incorporating knowledge into what and how you produce creates the real competitive edge. If managers play a role in the creation and application of knowledge (a key element of human capital), it then follows that they also have a part to play in achieving competitive success. In the next few sections, we will examine the manager's contribution to strategy in three different industries: a semiconductor manufacturer, an airline, and a software producer. Our assessment will reveal how, and how strongly, managers can help create a competitive difference for their organizations.

A Semiconductor Example

Although classified in the glamorous high-tech sector, semiconductor production is essentially a highly competitive, cost-intensive activity. Computer chips and potato chips have a lot in common, economically. Both come in a variety of flavors, but both are essentially commodities. At the same time, product features can represent points of differentiation (baked or barbeque flavor, for instance). It's been a fact of life in the semiconductor world that competition pushes for ever smaller, faster, transistor-dense devices. Companies must innovate or go out of business. Innovation creates better, more effective chips, and manufacturing efficiency ensures that they get to market at the lowest possible cost. The best semiconductor makers thus have the rare opportunity to inflict a competitive double-whammy on their rivals.

Cost competitiveness in the semiconductor business has conventionally been viewed as a classic learning-curve situation. Learning-curve theory says that cost per unit produced declines as the cumulative number of units increases (that is, as manufacturers amass learning about how to do it right). A theorist of classic learning curves will tell you that accumulating experience requires a gain in market share. Become the dominant producer and your greater production experience will yield insights that can make you more efficient than your competitors.

But piling up manufacturing experience isn't the only way to create a learning-curve advantage. A study by Nile Hatch and Jeffrey Dyer of the Marriott School at Brigham Young University showed that the ways firms manage their human capital can also reshape the learning curve—make it decline faster (as cost per unit goes down) and stay at a low, flat level longer than the rivals' curves. Hatch and Dyer studied the experiences of thirty semiconductor fabrication plants operated by sixteen different companies. They found that:

- Fabrication facilities (called "fabs" in semiconductor lingo) that place the greatest emphasis on statistical process control training for equipment operators have fewer defects and lower cost

- Involving equipment operators in problem-solving teams, rather than relying solely on engineers for troubleshooting, reduces defects and transforms the operators into "quasi-engineers" whose learning pays big performance dividends

- Conversely, costly defects increase significantly as the rate of employee turnover rises—that is, as an organization's human capital is depleted.[3]

In other words, even in a technology-heavy business, people matter as much as process.

While talking with the managers of the semiconductor companies they studied, Hatch and Dyer observed that, over time, the equipment operators developed a stock of specific knowledge about the intricate processes they use. Savvy managers put this human capital to good advantage by assigning equipment operators to troubleshooting teams. The teams could then implement quality-improvement processes, allowing the fabs to reduce semiconductor defects dramatically. Hatch and Dyer said, "Effective deployment of human capital integrates the entire manufacturing staff into one large problem-solving organization."[4] Effective deployment happens, in turn, when managers encourage growth in knowledge and skill and look for ways to help employees spread their learning around the organization.

Some of the knowledge transfer involves production factors so small that they seem trivial. For instance, while studying quality differences between two identical tools in different Intel factories, someone discovered that one group was cleaning the tool by wiping a towel in a circular motion. Another group wiped back and forth. The back-and-forth motion went against the grain of the metal, spreading debris particles rather than removing them. Circular polishing became the adopted procedure, and quality improved. Transferring these kinds of procedural insights is the responsibility of what Intel calls "seeds." These are technicians designated by their managers to transfer and replant manufacturing know-how from one Intel chip factory to another. Though the company prohibits willy-nilly changes, Intel managers encourage workers to present ideas to boost productivity or improve chip features.[5] Through this process, managers not only give employees valued control over key production decisions, but also help transform human capital into knowledge capital that others can use. The embedded wisdom about the big and small drivers of efficiency supports Intel's cost advantage.

Increasingly, however, innovation at Intel means more than just faster chips or lower production cost. Under CEO Paul Otellini, Intel is in the process of transforming itself from an engineering-driven organization (where, according to former CEO Andy Grove's famous aphorism, "only the paranoid survive") into a place where innovation requires heightened collaboration. In the past, engineers worked on creating speedier chips and letting marketers try to sell them. Now, cross-discipline teams (engineers, developers, marketers, and market specialists) work together to create compelling offerings. The organization has reached well outside the technical disciplines—to the medical profession, for example—to attract people who can work on technologies for health monitoring and data tracking. Although Intel has historically struggled to break into markets outside of PCs and server computers, the company has made a commitment to bringing out new chips for cell phones, consumer electronic products, and manufactured goods like cars. All of these will require Intel to make a change in the performance of its products.[6]

Intel managers must play their part in executing a strategy combining product differentiation, market expansion, collaborative product development, and cost efficiency. We would observe that, to succeed, they must perform well in four areas:

- See to it that employees have the right amount of both freedom and direction in executing work so they can function efficiently and with an orientation toward solving problems

- Make sure that people have a chance to learn and to pass on that learning to benefit other employees as well as the organization at large

- Encourage significant process change when needed to make a better, lower-cost product

- Expand their definition of teamwork and collaboration to include disciplines and perspectives hitherto foreign to hard-core engineers

These themes foreshadow elements of what we believe is a comprehensive model of manager performance. We will see them repeated, in different forms, in the next two company examples.

An Airline Example

Though it competes in an entirely different business, Southwest Airlines also pursues an efficiency-focused business strategy. To achieve and maintain a cost advantage, the company must do many things right—which it has for three and a half decades. Through 2009, Southwest had recorded thirty-seven consecutive years of profitability, a feat unequalled in the commercial airline business.[7] What does the airline do so well? Simply put, Southwest keeps things simple. The company flies one plane type (the Boeing 737), employs a pared-down boarding process, and gives no-frills (albeit friendly) service. This focus on streamlined operations has found favor with fliers. Southwest routinely scores among the better performers in on-time arrival, avoiding mishandled baggage, and minimizing customer complaints.[8] In effect, Southwest double dips—tactics that support operating efficiency also produce results that please customers.

Southwest has also implemented a set of practices that keep its planes in the air, where they earn revenue, rather than on the ground, where they don't. Many factors, and contributions from an array of employee groups, make this kind of performance possible. An analysis conducted by Jody Hofer Gittell, then of the Harvard Business School, identified coordination among those groups as one critical factor. Gittell and her team studied how airport supervisors in nine different work groups at four major U.S. airlines make connections among ticket agents, gate agents, baggage handlers, ramp agents, and operations agents. These are the folks who get you onto the plane, get your suitcases loaded, and get the aircraft off the ground. When they move quickly and in sync, you and your baggage have a much higher chance of reaching your destination on time, and at the same time. Sometimes it's as simple as a baggage service planner's anticipating a late flight and requesting a second set of stairs. This allows arriving passengers to exit from the front of the plane while departing passengers board using the rear stairs, accelerating the aircraft's turnaround. For that strategy to work, the baggage service planner must alert the lead gate agent, who can then manage the onboarding/offboarding procedure.

The researchers focused particular attention on this kind of cross-group teamwork, which they called relational coordination. Relational coordination encompasses elements like sharing knowledge within and across functions, mutual problem solving, establishment of shared goals, and assistance with tasks when time pressure becomes a concern. Southwest supervisors stand out for their performance in forming relational connections within and across work groups. When necessary, they work side-by-side with their teams. This gives them the legitimacy and knowledge they need to provide effective coaching and feedback. Southwest supervisors also spend more time advising and jointly solving problems with employees than do supervisors from the other airlines in the study.[9] In this way, Southwest managers achieve a human capital and employee engagement trifecta: increase employee involvement in decision making, help them build the skills and knowledge required to make those decisions effectively and, through both channels, enhance employees' rational and emotional engagement in their work.

The Southwest supervisors who participated in the analysis had a remarkable term for the people who reported to them. Not employees, subordinates, associates, team members, or even "most important assets." They referred to their people as their *internal customers*. At Southwest, the airport supervisor's main job is not to direct, monitor, assign blame, or ensure compliance, but rather *to serve*. Said one supervisor, "We are accountable for what the agents do...the agents are our customers. We are here to help them do their jobs."[10] Little wonder people want to work for this airline. In 2009, Southwest received more than 90,000 résumés and hired 831 new employees.[11]

It came as no surprise to the researchers that, across the nine airport groups studied, the two Southwest groups generally outperformed teams from the other major carriers on a variety of performance measures. By one estimate, for example, Southwest can turn a plane around from landing to takeoff in 23 minutes. That's about half the time it takes other airlines.[12] This kind of performance enables Southwest to produce consistently superior financial results. Indeed, even among other low-cost carriers, Southwest's advantage stands out. On an arcane measure called *average monthly revenue aircraft minutes per full-time equivalent employee*, Southwest hit 256 as of the first quarter of 2007. The overall average for low-cost carriers was 238.[13] In other words, in part because its supervisors keep airport teams informed, connected, and supported, they perform efficiently. Their efficiency, in turn, enables the airline to generate more flight-time revenue per employee than do most of its peers.

Managers at Southwest act in some noteworthy ways to help give the airline its clear and sustained performance advantage. Three areas stand out:

- Managers configure work efforts in efficient teams that coordinate to deliver service and share knowledge.

- They make coaching employees a high-priority part of their work, and ensure that people share knowledge within and across their department boundaries.

- They make certain that teams focus their attention on problem solving, so that procedures can be changed and improved, in the interest of maintaining Southwest's competitive edge.

A Software Example

SAS, a leader in business intelligence software, relies on innovation and tight relationships with customers to carve out a marketplace advantage based on product superiority and customer focus. In 2008, the company's fraud management software (which helps banks score individual transactions, including those at the point of sale, to catch credit cheaters) won a Technology Innovation of the Year Award from Frost & Sullivan, a research and consulting firm.[14] The company's success has produced impressive marketplace results: a nearly 100 percent subscription renewal rate among customers and thirty-three consecutive years of revenue growth through 2009.[15] Dr. Jim Goodnight, CEO of SAS, attributes the company's success to its development and investment of what he calls "creative capital." He means the innovative thinking and new ideas generated by engaged employees.

Over the past three decades, SAS has developed a creativity-management framework that incorporates three key principles:

- Keep employees intellectually engaged by removing distractions that interfere with their ability to come up with new ideas

- Make managers responsible for sparking creativity and eliminate arbitrary hierarchy that separates "suits" from "creatives"

- Involve customers as partners, so smart people can develop superior products that customers are certain to want to buy (another example of strategic double-dipping)[16]

To play their role in the creative process, SAS managers do a few simple things: bring groups of engineers together to encourage the exchange of ideas and spur innovation, handle some of the hands-on work themselves, and ask a lot of questions. Getting work done but not controlling it requires managers to find the sweet spot between being too distant and too involved. As one SAS director put it, "If you tell everyone, 'Here is how to do it,' then all you are really measuring is their typing skills."[17] Instead, managers create an environment in which technically skilled employees can take on substantial decision-making authority. Our research consistently shows that this is a key stimulus of engagement in high-technology companies. Managers also clear obstacles by acquiring the resources employees need to keep the creative energy flowing. Employees must trust that managers will get them what they need to do their work without putting them through a burdensome process of requests and requisitions. A manager heading up an SAS software testing team described this aspect of his job as "Go get it, go get it, go get it."[18] In turn, managers must trust that employees won't ask them to pay for something that doesn't contribute directly to performance.

SAS engineers forge connections with customers, and get direct customer feedback on product functionality, at the company's annual users' conference. There, consultants and technical support staff collaborate with users to define new products. This is how SAS developed its award-winning fraud management product, in collaboration with the global bank HSBC. The company says that 80 percent of the product improvements that customers suggest most frequently find their way into product offerings. Customer loyalty and repeat purchases are so high that the company can economize on customer acquisition investments, such as advertising and promotion. SAS puts the money it saves (about 30 percent of revenue) into research and development that drives innovation. The average for high-tech companies is about 10 percent. The stimulating, highly connected work environment pays off in another way: annual turnover at SAS runs between three and five percent, compared with a software industry norm of more like 15 percent. In other words, the company holds on to the human capital it builds.[19]

In a knowledge-intensive organization like SAS, the managers' job is essentially to help build human capital and then get themselves (and all other potential encumbrances) out of the way of its profitable investment. They accomplish this by:

- Clearing organizational obstacles so that the owners of creative capital can create

- Doing enough hands-on work to prove that they understand and appreciate the efforts of their employees and have the technical credibility required to coach effectively

- Calling on multiple sources of learning, from peers and managers to customers, so that creative capital constantly grows

- Helping developers turn their learning, especially what they derive from customers, into rapid product innovation

WITH HUMAN CAPITAL, IT'S BUYER BEWARE

The growth in importance of intangible assets over the last two decades is well documented. A study of the financial performance

(Continued)

of approximately nine hundred publicly traded electronics companies from 1996 through 2005 showed a significant relationship between human capital and the companies' market value. The author of the study concluded, "It is important to realize that IC [intellectual capital] is a main driver of competitive advantage.... In assessing the real value of a company, investors have to consider intangible assets, such as the human resources, skills, knowledge, processes, and innovation capabilities of an organization."[20] Although we would take issue with the characterization of human resources as assets, we otherwise agree with the statement.

In their semiconductor industry study, Hatch and Dyer found that costly manufacturing defects increased significantly with a rise in employee turnover. Turnover depletes valuable human capital, and that loss hurts organizational performance. They also found that the knowledge that mattered most was both tacit and idiosyncratic to individual organizations: understanding of particular equipment; skills at identifying and solving specific production problems; manager-supported team structures that saved time in addressing quality issues; culturally embedded managerial techniques for deploying workers; organizational dedication to heavy investment in learning. An organization's processes for hiring, developing, deploying, and leading people produce this firm-specific human capital.[21] These processes differ across the population of competing companies—some organizations do them effectively, some don't.

Can a company avoid costly investment in human capital development systems by hiring capable people away from its rivals? In general, the answer is no. In manufacturing, the data show that product defects tend to rise when manufacturers hire more workers with prior manufacturing experience, even from within the same industry.[22] Experience in another organization's manufacturing environment appears actually to slow learning in a new organization. When companies hire experienced workers from competitors, they acquire not only general knowledge about an industry or a profession, but also what one researcher calls the "schemas and scripts" that individuals construct to do their jobs.[23] When transplanted from the source to another organization, the knowledge of how things were done in the old organization appears to act as baggage. It slows new learning, impedes responsiveness in a new environment, and inhibits the ability to reflect and to reconstruct a new way of doing things.

The finding that the most important human capital is firm-specific also emerged from analyses done in the service sector. A research study of insurance company call centers confirmed that, among claims adjusters, claims assistants, and customer service representatives, prior experience in similar jobs detracted from performance in a new company.[24] Experienced workers were unable to transfer to another organization the portfolio of knowledge and behaviors established in prior jobs. This knowledge might have enhanced performance on their old jobs, but employees found it an anchor to performance in the new company.[25]

Human capital, it seems, is not an infinitely transferable asset. Its company-specific form, nurtured and supported by executive leaders and line managers, can create a competitive advantage that other organizations can neither acquire readily nor replicate easily.

The Manager Performance Model[26]

In the three company examples, we see consistent patterns of manager actions, fundamental performance requirements that cut across strategy categories and industry environments. With this foundation, we analyzed our consulting experience in manager role definition and reviewed employee survey results from companies around the world and across thc performance spectrum. Using all this information, we developed a performance model that we believe depicts how managers contribute most directly and significantly to sustainable competitive advantage. The model contains four categories of manager performance requirements.

Executing Tasks

This element comprises planning work, clarifying job-related roles, structuring specific job tasks, monitoring performance, and making the necessary adjustments to ensure that work meets organizational needs and supports business strategy. Overseeing task execution is, in many ways, the most traditional aspect of the manager's job. Of the four performance categories, it focuses most directly on the asset deployment, process oversight, and systems implementation elements that most people think of as integral to managing. Task execution comprises the fine-grained aspects of a manager's efforts to help a unit plot a path toward, and achieve, its strategy-contribution goals.

A manager's task-execution responsibilities will naturally take different forms in different organizations. When it comes to task execution at Intel, for example, managers stop short of solving quality problems for equipment operators. Instead, they let the operators work out their own solutions, making problem solving a core part of the job. Managers also involve people in making decisions about how their work will be done. They extend this job element to the organization more broadly by identifying efficiency advocates who can promulgate the organization's "copy exactly" philosophy. Managers structure work to move quickly from idea to implementation. At Southwest, managers know that to meet the competitive requirements of fast aircraft turnaround you need savvy people whose jobs are part of a team structure. Therefore, Southwest managers keep people focused on finding and executing the most efficient work processes. They build well-coordinated teams that make hand-offs smoothly and with minimal wasted time, effort, and resources. Managers at SAS create a work environment in which software designers can focus their efforts on creativity and customer familiarity. They encourage teamwork so employees can draw on each other to meet customer needs. They also provide flexibility for individuals, teams, and units to respond to customer needs, even in ways that may extend outside conventional operating procedures. Thus, even when the descriptors sound similar (all three organizations encourage teamwork, for example), the expectations and goals of task-execution approaches will vary: teams at Intel share quality improvement ideas; teams at Southwest scramble to serve customers; teams at SAS work with users to create new products.

Developing People

The next element of the performance model calls for managers to create opportunities for each employee to add to her storehouse of human capital. In doing so, managers create the ability for people to carry out their jobs and achieve their goals. Intel managers leverage diversity of thought and encourage the sharing of new, even unconventional, ideas around the organization. They ensure that on-the-job learning occurs consistently, so that equipment operators can play their roles on problem-solving teams and become almost-engineers. Their learning makes significant contributions to improved quality and lower production cost. Southwest managers focus learning on both individual task elements and on cross-functional training so that people understand fully what others do and so the team as a whole can function better. In the innovation-intense world of SAS, managers bring together teams of both engineers and customers to share ideas and make everybody smarter. They also give engineers substantial latitude to apply what they know, allowing them to approach their work in the way that yields the best performance.

Managers' roles in fostering learning and building performance capability will appear similar regardless of the competitive strategy adopted by their companies. Nevertheless, what seems common across strategy categories will exhibit important, if sometimes subtle, strategy-specific variations. Take learning and knowledge transfer approaches as an example. In a differentiation-intensive organization, learning programs will incorporate knowledge acquisition to keep people at the technical edge of their respective crafts. Companies with a differentiation strategy can't afford for their people to be left behind by market advancements. In a company that competes on cost control and efficiency, on-the-job learning efforts will often emphasize cross-training to ensure staffing efficiency and smooth interfunction handoffs. When customer focus is the driving strategic theme, managers will work to ensure that service delivery employees continuously improve their understanding of customers and their ability to anticipate and respond to buyer requirements ever more accurately.

Delivering the Deal

Managers play a central role in brokering the exchange of each employee's investment of human capital for the portfolio of financial and nonfinancial, intrinsic and extrinsic rewards that constitute a return on that investment. We refer to this reciprocal arrangement as *the deal* between employee and enterprise.

Intel, Southwest, and SAS all understand the importance of providing an appealing deal to employees as compensation for their contributions to strategic success. Naturally, financial rewards play a part in the organizations' overall reward portfolios. The Intel jobs Web site, for example, proudly tells prospective candidates about the organization's incentive philosophy: "Bonuses are the major element of Intel's variable pay and are central to Intel's approach to compensation. Our philosophy is to offer a greater portion of variable pay than the market average, because this provides a strong link between employees' compensation and company performance."[27]

But people work at companies like these for reasons that go much deeper, energized by intrinsic motivations that financial rewards can't address. Historically at Intel, intrinsic fulfillment came from being part of an organization that continuously innovated in technical ways. If you were an Intel engineer, you were inspired and energized by the chance to build ever-faster chips. In the evolving, marketing-oriented Intel, your internal motivation may come from helping to build a more diversified array of compelling consumer products. A manager who gets you involved in this kind of opportunity has made an important contribution not only to your personal satisfaction, but also to your career trajectory.

If you work at Southwest, what energizes you is the chance to exercise your individuality in serving customers. "One of the most important and significant freedoms we allow our employees is the freedom to be an individual," said Colleen Barrett, former Southwest president.[28] It takes astute, observant, and caring managers to encourage freedom but still keep people focused on what the customer needs and will pay for. Moreover, Southwest trusts employees' judgment not only in handling customers, but also in operating efficiently. The airline considers employees experts in how to save money, for instance. Pilots know the routes that save on fuel consumption; flight attendants make suggestions to economize on in-flight operations (such as using regular trash bags rather than logo-imprinted ones); IT technicians suggest that building computers is less expensive than buying them. It's all part of an environment in which contribution is rewarded not just with pay, but also with personal satisfaction and recognition.[29]

SAS rewards its employees with a variety of impressive benefits. They include an on-site exercise facility (where they launder your sweaty workout clothes and return them ready for use the next day); on-site child care; no limit on the number of sick days employees can take; and a seven-hour workday. But there's a strategic rationale for all this apparent largesse: to make it impossible for people not to do their work. And what if people took unfair advantage of the policies, and spent all day on the treadmill or playing Ping-Pong instead of working at their desks? Says John Sall, owner of one-third of SAS's equity, "I can't imagine that playing Ping-Pong would be more interesting than work."[30] According to one employee, "You're given the freedom, the flexibility, and the resources to do your job. Because you're treated well, you treat the company well. When you walk down the halls here, it's rare that you hear people talking about anything but work."[31]

In effect, SAS operates on the belief that intrinsically interesting work leads to satisfaction, superior performance and, ultimately, better products. Unlike most technology organizations, SAS offers no stock options, and never has. But the company is known for going to uncommon lengths to find the right intrinsic motivation for its employees. Software developers, for instance, value the opportunity to create elegant programs. The company sends them to technology conferences where they can hone their skills and create contacts within their professional disciplines. Sales people respond to the thrill of the hunt and the adrenaline rush from closing a big deal. For them, SAS created a technical support position to answer staff questions and solve engineering problems. This allows sales reps to spend more time finding prospects and making sales.[32] Managers have responsibility for bringing these kinds of intrinsically fulfilling elements into alignment with what the organization needs to achieve strategic success.

Energizing Change

Effective managers look ahead in time and outside the boundaries of their units and their organizations to anticipate and respond to environmental shifts and to envision, plan for, and create the future. Sometimes, this requires managers to respond to change that is imposed and unavoidable—reorganization, strategic redirection, or downsizing, for example. In other cases, innovation and creativity may spark the change, as people develop new offerings or find better ways to work. These forms of change call for varying levels of reactivity or proactivity, adaptability or resilience.

At Intel, innovation-inspired change historically emphasized balancing new technology and chip performance features with a constant search for ways to cut production cost and raise quality. The definition of innovation has broadened to include new offerings in consumer product categories that have been, until recently, foreign to Intel. Managers must now combine technical intelligence with social intelligence to create ways for employees to master their design and production challenges and share their wisdom with their (sometimes unfamiliar) teammates. In effect, energizing change has morphed from a technical challenge to an organizational and social one. Within the Southwest Airlines organization, managers must build efficiency-improving relationships among employee teams, and then reinforce the results with one-on-one employee coaching. Managers at SAS promote change by fostering social learning with stakeholders from the company's external environment. Managers and employees also make external connections to ensure that new product designs meet evolving customer needs.

These examples chiefly emphasize affirmative, forward-looking (though not necessarily gentle or easy) forms of change. But change has a dark side as well, when economic conditions, competitor success, or unexpected shifts in customer behavior make change a requirement merely for survival. In those scenarios, the manager's job calls for building employee resilience and flexibility. We will go more deeply into both aspects of change in Chapter Eight.

We believe this four-part model—executing tasks, developing people, delivering the deal, and energizing change—balances individual interests with those of the group. We think it also reconciles operational realities with social requirements and acknowledges the possibility that what worked yesterday can be improved upon. Although the four performance components represent discrete categories, the boundaries between them are highly permeable. For example, in performing their task-related responsibilities, managers can help people craft jobs that contribute to skill-building and, often, to customer relationships. Likewise, managers can ensure that employees' developmental efforts focus on the creation and implementation of new and improved work systems and technologies. Learning opportunities can also be framed as rewards in themselves, especially for high-performing employees who want to get ahead. Managers who recognize a particular employee's risk-seeking propensities can provide opportunities for the individual to introduce changes that bring about radical new ways of doing the unit's work.

Our four-element manager performance structure needs just one more component: a foundation.

The Foundation—Authenticity and Trust

The discussion to this point has presented an outside-in look at the manager's job. We've described manager performance requirements that employees, and the rest of the organization, would observe and experience. But effective managers don't define themselves and their roles solely through the eyes of others. Instead, each looks as well to an internal, self-defined standard of acting and speaking to which he holds himself, regardless of the requirements imposed by the external world. This notion, which scholars of leadership call authenticity, forms an attitudinal and behavioral foundation for the manager performance model.

Two ideas—that high-performing supervisors and managers both develop self-knowledge and adhere to high standards of integrity in thoughts, words, and deeds—constitute the underpinnings of authentic behavior. Researchers who study authentic conduct define it with four components. We list them here and elaborate further in Chapter Nine:

- *Self-awareness.* Having an understanding of one's strengths and weaknesses and knowing how one is affected by external events.

- *Relational transparency.* Presenting one's true and honest self to the world, without pretense, manipulation, or intentional distortion.

- *Balanced processing.* Objectively analyzing all relevant information, including data that are challenging or uncomfortable, before reaching a decision.

- *Internalized moral perspective.* Adhering to one's personal (presumably high) ethical standards, in spite of group, organizational, or societal pressures.[33]

Adherence to high standards of authenticity endows managers with the humility, intellectual honesty, interpersonal sensitivity, and behavioral consistency required to perform effectively across all core elements of the manager model. For instance, a manager can demonstrate self-awareness in the way she steps back from a do-it-yourself approach and allocates more fulfilling work to her subordinates. Her efforts to provide honest, constructive, but accurate performance feedback to an employee can demonstrate relational transparency. The ability to make a balanced consideration of all available input, including information that challenges current ways of doing things, can help a manager decide that it's time to change a traditional work process. A manager who accepts blame for a performance shortfall, perhaps because of unclear direction to employees, is demonstrating a strong moral perspective.

Much as authenticity and trust together form a behavioral foundation for the manager performance model, authenticity itself acts as a basis for establishment of a trusting relationship between manager and employee. Trust denotes the faith we have that another will act reliably in ways consistent with, and supportive of, our best interests. People who trust each other are willing to be vulnerable. They know that their trusted partners will not exploit their vulnerability.

Like other aspects of the social interaction among people, trust exists for a simple reason: it benefits those who exercise it. As he applied game-ending pressure on the Soviet Union, "Trust, but verify" (an old Russian proverb) became one of Ronald Reagan's favorite phrases. He incorporated it into his comments at the December 1987 signing of the Intermediate-Range Nuclear Forces Treaty, prompting the exasperated Mikhail Gorbachev to complain, "You repeat this phrase every time we meet." Reagan reportedly replied, with characteristic confidence, "I like it." Reagan knew that if we could trust the Soviets (and they us) to reduce investment in nuclear weapons, everyone would gain from the redirection of military resources and the reduced danger of global annihilation. "No nasty surprises" is the expected outcome of a trusting relationship.

Managers who demonstrate trustworthiness produce valuable benefits for their organizations. Researchers who studied a group of restaurant workers discovered that employee trust in their managers correlated significantly with higher restaurant sales, higher profits, and somewhat lower employee turnover. Employees who trusted their managers—and whose trust was consistently reciprocated through behaviors like delegation and broadening of employee decision authority—were more likely than others to acknowledge the legitimate needs of the organization and the individual unit. They also expressed a higher inclination to take on challenging and important jobs, cooperate with their peers, and display creativity and resilience in the face of change. As a result, customer service improved, waste and theft declined, and turnover dropped. The researchers concluded, "A (restaurant manager) who can garner higher trust from the firm's workforce gains a competitive advantage over rival firms."[34]

Managers can build trust with employees in ways that span all aspects of the performance model. Keeping people honestly informed about the unit's task performance builds manager credibility. Using consistent performance assessment standards from period to period and person to person gives people confidence in the manager's predictability and reliability. Managers who pay close attention to what motivates individuals and drives their engagement can make insightful decisions about individuals' jobs and rewards. And managers who let go of their comfortable, dearly held ways of doing things when it's time to change can demonstrate their authentic willingness to sublimate self-interest for the greater good.

Exhibit 3.1 illustrates the full manager performance model.

Exhibit 3.1: The Manager Performance Model

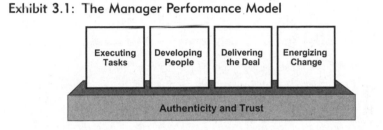

THE LEADERSHIP DEBATE

Much of the dialogue about leadership over the last two decades has focused on the differences between transformational leadership and its presumably inferior cousin, transactional leadership. Transformational leaders offer employees a purpose that transcends short-term goals and focuses attention on loftier intrinsic needs (and big organizational objectives). They project charisma, build inspiration and motivation, stimulate followers intellectually, and attend to each follower's individual needs. Transactional leaders, as the name implies, focus on the exchange of resources—leadership by *quid pro quo*, if you will. They concentrate on rewards and recognition for achievement.

Most effective managers, of course, use elements of both transformational and transactional leadership. The transactional type, while more limited in intellectual and emotional scope, can form the operational basis for transformational leadership. Consistent

(Continued)

honoring of agreements demonstrates to employees that their managers act predictably and dependably. These beliefs, in turn, lay the foundation for the high levels of trust and respect associated with transformational leadership. Without the foundation of an exchange agreement, transformational leadership may seem more idealistic than effective. Conversely, a purely transactional deal between manager and employee may produce short-term results, but will fall short in building the emotional energy and future competency required to improve and sustain performance.

A study of Army platoon leaders reinforced the conclusion that transactional, reward-focused leadership and transformational leadership can support and augment each other. A smoothly functioning platoon requires coordination among tasks and clarity of responsibility for achievement of targets and goals. This makes Army platoons like any company department, except that when a platoon performs poorly, people end up injured or dead. The research team pinpointed the importance of setting clear performance standards and recognizing success at achieving specific goals. "Specifically," the researchers said, "the performance context may elevate the importance of the role transactional leadership plays in contributing to effective leadership."[35]

The team concluded, "Transactional leadership can build a base level of trust in the leader.... Transformational leadership may build on these initial levels of trust by establishing a deeper sense of identification among followers with respect to the unit's values, mission, and vision."[36]

We constructed the details of our manager performance model using data from our 2010 global workforce study. The analysis encompassed data from a total population of more than twenty thousand employees in twenty-two countries. We performed a factor analysis to determine whether the manager effectiveness items in our survey would yield one coherent manager performance factor with high internal reliability. We found that a cluster of manager effectiveness items did indeed adhere together to form a strongly coherent index consistent with the performance model we've described.[37] Examples of those items appear in Table 3.1.

In some cases, the gaps between item scores for highly rated managers and those with lower ratings are remarkable. For example, among respondents who say they have an effective manager, 81 percent also agree that the manager consistently assigns tasks suited to the individual's skills and talents. Among those who disagree that their managers are effective, only 27 percent say their managers effectively match tasks with employee abilities (a gap of 54 percentage points). Several such gaps exceed 60 percentage points. These results suggest that the categories in our performance model do indeed define manager effectiveness and provide a way to differentiate between managers who do their jobs well and those who don't.

We also used the survey data to determine whether frequency of manager contact with employees was correlated with perceived manager effectiveness. As Table 3.2 indicates, we found a remarkable result: more frequent manager contact was associated with higher effectiveness ratings.

Manager effectiveness, in turn, was correlated with greater employee comfort in working autonomously. This finding suggests, paradoxically, that employees who have *more* manager contact feel more capable than other employees working with *less* manager oversight. Evidently, more manager contact (an element commonly included in the definition of micromanagement) isn't necessarily bad. Some managers, it seems, are particularly effective at using the time they spend with employees to create the circumstances and ability for individuals to work with high independence and self-determination. How do effective managers use this time? We think a close examination of our performance model will answer that question.

Table 3.1: Employees with Effective Managers Give Higher Scores for Performance Model Items

Performance Model Category	Survey Item—My Immediate Manager:	Percentage Who Agreed with the Survey Item and Who Also:	
		Agree That Immediate Manager Is Effective (%)	Disagree That Immediate Manager Is Effective (%)
Executing Tasks	Assigns tasks suited to my skills and abilities	81	27
	Provides clear goals for the work of the team	78	18
	Always knows how well our unit is performing its work activities	78	22
Developing People	Provides me opportunities to develop my skills	72	17
	Helps me with career planning and decisions	58	10
	Helps me to access learning opportunities outside my organization	57	12
Delivering the Deal	Provides frequent recognition for a job well done	73	17
	Makes fair decisions about how my performance links to pay decisions	66	11
Energizing Change	Encourages new ideas and new ways of doing things	73	17
	Keeps me informed about changes in my organization that affect my work unit	77	17
	Is good at explaining the reasons for changes that happen in the organization	73	12
Authenticity and Trust	Recognizes his or her own strengths and weaknesses	69	14
	Listens carefully to different points of view before reaching conclusions	76	15
	Acts in ways consistent with his or her words	85	11
	Is a trusted source of information about what is going on in the organization	76	14

Source: *The New Employment Deal: How Far, How Fast and How Enduring*, Towers Watson, 2010.

Table 3.2: Effective Managers Have More Contact with Employees

Frequency of Contact with Immediate Manager	Percentage Who Specified a Contact Frequency and Who Also:	
	Agree That Immediate Manager Is Effective (%)	Disagree That Immediate Manager Is Effective (%)
Once a day/several times a day	75	62
About once every few days/once a week	20	24
About once every two weeks/once a month or less often	5	14
I feel comfortable managing my work on my own, with little direct oversight	89	68

Source: *The New Employment Deal: How Far, How Fast and How Enduring*, Towers Watson, 2010.

CULTURAL DIFFERENCES IN MANAGER-EMPLOYEE RELATIONSHIPS

One of the authors (Stephen) grew up in the United Kingdom but has spent much of his career as a consultant working with organizations in other countries throughout Europe and parts of Asia. Recognizing and responding to cultural differences come with the territory.

(Continued)

Picture the scene, for example, of a Dutch bank acquiring an Italian one. Stephen studied this integration of two established companies as they moved from "talks about talks" to operational reality. Getting these two organizations to collaborate required a lot of work, including culture sensitivity training for managers from both banks.

They had plenty of real-life examples to work from, such as the time the Dutch sales director took his regional managers out to dinner following their first operational away-day. Immediately upon sitting down to dinner, the Dutch manager took off his jacket and tie. He assumed the relaxed informality of his home culture, and so did not expect the looks of surprise from his new Italian colleagues. Dining in an upscale restaurant in Italy is still a formal affair requiring correct behavior. The Italians saw his casual approach as bad manners verging on disrespect.

On the one hand, our model proved to be robust across the twenty-two countries we analyzed.[38] On the other, we know that manager actions and employee reactions, behavioral expectations and resulting responses will inevitably vary across cultural boundaries. No model structure, regardless of how statistically strong, can predict every nuance of manager and subordinate relationships. Only real-life experience can do that.

SUMMARY: MANAGERIAL METAPHORS

In one study of manager roles, a participant used an automotive metaphor to describe his job: "I try to keep things running smoothly. Basically, we have this really high-powered technical engine—a Maserati—and when you see that Maserati running and racing and really impressive, you don't see me driving it, you don't see me as the car or the engine. I'm the mechanic that comes in at night that does the tune-ups so that the next day it's running smooth."[39]

This idea conjures up images of high performance and winning races, themes consistent with the manager's contribution to organizational effectiveness and competitive success. But notice that the manager-as-mechanic, who makes sure the machine runs flawlessly, works so subtly that he makes his contribution not only off-hours, but also off-stage. This metaphor reminds us of the motif introduced in Chapter One, the idea that, for a host of reasons, twenty-first-century managers must do what they do away from center stage. With this in mind, we might also think of the effective manager as:

- *Sculptor,* crafting job roles that fit both individual needs and organizational requirements

- *Catalyst,* initiating action in the workplace but doing so without direct involvement

- *Conductor,* orchestrating the efforts of others and the environment in which they perform for maximum effect, while not actually playing the music

- *Broker,* acquiring resources and creating internal and external relationships that make people more effective

These forms of manager behavior don't just produce good feelings among employees, nor do they merely improve a manager's ability to contribute to strategic success. Ultimately, they represent the only feasible approaches for responding to the inherent ambivalence people harbor toward leaders. Our analysis of employee commentary about their managers tells us that people want managers to spend the right amount of person-to-person time (not too much, not too little) and make the time valuable for the employee (whether gratifying to the manager or not). Managers who strike this balance give people the ability and the confidence needed to work autonomously.

Managers benefit their people most when they manage the task environment, the learning environment, the reward environment, and the change environment. They manage everything *except* the people (who aren't assets to be managed anyway, as we said in Chapter One). These effective supervisors are indeed environmental engineers, constructing the organizational landscape to create a fertile ecosystem in which employees can flourish. Gary Hamel and Bill Breen, in the *Future of Management*, echo the manager paradox when they describe the need for a light-handed approach to management and leadership: "The most valuable human capabilities are precisely those that are the least manage*able* [italics original]...getting the most out of people seldom means managing them more, and usually means managing them less."[40]

To be sure, managers must exercise power—but not in the way usually ascribed to the manager's job. Rather than *power over*, a manager who effectively leads from offstage will focus energy on *power to*—to obtain resources, to clear obstacles, to build network links, and to identify information sources.[41] An employee at a high-tech client of ours said it succinctly in written comments he gave on a survey: "My manager's success should depend on my success. He should be held more seriously accountable for focusing 'down' than focusing 'up.'"

We took pains in Chapter One to differentiate managing from leading. We emphasized the difference to make a point: that they are separate disciplines, each necessary for enterprise success, but not to be confused with each other. So, you might ask, as they oversee the execution of tasks, build employees' ability to perform, deliver an engaging deal, and energize change: are managers managing or leading? The answer, no surprise, is both, often seamlessly. For example, a supervisor who involves employees in deciding how work will get done must focus both on the process (a managerial task) and the person (a leadership activity). By crafting a job with high autonomy for an employee, she is practicing both one-person-at-a-time leadership and managing the improvement of work processes. On the one hand, a manager's efforts to energize change could focus on improvements to procedures and systems (managing). On the other, those improvements will likely falter without involvement from employees who have the practical knowledge to help plot the way to the future. In these situations, an effective manager entwines the strands of management and leadership to create a single cord. The two threads remain distinct but combine for added strength.

Although we find this configuration of elements logical and compelling, we continue to see that, from the employee perspective at least, managers often fail to deliver the full benefits of this way of managing. What goes wrong? Why can't managers consistently live up to their potential as sources of competitive advantage? What must organizations do to give their managers a fighting chance to do their best work and make their greatest contributions? We will tackle those questions in the next chapter.

CHAPTER OUTLINE

Manager Contribution—The Player-Coach Job

Manager Competency—The Technical Skill Dilemma

The Size of the Job—Span of Control
> Because They Thought They Had To
> Because They Thought They Should
> The Truth about Spans

Building the Role System

4

Constructing the Manager Role

In the wild, the lives of vervet monkeys are like one big soap opera. Some sit at the top of the social hierarchy, with better access to food, mates, and grooming opportunities than lower-ranked troop members. But subordinate monkeys, like soap opera characters, can be a deceptive lot, using trickery to improve their position in life. For example, vervets have been observed using a warning call (intended, say, to alert the troop about a specific approaching predator) to send the other monkeys scrambling up a nearby acacia tree. This strategy leaves the lone monkey with sole access to the juicy berries, a food source he would have to share with higher-ranking animals, if they weren't busy hiding from a nonexistent leopard.

Studies of vervet monkeys have enlightened psychologists about how dominance works. One interpretation of dominance—high social status achieved and preserved through skillful connection—has important implications for the manager position. How is it, exactly, that individuals ascend to manager and executive jobs, where they have authority over others? Is the process as rational as we would like to think, or are other forces at work?

We have considered some of the organizational phenomena that make the manager's job difficult and cause no small amount of resentment against the people who hold manager positions. In Chapter Three, we laid out a manager performance model that aims to address these concerns, to transform managers into a competitive advantage rather than merely an inert layer in the organizational hierarchy. We ended the chapter with a question: why don't managers more consistently execute these performance requirements? We will address this question by considering key elements of the manager's role and exploring how the construction of the job affects the execution of the performance model. We will focus on three major elements of the manager's position:

- What the job is supposed to accomplish (the determination of how managers do and should spend their time and how they ought to contribute to the organization's quest for better product and service offerings, lower process cost, or stronger customer relationships)

- How managers are expected to do what they do (the balance of relational competencies and technical skills and how that balance determines the way managers go about their work)

- How the reporting scope of the manager's job affects performance (the number of employees the manager oversees and how that number renders the job feasible, impossible, or somewhere in between)

Manager Contribution—The Player-Coach Job

Sometimes, in a team sport like basketball, a single person will play the dual roles of player and coach, analogous to an actor-director in movies or a musician-band leader in a 1940s swing orchestra. In 1967–68, Bill Russell, in the player-coach role, led the Boston Celtics to the championship of professional basketball in the United States. He may have been the last truly successful example of that approach, at least in professional sports. Those who hold him up as an example of how a player-coach can succeed forget that, in the prior season, the Celtics led by player-coach Russell had failed to make the playoffs for the first time since 1956. His success the next season came only after he cut back his playing time and concentrated on coaching.[1] Even Bill Russell, who had exceptional ability in both disciplines, couldn't do both jobs equally well at the same time.

Although the player-coach structure has produced only mixed results, American business has virtually institutionalized it. Across a range of industries and functions, organizations consistently expect line managers, especially those at the first supervisory level, both to perform and to oversee work. In a Webcast we did in partnership with the Human Capital Institute (HCI), we asked the participants (102 human resource managers and executives) what percentage of their managers spend at least half of their time doing the work performed by their units. More than half of the survey respondents said that a majority of managers spend at least half their time in direct personal production. Almost one-third of the respondents said that 80 percent of their managers concentrate more than half of their time on personal output.[2]

When we did focus groups with sixty-three managers in a midsized commercial bank in the United States, the participants told us clearly how the push me–pull you aspects of their jobs diffuse their attention. Their greatest frustration, they said, comes from having to adopt a player-coach role, juggling demands for personal production with the responsibility for leading people and managing work processes. They said they spent almost 40 percent of their time doing hands-on work, and less than one-third focusing on people. Almost 60 percent said that solving this problem would be one of the best ways to enhance their effectiveness as managers. As one put it, "Managing people is a small piece of what I do. Our managers are working managers, and they own the projects they're responsible for." Another pointed out one underlying cause of the problem: "Ideally I'd concentrate on managing, but as it is I don't have enough resources, so I have to get in there and help." They lobbied for a job structure that would decrease hands-on time to 30 percent and increase people-related time to more than 40 percent.

We got comparable results from a similar-sized study we did of a U.S. utility company. Almost 60 percent of the utility managers said that one of the best ways to improve their managerial effectiveness would be to reduce the time spent juggling personal production tasks and oversight responsibilities.

Table 4.1 shows some of the reasons organizations cite for instituting player-coach structures, points out the flaws in those reasons, and suggests another way of thinking.

The player-coach construction has links to the all-too-common tendency to promote people to supervisory roles chiefly for their technical abilities. After all, doesn't it stand to reason that a technically proficient supervisor should spend most of her time selling farm supplies, designing communication networks, or writing copy? Isn't that how the organization can achieve the highest possible return on the compensation it pays that person? In fact, it's rare to find a supervisor or manager who does no hands-on work. Virtually all must balance some amount of playing and coaching. At Southwest Airlines, for example, supervisors work next to their employees. But they do so not because they perform better than the people on their teams. Instead, they do so because it provides the experience they need to give effective coaching and performance feedback. At SAS, managers do some of the work to free up highly skilled programmers to focus on what matters to them. The issue is not one of absolutes, but rather of optimal balance for the highest productivity of the unit as a whole, not just the highest manager output. As one consultant notes, "Most managers in the technical fields were superb individual contributors, which makes sense—it's how they got identified as 'management material' in the first place. Still, being good at doing something doesn't mean you'll be good at teaching others to do it or motivate them to get to it done even if they know how."[3]

Manager Competency—The Technical Skill Dilemma

The predisposition to attach leadership responsibility to domain-specific abilities is a ubiquitous organizational phenomenon with deep psychological underpinnings. At least one CEO, Indra Nooyi of PepsiCo, has

Table 4.1: Player-Coaches—A Losing Game

Reason for Creating Player-Coach Roles	Problems with the Reasoning	A Better Approach
We don't want a full-time manager overseeing a small group of employees.	Narrow spans of control* may be inefficient, but creating player-coach structures is not the best solution.	Restructure units and consolidate activities differently to create reasonable spans of control.
We have no choice—we can't afford to have managers who only manage.	The math is wrong. It overlooks the additional employee productivity managers can generate if they concentrate more time and energy on leading and managing and less on personal production.	Make careful decisions about who should manage and who should function as an individual contributor. Put people where they can be most successful and don't mix roles.
We reward our best employees by letting them oversee one or two other employees.	This makes promotion more about reward than about competence in a manager role.	Introduce dual career paths and richer reward and recognition opportunities. Make promotion about ability to perform well in the next job, not technical skill in the last one.
We don't allow first-time managers to supervise more than three subordinates.	Transitions may make sense, but they should be carefully planned and short-lived. Properly selected and trained, first-time managers don't need to be constrained for long periods to artificially narrow spans of control.	Define spans reasonably and help people make speedy transitions to spans that make sense.

*By "span of control" we mean the number of people who report directly to the manager. This may include part-time, temporary, and contract workers as well as full-time equivalent employees.
Source: Adapted from *The Fallacy of the Player-Coach Model,* The Boston Consulting Group, Inc., 2006.

said that this is part of a successful corporate culture: "PepsiCo is a meritocracy. Hard work gets recognized.... There are some skills that I believe are the hallmarks of a good leader. [One is] competence. You must be an expert in your function or area of expertise. You will become known for that."[4]

People must strike the difficult balance between the need for effective leadership and the innate drive for personal autonomy. Moreover, we must choose when to tolerate leadership and enjoy its benefits and when to avoid elevating someone to a position that might lead to exploitation. We can sometimes mitigate the danger of being dominated by making leadership situational. This means choosing leaders for the abilities required to deal with immediate threats or to capitalize on near-term opportunities. Under this strategy, a clan will delegate temporary responsibility for finding the nearest water hole to the most geographically knowledgeable person. They will choose the wisest and most impartial to restore peace or to render a fair judgment in a dispute. The most aggressive and strongest member will lead them into battle and then humbly return, like Cincinnatus, to membership in the group.[5]

In our HCI Web survey, we asked the participants to tell us how much weight their organizations place on technical and operational skills (as opposed to social and relational abilities) when they promote employees to the first level of supervision. About three-quarters said their organizations place significant weight on technical and operational skills.[6] A researcher who studied supervisors overseeing engineers in petrochemical and engineering organizations summed up her observations this way: "Technical skill is a common criterion used to promote technical professionals into management. Often the 'best and brightest' are rewarded for their technical performance with a supervisory or management track promotion. The underlying assumption of this practice is that individuals who excel in a given position (e.g., engineers) will also excel at supervising individuals in that position." She concluded, with admirable understatement, "This assumption, however, is largely untested."[7]

The tendency to elevate skilled practitioners into managerial positions also occurs in professions less technical than engineering. For example, a study of promotion decisions in large accounting firms showed that technical skills were by far the major criterion for moving from senior accountant to manager.[8] Similar weighting for function-specific abilities also occurs in nursing. In one study of advancement criteria, the data showed that promotion from clinical nurse to assistant nurse manager depended most heavily on clinical competency and knowledge. Demonstrated teaching and supervisory experience and overall communication skills fell further down the list. Clinical competency and knowledge remained a dominant promotion criterion in moving up one more level to nurse manager, tied in importance with communication skills. As the researchers noted, "The fact that managers need very different skills than workers on the front line is not always recognized.... Exceptional nurses may not always make exceptional managers."[9]

At play here is the eponymous phenomenon defined in the late 1960s by Laurence J. Peter, a professor of education at the University of Southern California. The "Peter Principle" states that people advance until they reach their levels of incompetence. As it's often expressed, the cream rises until it sours. In many organizations, the Peter Principle manifests itself as the promotion of technically skilled employees into manager positions for which they are unskilled. In some cases, technicians and scientists actively seek these promotions, even knowing that they lack the needed competencies. They do so because organizations afford no other path to greater prestige and higher earnings. In other cases, organizations either overemphasize the importance of technical ability in the equation of managerial performance, or believe that there are simply not enough people with sound leadership and managerial abilities to fill the available managerial slots.

But just what is the relationship between technical skill and the interpersonal, social, and emotional competencies required for successful manager performance? Is it an either/or situation—you can have one, but not the other? Or are they merely contrived opposites, juxtaposed to depict a simplicity that doesn't reflect reality? As with all things concerning human talents and abilities, the answers are complicated. Economists who study how the Peter Principle plays out assume a negative correlation between the two sets of abilities. They postulate an implicit tradeoff—the best technician is a social misfit, the most socially adept are technical goofballs, and you must choose between the two. Of course, the manager ranks may contain members who are incompetent on both dimensions. One academic uses the term "the Dilbert Principle," referring to the pointy-haired boss created by cartoonist Scott Adams, for the tendency of an organization to promote the doubly incompetent.[10]

And what does the research say about the relationship between technical skill and the leadership and management competencies required for successful manager performance? Are they utterly unrelated, negatively correlated, or in some way connected? One study concluded that a small but positive and significant correlation existed between the subject group's average technical and managerial evaluations (0.361, where 1.0 would mean a perfect correlation).[11] These findings suggest that, while not highly connected, the two bundles of competencies need not be considered completely disconnected. Exhibit 4.1 illustrates the array of possible combinations available to an organization.

In looking for candidates to promote into managerial positions, organizations should search for people who have high levels of interpersonal and emotional skills and at least moderate levels of technical competence. People who have this profile of dual competence can avoid both the Dilbert and Peter Principle zones. We find them in the S-Zone ("S" for strong on both dimensions). Who occupies the S-Zone? Managers who have a sound technical foundation to go with well-developed leadership and management qualities. They have recorded strong performance as engineers, scientists, and salespeople. They may not be the top technicians, but they have enough ability in their disciplines to act as credible sources of advice and guidance for their technical

Exhibit 4.1: Finding the S-Zone—Considering Competencies on Two Dimensions

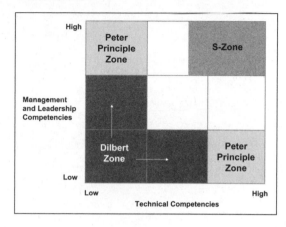

subordinates. They have also demonstrated the ability to connect with people, analyze and improve ways of working, and plan for (and achieve) better performance in the future. As a result, they can effectively help people craft engaging jobs, set and achieve goals, become more proficient, and develop the resilience required to weather change. In other words, they can lead (and manage) a unit.

IS YOUR MANAGER JUST BLUFFING? (PART 1)

Effective leaders understand and deliver what followers want. As one social psychologist has said, "An ability to estimate the pay-offs for followers is necessary for leaders to be influential. This would explain the empirical links between leadership and social intelligence, political skill, empathy, perspective taking, and nonverbal sensitivity."[12]

(Continued)

In practice, however, groups tend to grant leadership status for reasons that suggest at best a questionable ability to discern genuine leadership competence. A team of researchers from the University of California, Berkeley, ran an experiment in which they assessed how college students achieve status in three familiar venues: a fraternity, a sorority, and a mixed-gender dormitory. They measured the effect of physical attractiveness and personality on the achievement of status (defined as factors like prominence, influence, social position, and formal leadership roles). They discovered that, in the male-only environment of the fraternity, three factors correlated strongly with status:

- Physical attractiveness, as rated by both male and female students who were not acquainted with the fraternity members and knew nothing of their backgrounds.

- Extroverted personality, assessed through a self-evaluation by the subjects using a standard personality inventory. Extroversion implies an energetic and outgoing approach to the world. It incorporates such traits as sociability, assertiveness, and enjoyment of the company of others.

- Low neuroticism; neuroticism reflects vulnerability to stress, anxiety, depression, and guilt.[13]

Some of these findings seem intuitive, others more puzzling. For example, it makes sense that outgoing young men would be more inclined than their shy brethren to seek status and to achieve it. But what to make of the importance of physical attractiveness in an entirely male, overwhelmingly heterosexual environment? Perhaps they viewed physical attractiveness as a proxy for likely success on the social scene, which in turn engendered admiration.

The mysterious importance of male attractiveness among males only grew deeper when the research team conducted a second analysis to look at the female-only world of a sorority. Using a similar research approach, the team found that, as with the men, extroversion related strongly to status. But neither neuroticism nor physical attractiveness showed any significant correlation with status. Apparently, women don't worry as much as men do about either looks or emotional stability, at least when it comes to granting status to their same-gender peers.[14]

In the third study, the researchers analyzed status in the mixed-gender environment of a dormitory. The research confirmed the findings from the two earlier analyses: extroversion is positively correlated with status; neuroticism has a negative correlation for men but not for women; and physical attractiveness has a positive relationship with status among men (regardless of whether men or women are doing the judging) but no relationship among women.[15]

We all know of managers who received promotions because of their outgoing personalities, reassuring self-confidence, or movie-star looks. But, you might protest, this research study looked at social groups, not work groups. Fraternities, sororities, and dorms have few clear competence criteria aside from social skill, which extroverts project effectively, and emotional stability, to which we all aspire. Surely things work differently in groups that actually have to accomplish something.

Or do they?

The Size of the Job—Span of Control

Span of control (the number of people reporting to a manager) represents a fundamental architectural element of organization structure. From the top of the organization to the bottom, span of control speaks to the organization's philosophy about power, accountability, prestige, and rewards. In the last decade and a half, organizations have tended to broaden spans of control for two reasons: because they thought they had to and because they thought they should. Let's examine these two motives.

Because They Thought They Had To

As we saw in Chapter One, the recession of 2001 and the years following brought widened manager spans as organizations responded to the economic downturn by cutting costs. The logic of cost saving through broadened spans is seductive; flattening organizations by reducing the number of managers lowers operating expense by the dollar value of all of their salaries, benefits, and the variable elements of overhead. But the relationship between wide spans and financial performance is ambiguous at best, as the data in Table 4.2 suggest.

The table shows that firms losing money tend to have relatively narrow spans. As revenue performance improves, spans begin to widen. However, as performance improves further, the widening stops. In fact, spans narrow, from an average of about eight direct reports per manager to about seven and a half. Moreover, the data on organizational layering suggest that flatter structures don't track consistently with better performance. European data paint a similarly ambiguous picture. Overall, money-losing firms have about 8.5 subordinates per manager. The number increases to 10.8 for firms with revenue growth of less than five percent, but drops to 9.0 for companies in the 5–20 percent revenue growth category.[16]

We must be careful about interpreting these data. First of all, the analyses don't trace one group of firms as performance increases or declines, so we can't necessarily infer a trend. Also, we must exercise caution in assigning cause and effect. Do narrowing spans and heightening the organization drive performance, or do better-performing firms simply tend to become (or remain) narrower? These are interesting questions, but the more important question for us is: what really happens

Table 4.2: Span of Control and Company Performance—Any Connection?

Revenue Growth	Median Manager Span of Control	Median Organization Layers
Loss	6.4	9
Less than 5%	8.1	8
5%–20%	7.5	8

Source: *Organization and Operations Results—U.S. Human Capital Effectiveness Report 2009/2010*, Saratoga, a service offering of PricewaterhouseCoopers, LLP, 43, 59, 72.

to employee attitude and organizational performance as spans change? More on that later.

Because They Thought They Should

Some observers would say that the widening of spans of control and the pancaking of the organizational pyramid are the inevitable results of commercial evolution. Modern organizations, they would say, have evolved beyond the bureaucratic form. Hierarchy (and, consequently, supervision) has become obsolete.[17] Moreover, a workplace with less supervision would be more in sync with the evolving context of work— greater demand for quality, shorter product life cycles, consistent pressure to adapt to a shifting external environment, increased foreign and domestic competition, and related pressures on trade, communication, and transportation costs. Organizational architects have assumed that layers in the hierarchy slow decision making and raise cost—bad things in an increasingly competitive marketplace.

Organizational flatteners also hailed advances in electronic communication as enablers of hierarchy reduction. According to one commentator, "We used to need hierarchies because we had only primitive communication and information processing capability. Computers, electronic communication, and particularly the Internet have made it possible to flatten almost everything. Flat organizations ... are necessary to deal with accelerating change."[18] The flatter the organization, the easier it becomes for work groups to communicate horizontally with each other. Information moves faster because it doesn't have to go up the chain of command to a supervisor, across to another supervisor, and then down. Eliminating kinks in the communication lines means direct, horizontal, individual-to-individual, group-to-group connection: "Direct communication between individuals is both quicker and more accurate than nodal information flow."[19] And everyone lives happily ever after. At least that's the theory.

The Truth about Spans

The only way to determine the right span of control for any managerial position is to take a hard-nosed look at what you really want managers to accomplish, in the context of competitive strategy. If you believe that managers have existed merely (or even mainly) to disseminate orders and collect information to pass up the hierarchy, then you will surely find better ways to perform these tasks. You will remove managers from the organization, broaden spans, flatten structures, and give everybody direct access to information. If, however, you believe that effective managers do a host of other things that make employees more productive and organizations more successful, then you will take a different course. You will decide how you want managers to contribute and structure their jobs accordingly.

In Chapter Three, we defined manager performance in four action categories: executing tasks, developing people, delivering the deal, and energizing change. Performing well in these areas requires time and ability. It becomes impossible if spans are too wide. Consider examples from four industries: transportation, health care, chemical manufacturing, and call center service.

We saw how managers at Southwest Airlines view their employees as customers. Within this guiding perspective, supervisors do all they can to make their people successful at satisfying customers and keeping airplanes in the air. Southwest's competitive and financial success stems in part from this managerial role definition. This role, in turn, relies largely on creating close relationships between employees and supervisors, which requires comparatively limited spans. In the highly connected team environment of Southwest, supervisors have responsibility for staying close to employees, working side-by-side with them when necessary, coaching them, and giving constant feedback. The organization expects each supervisor to do all this for a group of about nine people. Spans of control at the other airlines included in this study ranged as high as forty. The researchers found a strong relationship between narrow spans and high performance in minimizing customer complaints, handling baggage efficiently, and avoiding late arrivals.[20] The lead researcher on the Southwest project concluded, "My quantitative findings suggest that, overall, large spans are not conducive to high performance in this setting. My qualitative findings further suggest that it is the combination of small spans and facilitative supervision that offers the greatest long-term promise....It is also difficult to see how high performance can be sustained if, notwithstanding a more facilitative style of supervision, large spans deprive teams of the support they need to sustain strong group process."[21]

In a broad study of seven Canadian hospitals, a group of researchers from the Canadian Health Services Research Foundation studied nurses' spans of control. The team, headed by principal researchers Dr. Diane Doran and Dr. Amy Sanchez McCutchen, looked at how spans interact with leadership style to affect both work experience (as reflected in job satisfaction and turnover) and operational outcomes (measured by patient satisfaction). The researchers confirmed that the two classic leadership styles (transformational and transactional) produce high job satisfaction among employees. They also found that wider spans of control decrease the positive effect of these styles on nurse job satisfaction. Moreover, they discovered that wider spans were associated with lower patient satisfaction and higher nurse turnover.[22]

These findings raise an interesting question: what happens if spans of control are wide but managers nevertheless adopt a transformational leadership style? Doesn't manager behavior trump number of employees? The Canadian researchers found that it doesn't—or, more precisely, it can't. As they wrote in their study summary, "There is no leadership style that can overcome a wide span of control. More specifically, the wider the span of control, the less positive the effect of transformational and transactional leadership styles on nurses' job satisfaction.... As well, wide spans of control decrease the positive effect of transformational and transactional leadership styles on patient satisfaction."[23] Evidently, the effects of even the most enlightened leadership become diluted if managers have too many direct reports. They proposed a simple explanation: "It is not humanly possible to consistently provide leadership to a very large number of staff, while at the same time ensuring the effective and efficient operation of a large unit on a daily basis." They went on to say, "Even if managers possess the desired leadership style, their span of control may interfere with their ability to influence desirable outcomes for their subordinates, patients, and their unit. To succeed, nurse managers must have an optimum span of control that will allow them time to develop relationships with staff."[24]

The same conclusion—that overly broad spans make it difficult for even relationship-focused supervisors to manage effectively—emerged from a research study that looked at production work teams in a U.S. chemical company. Several years prior to the analysis, the organization had undergone a delayering and reengineering program that eliminated management levels. The company had also undertaken efforts to increase employee empowerment, all part of a move toward a lean production mode of operation. As the management structure became sparser, employees took on more responsibility for the actions of the safety committee. This benefit was undercut, however, by the effects of increased spans of control. Wider spans were correlated with more unsafe behavior and more accidents. The researchers concluded, "The potential beneficial impact of empowerment may be tempered by the negative impact of work group size.... Empowering employees may not be enough if leaders have too many members to handle."[25] Towers Watson's research supports this conclusion. We studied human capital metrics from about 150 companies around the world. We found that, as spans of control grow broader, employee engagement, people's willingness to invest discretionary effort in their work, perceptions of learning and career development opportunities, and commitment to the organization all decline.

But what about organizations that have narrower spans of control than others they compete against? Do they derive any benefits from bucking the industry trend? Southwest gave us one example—are there others? A Philippines-based call center organization, eTelecare, provides another instructive case. Spans of control as high as twenty employees per supervisor are not uncommon in call centers. It's a competitive, cost-pressured business; minimizing operating overhead is high on the strategic agendas of call center companies. But eTelecare has a ratio of customer service representatives to team leaders of just 8 to 1, less than half the industry norm. Employees report that team leaders, freed up from the burdens of wide spans, have more time to help employees develop their service skills and technical knowledge. This investment in staff development enables eTelecare to build the skills of its representatives quickly. Some staff make the leap from entry level to licensed securities sales representative in just eighteen months.[26] By narrowing spans of control and focusing on human capital, eTelecare has been able to reshuffle the competitive deck in its business, delivering a differentiated offering in an industry that usually cares mostly about cost.

IS YOUR MANAGER JUST BLUFFING? (PART 2)

The line between technical skill and leadership competence would seem clear enough. We should be able to decide who resides in the S-Zone and who falls short on either the relational or technical spectrum. But can we? How do personality, technical skill, and status interact to affect position in work groups that have a specific assigned task? To answer the question, two University of California researchers (one of whom, Cameron Anderson, had been on the team that studied status in the fraternity, sorority, and dormitory settings) analyzed how having a dominant personality affects one's perceived technical prowess. They found that an individual's personality strongly influences the group's assessment of the person's technical skill.

The researchers asked groups of students to create an imaginary organization and outline its strategy. The study design called for both team members and outside observers to evaluate collective participants on influence in the group, competence demonstrated on the group task, and personality traits. One of the study results had been expected: people with dominant personalities got high ratings for influence. The study also produced a more surprising outcome: dominance predicted group members' perceptions of both task competence *and* social competence. That is, people who exude self-confidence and a take-charge attitude convey the appearance of both social and technical skills. As the researchers said, "Dominant individuals seemed truly to appear more competent than their less dominant teammates."[27]

To be sure, self-confidence and social skills are critical to successful leadership (as is a low tendency toward neurotic worrying). But don't we want and deserve more from leaders than just a confident façade? Don't we prefer managers from the S-Zone, where true management and leadership competencies combine with significant task-specific know-how? Maybe extroverted people can bluff their way to the head of the group when there's no easy way to measure occupational skills and knowledge. But what about situations where there is a specific measure of competence in a discipline? Surely in those cases a group can sort out who has real functional knowledge and who is merely acting?

It turns out they can't.

Building the Role System

It is probably obvious by now—though surprisingly few companies we know think of it this way—that the manager's job is a system. It comprises a set of interconnected activities that complement each other and ultimately drive individual and unit performance. Some of you may be thinking, "You seem to be dumping all manager positions into one bucket. Anyone who works in the real world knows that managerial jobs differ across professional disciplines, industries, companies, and functions." True enough—occupation and function matter. Legal department managers, sales managers, and aquaculture managers may have many common job requirements, but their jobs also differ in many ways as well. Researchers from DePaul and Michigan State looked across a range of occupations to see what factors affected the job requirement variations in three categories: conceptual (analytical and general cognitive strength), technical (function-specific operational expertise), and interpersonal (interacting with and influencing others).[28] They found, intuitively enough, that specific technical tasks required by an occupational group— from filing briefs to feeding fish—varied the most among job types. Conceptual and interpersonal requirements, however, varied far less across occupations. The researchers called these two categories "universally important."[29] Thus, although manager skills, work processes, and outputs clearly differ across industries and professions, the basic requirements (and challenges) of the job remain fundamentally consistent. Therefore, we will proceed to propose a managerial system that encompasses a set of central elements with more similarities than differences across the spectrum of manager jobs. We will incorporate the flexibility required to define the role and its components in ways that respect the unique requirements of specific disciplines and organizations.

To construct our model of the manager's role, we need first to define the elements and then set forth some assumptions for how the elements work. Table 4.3 summarizes the manager job elements.

Table 4.3: Elements of the Manager Role

Job System Elements	Definitions
Net outcomes	Revenue generated by products and services a unit provides, net of the people-related cost (chiefly pay and benefits) required to make and deliver those offerings
Role elements	Time allocated by the manager to:
	Direct production: Hands-on effort to produce and deliver goods and services
	People focus: Creation of a productive work environment for employees in the unit; this encompasses activities like guiding, coaching, developing, rewarding
	Work process oversight: Monitoring procedures and looking for ways to improve how work gets done in the unit
	External contact: Making connections outside the group, either with other units inside the company or with external organizations, to improve unit performance (for example, by acquiring information, assets, and assistance)
	Administration: Handling a potpourri of support tasks, including planning, budgeting, monitoring, and reporting

Table 4.3: (*Continued*)

Job System Elements	Definitions
Manager competencies	*Management:* The human capital needed to acquire, develop, and oversee the assets, processes, and systems of the unit
	Leadership: The full panoply of knowledge, skills, talent, and behavior necessary to develop a vision, plot a path to achieving it, energize others to follow the path, and clear obstacles along the way
	Technical: The skills and knowledge needed to perform well the function-specific, output-producing work of the unit
Employee competencies, roles, and resources	The human capital employees have to execute their roles, the structure of their jobs, and the freedom afforded them to decide how their work will be done
	Also the information, tools, funds, and other assets available to them
Span of control	The number of employees reporting to the manager
	This encompasses full- and part-time employees, temporary workers, contractors, and consultants

The variables in the analysis can be manipulated according to these assumptions:

- Time is a zero-sum element. A single hour can be invested only once. Tomorrow's time allocations can differ significantly from today's, but once spent, hours are gone.

- When managers concentrate on direct production, intuitively enough, they produce more than managers who spend their time elsewhere. Plus, their technical expertise grows with practice, so they'll improve their production over time, to a maximum point.

Managers with the greatest technical abilities have the highest personal production.

- However, when managers focus more attention on people and less on production, several things happen. The manager's individual production drops as his investment of effort in that area diminishes. But then the magic starts to happen. Employees become more capable as the manager spends more time coaching and developing them. Their engagement goes up as well, for the reasons discussed in Chapter One. As the manager's experience with these relational elements increases, so do his leadership and management competencies. All of this produces an important increment in employee productivity and, therefore, in unit output.

- The time that managers spend in work process oversight and forming external contacts can contribute to employee productivity in several ways: improved means of doing things, better access to useful information, and periodic injection of fresh ideas, for example. Hours invested in this element can add an important increment to unit productivity.

- Administration is a necessary activity, but one best circumscribed. Planning, monitoring, reporting, and budgeting are important, to a point. Most managers would say they want to reduce the time spent in this category. Organizations should accommodate them to the extent possible.

- For the sake of simplicity, all manager competencies fit into three categories: management (the wherewithal to handle assets, processes, and systems); leadership (the relational attributes required to connect with people and help them move toward a specific goal); and technical (function-specific, output-producing skills and knowledge). Of course, these three categories could be infinitely subdivided. Plus, one could argue that they overlap in more than a few areas. Coaching employees in specific technical areas, for instance, might require abilities in all three domains. Increasing the manager's technical prowess affects only his own personal output. Increasing his leadership and management competencies, however, affects the engagement and human capital, and therefore the productivity, of every employee.

- A similarly simple three-part cluster describes the employee's place in the system. Competencies encompass the knowledge, skills, talents, and behaviors people use on the job and build over a career. Roles refer to the tasks and responsibilities contained within a job, along with the degree of workplace self-determination available to employees. Resources incorporate the physical, financial, and informational assets required to get the job done. These three elements come together most effectively when managers pay attention to individuals' needs—crafting engaging jobs, recognizing competency with incremental freedom and responsibility, and providing access to experience and wisdom. As the employee role becomes richer, employee productivity rises. Also, people with improving competencies become more capable not only of performing their own work, but also of extending their contribution to intraunit and interunit work planning. In essence, they become able to do some of the work conventionally allocated to the manager.

- Span of control affects a manager's ability to spend time with and invest attention in each individual in the unit. Beyond a certain point, spans become so large that the manager can barely say "good morning" to someone as he sprints down the hall to put out the latest fire. Conversely, spans can be too narrow. In one insurance company client of ours, one-over-one structures proliferated because many middle managers had assistant managers. They needed someone to stay behind and mind the store while the managers attended meeting after meeting. The organization chart was a forest of narrow spans, pointed at the top and slender all the way down. Obviously, the output of any unit is the sum of each individual's production. More people in the unit means more product and service output. Moreover, as noted earlier in the chapter, faster and better information flow permits flatter organization structures and broader spans. But let's make sure we have the horse and the cart in the right order. Freer information flow makes wider spans possible; wider spans don't, by themselves, cause information to flow more freely. Likewise, a manager with a narrow span isn't necessarily required to handle every data bite before it gets to employees. The challenge, in other words, is to optimize span of control—as wide as possible, so that the unit has more people producing; as narrow as necessary, so that the manager can help each person become optimally productive.

As with any system, factors affect other factors, and there are many tradeoffs to be considered. Choosing between tradeoff options is, of course, an it-depends game. How much will diverting manager attention from personal work to coaching employees and improving work methods actually increase unit performance? It depends on the specific function. Manager investment in these areas may have greater leverage in departments that have higher complexity and skill requirements than in areas with simpler work processes. How much leverage can a manager get from time spent fostering connections outside the unit or external to the company? It depends on the value that outside information and support can add to any unit's performance. Great insights from the market research function may provide an important boost to the performance of a sales group, for example. R&D needs an external network with which to share research findings. We find, however, that HR functions are sometimes distracted and deflected by an endless search for external benchmarks and best-practice information. How much added value comes from the increases in employee performance that arise from growth in knowledge and abilities? It depends on the job and the learning curve associated with it. In some functions (receptionists, for example), performance peaks after a few months or weeks of experience. Coaching from a manager in the critical early period therefore has a greater influence on learning speed and proficiency than coaching later on. Learning curves for materials scientists are much longer. A manager who can help a young scientist focus his attention on the most fruitful research paths and get ideas more quickly to a revenue-generating stage can add significantly to the financial contribution of a research group. And what about the engagement effect of manager attention to elements like individual development, on-the-job autonomy, and participation in decision making? Again, it depends—on how high engagement is to begin with and on the status of other engagement-driving factors (for instance, the concern senior executives display for employee well-being).

With these dimensions and provisos in mind, consider the two jobs depicted in Exhibits 4.2 and 4.3. The points and lines show the architecture of the manager's role: time allocation; competency and resource balance for manager and employees; and span of control. Exhibit 4.2 shows the job of a manager who has a strong technical focus. Call her the Widget Wizard. She's the most skilled producer on the team, and

Exhibit 4.2: The Widget Wizard

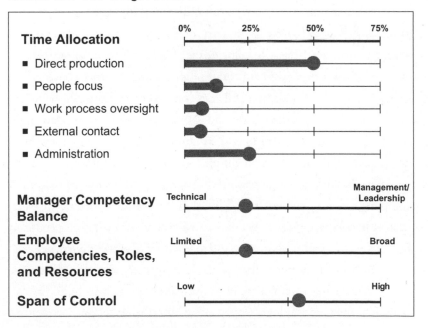

Exhibit 4.3: The People Powermeister

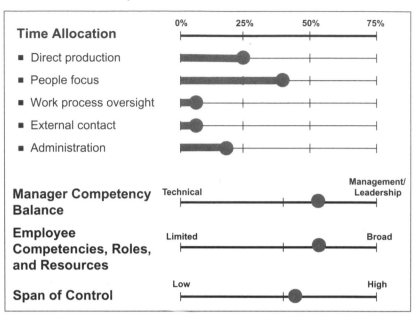

she spends her time accordingly. Half of her working hours go to directly producing output. The biggest part of the rest (25 percent) goes to administrative activities. She allocates what's left to focusing on people, overseeing work processes, and maintaining some external contact. Her span of control is moderate and her competencies lean clearly to the technical side. Little time investment goes to people (with, say, eight direct reports, an average of only thirty minutes each during a forty-hour week) and to work process oversight. Consequently, employees in the unit perceive limits to their roles and to their ability to improve their competencies and performance. This manager will seem successful, especially if her goals and rewards focus chiefly on what she herself produces. But the people in the unit will suffer. In effect, she has traded her productivity for that of her work group. It is unlikely that this job profile will maximize net revenue. It certainly won't do much to build human capital or enhance employee engagement. Increasing the span of control would only make things worse. At some point, the dilution of manager attention to employee needs ultimately diminishes individual productivity and overall group output falls.

In contrast to the Widget Wizard, the People Powermeister (see Exhibit 4.3) spends one-fourth of his time on direct personal production, enough to keep technically current and professionally credible. A full 40 percent goes to people focus. This allocation yields a generous two-hour allotment of development time per week for each of eight direct reports. Not all of this time goes to one-on-one coaching; some could be invested in group discussions of goals, team learning sessions, and quiet time to plan development strategies for each individual. Equal 10 percent allotments go to improving the work systems used by the group and to building network contacts outside the unit. What chiefly distinguishes this manager role is the more than 50 percent time allocation to activities (people focus, work process oversight, and external contact) that add to individual and group productivity.

We've developed an approach for analyzing the impact of changing the relative weights of these manager role elements. Our calculations suggest that this manager profile could yield a 15 percent increase in revenue production over the Widget Wizard role structure. Expand the manager's leadership and management competencies and figure that commensurate growth in employee competency and autonomy will produce an even more dramatic jump in unit performance.

The real question is: what role structure makes the most direct contribution to competitive advantage? What formula for designing a manager's job makes task execution more productive, people more competent and more suitably rewarded, and change more readily adopted and beneficial? The People Powermeister structure is set up to accomplish those goals by concentrating the manager's time and ability on improving employee performance and growth. The potential for competitive advantage is obvious: for every dollar invested in employee salaries and benefits, this approach can produce higher output than one that relies more heavily on a manager's personal production.

But how do we really know that one role structure produces more than the other? Of course, the results of this analysis depend on the assumptions that go into it. In particular, the People Powermeister role definition requires a manager who has strong leadership and management competence. This means someone in the S-Zone, a manager who knows how to apply his analytical ability and relational savvy with a light touch. Nevertheless, fairly conservative parameters for the impact of additional manager attention to employee performance and work process effectiveness produce dramatic output improvements. Manager attention to employee needs produces a multiplier effect as employee knowledge and abilities increase and the work environment becomes more productive. The incremental production of individual employees soon swamps any output lost as managers shift their time away from hands-on work.

But don't take our word for it—do this business case analysis across various functions in your organization and see what job structure produces the best economic outcome. Autodesk, leading producer of 2D and 3D design software for manufacturing, building, construction, engineering, media, and entertainment, did just that. In 2005, the company set about to improve the productivity of its sales force. As part of the analysis, Autodesk conducted a survey to determine how high-performing sales managers spend their time. The analysis team discovered that the best performers differentiate themselves chiefly by spending more time than other managers on coaching sales representatives. For example, in the EMEA (Europe, Middle East, and Africa) sales region, high-performing managers spent about two hours per week more than other managers on coaching activities. Star managers also focused more attention on helping reps with pre-sales planning and deal closure and more time on internal coordination with other functions. The time allocation analysis revealed that some sales managers in another key channel, the value-added reseller group, also had challenges. They carried a heavy burden of administrative, compensation, and post-sale follow-up tasks. All of these are secondary to the goals of spending maximum time with the customers and their reseller partners.

Autodesk took a multipart approach to changing the time allocation strategies of sales managers and increasing their attention to coaching. The organization first set a goal for managers' coaching time: four hours per sales rep per month (an hour a week on average per rep). To help managers achieve that goal, the company collaborated with Inside Out Development, LLC to implement a sales manager coaching program called G.R.O.W. (goal, reality, options, and way forward). The program trains managers to establish a goal for each conversation with a sales rep, assess the current selling situation and pinpoint key challenges, identify alternative actions, and choose a course of action for the rep to resolve the challenge. Sales manager job descriptions have been modified to emphasize the importance of effective coaching. Manager compensation has been changed to focus more attention on coaching success. Not all managers have been comfortable with the increased quality and quantity of coaching expected of them. In response, Autodesk has also taken some managers (5–10 percent) out of their managerial roles. Most, however, are achieving the target of four hours of coaching monthly for each rep. And sales reps are noticing the improved focus as well. Survey scores for manager effectiveness in this area are on the rise. As the Autodesk experience confirms, improving manager performance starts with understanding how managers' time allocation choices drive their ultimate effectiveness.[30]

IS YOUR MANAGER JUST BLUFFING? (PART 3)

In another study, the U.C. Berkeley researchers looked at how well a group could solve a set of math problems. Here again, dominant personality traits (including extroversion and enthusiasm) predicted the attainment of influence in the group. And, here again, dominance predicted perceived competence. People with strong, outgoing,

(Continued)

assertive personalities tended to put forth more information about the problems, more initial answers, and more answers overall. Their behaviors suggested high levels of task-relevant competence.

As it turned out, however, these signals did not necessarily align with their actual abilities. The researchers found no correlations between dominance and either SAT math scores or the accuracy of the answers contributed during the group task. The team concluded, "Individuals higher in trait dominance were perceived as more competent even when controlling for their actual competence." They went on to suggest that the word *dominance* doesn't really capture the source of influence for this successful cohort of the population: "The term *dominance* [italics in original] implies behaviors such as bullying and intimidation.... Yet, we found that dominant individuals attained influence through a very different path, by displaying competence and signaling their value to the group. These findings suggest that dominant individuals may ascend group hierarchies by appearing helpful to the group's overall success as opposed to aggressively grabbing power."[31] They added a chilling note for those who assert that organizations can consistently make rational and accurate promotion decisions: "It seems that certain personality traits (in this case dominance) can distort perceptions of abilities and make it more difficult to detect who is more or less competent."[32]

In many ways, of course, the experimental situations described here don't resemble working life. In the real world of work, recruiters, employees, and senior managers typically have more time and more opportunities to assess people's true abilities. Still, these research findings sound a warning bell. We must be rigorous in testing our perceptions and challenging our social biases to ensure that promotion decisions rely on proven ability and performance and not on perceptions of competence reinforced by skillful bluffing. We're not vervet monkeys, after all.

SUMMARY: A BALANCING ACT

We work with many organizations whose promotion process frequently puts highly qualified technicians into managerial roles where they fail, or at least underperform. Managers, the Human Resources department, and executives all acknowledge the problem. There are many possible causal pathologies: expediency, believing that direct production is all that really counts, concluding that managers really don't matter if organizations have charismatic senior leaders. Sometimes, organizations program the manager's job to fail by promoting the right person but subsequently failing to define the job sensibly or support it effectively.

The goal of this chapter has been to propose a systems approach to defining the major elements of the manager's role. The analysis reflects sensitivity to the assumptions many organizations bring to their conceptions of what managers are supposed to do and how they are supposed to do it. Types of skills, reporting spans, and balancing work and leadership must all be considered. The point is to look at these factors together and consider how they influence each other rather than making decisions that rely too heavily on a single factor (the belief that flatter organizations are *ipso facto* better organizations, for example). The prize is a role definition that makes it possible for managers to execute the elements depicted in the manager performance model in Chapter Three. Some juggling and balancing are inevitable in the manager's job, but a thoughtful approach to defining the position can make managers' lives easier and maximize their contribution to the organization's strategic advantage.

Not long ago, one author (Tom) had the opportunity to hear a panel of millennials describe their actual and ideal work experience. They were in their early-to-mid twenties, most working at their first or second job out of college or graduate school. Someone in the audience asked them to describe their perfect supervisor. A young woman from Korea answered the question by defining both her worst boss and her best boss. Her definition incorporated two simple dimensions, shown in Exhibit 4.4.

Exhibit 4.4: Best Boss and Worst Boss

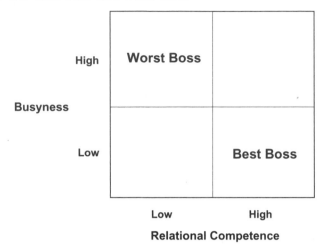

Her worst boss stayed too busy doing work to spend time with her. Also, he lacked the relational attributes necessary to make the time he did spend with her truly beneficial. Her best boss had freed himself from production pressure and increased his time available for personal connection. He also displayed the empathy required to coach her effectively. Empathy denotes the ability to comprehend what another person is experiencing and, on some level, to share the other's emotional state without having gone through the same causal events. The best boss represented the paradigm of the offstage manager: available when needed but not hovering; not too busy, either with increasing his own output or closely overseeing work, to have frequent employee contact; and qualified to make the most of the time spent with each individual.

The next step is to explore how managers in a well-structured role system go about executing tasks, developing people, delivering an engaging deal, and energizing change, all while fostering trust and acting authentically. We begin that exploration in Chapter Five.

Part II
Implementation

CHAPTER OUTLINE

Planning Work

Develop Causal Maps

Analyze Results from a Reference Class of Projects

Engage in Counterfactual Thinking

Clarifying Job Roles

Customize Individual Jobs

Recognize Who Can, Should, and Wants to Do What

Make Teamwork Work

Carefully Catalyze Self-Managing Teams

Monitoring Progress

5

Executing Tasks

What do the Egyptian pharaoh Cheops and the American psychologist Abraham Maslow have in common? Both are known for their pyramids. Cheops completed construction on his monument, the Great Pyramid of Giza, about 4,500 years ago. He intended to be buried in it, along with all the treasures and supplies he would need in the afterlife. How well he accomplished his intentions we'll never know; grave robbers stripped the Great Pyramid clean of all valuables long before modern archaeologists arrived on the scene.

Maslow's pyramid, which he described in a 1943 paper, has a purpose both loftier and more earthbound. Maslow created his pyramid to depict his conception of the hierarchy of human needs. At the base of his pyramid lie physiological needs—food, water, and air, for example. The pyramid extends upward four more levels, encompassing, in order, the need for safety, belonging, esteem and, finally, self-actualization. The pyramid form captures Maslow's notion that people don't (indeed, can't) attend to a higher-level need until they fulfill the requirements below it. Though he didn't invent the notion of self-actualization, Maslow's pyramid of needs brought it into the forefront of psychological theory. He defined self-actualization as the individual's striving to become more and more what he or she is, to become everything that one is capable of becoming.[1]

The decades have largely been kind to Maslow's concepts. Self-actualization remains a critical element in the design of engaging work. We will keep this in mind as we define the manager's role in the execution of tasks. We will also return to the principle established in the first three chapters—that the most effective managers work away from center stage—and see how it applies to the manager's role in the fundamental components of task execution. We will focus on three elements of task execution: planning work, defining and clarifying work roles, and monitoring progress.

Planning Work

Planning in a modern enterprise traces its roots back to methodologies and approaches developed by Frederick W. Taylor and Henry Ford in the early twentieth century. Their legacy includes an array of tools for doing the objective-setting, resource-allocating, and step-defining aspects of planning. Most of us would agree that the tools available for planning work provide more than enough functional support. The problem with planning isn't the tools, nor is it the intelligence of planners. When planning fails (that is, when work doesn't proceed as anticipated and workgroups miss deadlines, production quotas, or quality goals), the problem usually lies not in our tools, but in ourselves.

Psychologists know that we humans give ourselves far too much credit for our ability to perform rational analysis. In fact, our reasoning is fraught with deviations in judgment, cognitive faults that influence how we perceive the world and act on our perceptions. From the list of logical fallacies to which humans (and therefore managers) are heir, three have a direct effect on work and project planning:

- *The framing effect.* Drawing different conclusions or taking different actions from a single set of facts, depending on the how facts are presented or labeled. For example, do you feel better about the use of the same amount of taxpayer dollars for *economic stimulus* or for *bailouts*? Which career path would you rather your lawyer daughter pursue, *ambulance chaser* or *public protection attorney*?

- *The illusion of control.* Believing that we can direct, or at least influence, events over which we actually have no power. Those afflicted with this fallacy include gamblers who throw the dice harder to roll higher numbers and lottery ticket buyers who choose lucky numbers from among their children's birthdates.

- *The planning fallacy.* Consistently underestimating the time and cost required to complete a task. The planning fallacy seems particularly to affect public servants. It explains why infrastructure projects rarely come in on time and within budget.

These biases influence how managers and other humans instinctively approach planning. We all experience them to a greater or lesser degree. We must recognize and deal with them if we are to succeed at the basic tasks of goal setting, resource planning, and action taking, no matter what competitive strategy we hope to execute. Fortunately, the work of psychologists gives us tools we can use to battle our biases and inject an element of rational thought into work planning.

Develop Causal Maps

We can deal with the framing bias, for example, by recasting our language and by using a technique called causal mapping. A causal map (which can take a visual or verbal form—the term *map* is a metaphor) requires one to identify the true antecedents, actions, and consequences associated with a situation.[2] Reframing calls for a revised description of those facts. Here, for example, is one way of describing a research project:

> The client is a technology company that recently went through an initial public offering. The project involves an extensive customer survey to determine how well the organization is serving its business clients. The project will produce $1 million in revenue for the research firm doing

the survey. It has a 67 percent probability of generating a 40 percent profit and a 33 percent probability of producing a 40 percent loss. The firm normally wouldn't take a project without a virtual certainty of at least a 25 percent margin. The client organization is known for political infighting, which will make the project difficult to manage and not much fun to execute.

Here's another way to look at it:

The effort would be one of several similar projects the research company has going with this client. If the researchers can establish themselves as the client's provider of choice, they will have a unique understanding of the client's business and access to its data. This will enable the firm to put up barriers to exit for the client, and barriers to entry for competitors, and significantly increase the probability of securing repeat versions of the project. The research firm currently enjoys consistent 30 percent profits on other work for this organization. The relationship manager for this client has a personal goal of 25 percent margins on all of his projects. He made partner largely because of his successful management of this relationship.

The first framing leads to a no-go decision. The second calls for a different conclusion, particularly if the project manager has dreams of following the relationship manager's path to partnership.

If the firm should decide to proceed, the project manager and her team can then go through the causal mapping exercise. Doing so would help them determine how best to minimize the anticipated problems and increase the probability of a mutually satisfactory outcome. After reflection, for example, the team might conclude that the client organization's evolving, unstable, post-IPO culture poses the risk that internal politics could disrupt the project. The response might be to staff the project with consultants who have worked with this client on similar projects before. They know the methodologies required, understand the organization's cultural landscape, and have credibility with the client-side project manager. This combination should help the consulting team anticipate and deal with client politics that threaten to interfere with the project. Similarly, mapping the project would help the consulting team identify where in the project timeline lie the greatest risks that an undisciplined client could fundamentally redefine the project's requirements. Armed with this information—a map of virtual landmines, so to speak—the team might decide to price the project flexibly (time and expense) rather than rigidly (fixed fee) to protect their firm from unexpected scope changes. The team could also plot the key decision-making contingencies on the project time line. By doing this, they could highlight the financial and project quality implications of hitting, or missing, major project milestones.

Analyze Results from a Reference Class of Projects

Reframing and causal mapping take managers and their teams through a clarifying exercise that gets beneath the surface of the framing bias. Approaches like these help managers and their teams to identify the true risks associated with planned work. But even a carefully crafted causal map won't be worth the pixels it's printed with if it fails to produce a realistic estimate of the time and resources required to get work done. Managers also need a way to force reality into the project outcome estimates. One approach, called reference class forecasting, can help managers overcome the unjustified optimism that underlies the planning bias.

Reference class forecasting uses the actual outcomes of a group of similar actions to provide a context for a project under consideration. In effect, it provides an outside view that helps prevent some of the misestimation that often characterizes purely inside views. Reference class forecasting does this by taking the planner through three steps:

1. Identification of a group of similar past projects from a class large enough to be meaningful but also narrow enough to be comparable with the target effort

2. Establishment of a probability distribution for the outcome in question (say, profitability, minimization of defects, customer satisfaction) using results data from the reference class

3. Comparison of the specific project with the reference class distribution, to identify the most likely outcome[3]

The first use of reference class forecasting to challenge the planning bias occurred in 2004 as part of the budgeting process for a public transportation project in Edinburgh, Scotland. The promoter of the project, Transportation Initiatives Edinburgh, had submitted a business case estimating the project would come in at £255 million. With a contingency allowance of £64 million, the total project estimate came to about £320 million in capital cost. After considering a reference class of similar projects, a firm of consulting engineers recommended that the transportation authority raise its estimate to £400 million—a 25 percent increase—if it wanted to have an 80 percent probability of staying within the budget.[4]

Admittedly, most managers aren't dealing with financial numbers this big. Still, the need to budget accurately and then meet the budget remains central to managerial success. Avoiding an £80 million overrun just might save some politician his job. Techniques like reference class forecasting can enable a manager to suspend her natural (and often cognitively flawed) judgments and look for outside evidence that provides a more accurate context for planning.

In applying reference class forecasting to the research project, the team would begin by identifying the consulting costs to complete a group of similar past projects. They might discover, for example, a tendency to overrun consulting budgets by an average of 12 percent on those projects. Therefore, they might decide to raise their cost estimate by 15 percent, factoring in the vicissitudes of this particular organization's unpredictable politics. They could incorporate even more aggressive adjustments if they wanted to make doubly sure not to underestimate costs or overestimate profits.

Engage in Counterfactual Thinking

Techniques like causal mapping and reference class forecasting can help managers overcome framing and planning biases. But what should they do to deal with the illusion of control? Having a carefully crafted project map, complete with all the up-and-down topography of a challenging project, might actually heighten a manager's feeling of influence over circumstances and outcomes. But that confidence might be an illusion, just like thinking that throwing the dice harder will produce more elevens. Managers also need a way to reflect back on real events and to imagine what might have changed the outcomes. One way to do this is to engage in a mind experiment called counterfactual thinking.

Counterfactual thinking simply means comparing what actually happened in a situation with what might have been had past circumstances unfolded differently.[5] It involves reviewing a chain of events, mentally altering something in the action sequence, and imaging how the outcome would have differed. Often, reflecting back and creating "if-only" scenarios can compel a realistic reassessment that challenges an individual's illusion of control. In reviewing the outcomes of similar efforts in the reference class, the research project team might reaffirm a tendency for similar projects to produce cost overruns. A causal map might reveal that falling behind in producing the final analysis and report, and having to scramble to hit the deadline, consistently caused those overruns. Our project manager might start by looking for things she could have done differently. She might order a round of lattes, convene her team, and run through a set of if-only scenarios like these:

- "If only we had brought together larger project teams—perhaps we could have gotten more analysis and report production done more quickly. But that would only have added to our project cost and reduced our profitability even further. Plus we would have gotten in each other's way. After all, nine women can't have a baby in one month."

- "If only we had gotten the team to work longer hours early in the project so we could have avoided falling behind. But that would only have burned us all out sooner and made us more prone to errors that had to be corrected later. And imagine the cost of all that after-hours pizza."

- "If only clients would give us a cleaner file of survey participants' locations and e-mail addresses at the front end of the process. We could get surveys out in the field sooner, spend less nonproductive time correcting survey administration errors, and hit our deadlines."

The manager—and probably the team as well—would likely conclude that the last scenario provides the best solution to the problem. In the process, the project manager would realize that she never had complete control over the outcomes. And so the illusion of control bites the dust. In the future, she would have to work more closely and effectively with others who have influence over project results (specifically, the client's project manager).

Causal mapping, reference class forecasting, and counterfactual thinking complement each other. Reframing and causal mapping require us to challenge the way we look at facts and get beyond the labels that bias our judgment. Reference class assessments force us to look at relevant past outcomes and push us to revise our typically optimistic initial projections. Counterfactual thinking supports our causal mapping by providing scenarios that lead to outcomes different from those actually experienced. Each technique, in its way, reinforces the balanced processing element of manager authenticity—the requirement that a manager objectively analyze all available information, especially facts and insights that challenge assumptions. These approaches require a manager to have sufficient self-awareness (another authenticity element) to recognize and address his own cognitive weaknesses. They also call for no small amount of humility; a successful offstage manager recognizes that overcoming cognitive biases usually requires help from others.

By themselves, techniques like these won't magically turn managers into thoroughly rational thinkers. It will take a few million more years of evolution to accomplish that. Moreover, overcoming judgment biases is a necessary but not sufficient requirement for successful work planning. A manager's approach to planning must be part of a broader philosophy for how work should get done. That approach should acknowledge that the best (that is, the least cognitively biased) planning, like other aspects of the manager's job, happens when managers have a light hand and when they involve others. In the time allocation structure laid out in Chapter Four, planning activities falls into the work process oversight category. Of course, work planning efforts must dovetail with the manager's other responsibilities, especially those associated with people focus. Ensuring that these role elements mesh effectively provides a platform for unit and individual success.

MANAGER COMMUNICATION IN A MEDIA-RICH WORK ENVIRONMENT

For managers to play their task execution role—or any role, for that matter—requires constant communication with employees. The manager's role as communicator has coevolved with the burgeoning of media that connect people in the workplace. For some topics, employees express a clear preference for information sources other than their immediate managers. When it comes to getting fast-breaking news or fact-heavy information about benefit plans, employees choose electronic sources over conversations with their direct supervisors. However, for information about more personal topics—career development advice, explanation of how an individual's job contributes to unit and company success, details of incentive payouts—employees look to personal connections with their immediate managers. In these areas, explanation and context are important. Personal dialogue fills this need. As one employee communications expert says, "Employees still rely on their managers for direction and interpretation, but the intranets are displacing managers' role as human filing cabinets."[6]

(Continued)

As the communication landscape continues to change, driven by social networking and whatever technology follows that, how will the communications role of managers continue to morph? Social networking introduces a new inflection on an old issue: how to handle the overlap between work and personal life, between sharing information with workplace colleagues and staying in touch with friends and family during work hours. If a manager and employee together have created a challenging, fulfilling job, then isn't interpersonal contact through social media just another part of the landscape at work? One blogger refers to a few minutes of checking a social networking site as "the new cigarette break," a five-minute space for taking a deep breath and clearing the mind.[7] The growing ubiquity of social media doesn't fundamentally change the manager's responsibility regarding employees' personal connections at or away from the job. A manager should have no greater need to closely monitor employees' electronic conversations than she would the old fashioned face-to-face or telephonic ones. After all, why would a successfully contributing employee suddenly lose all self-control, time-management ability, and judgment just because a new way to gossip has entered the work scene? Conversely, if poor performance is an issue, is wasting time with Facebook or Twitter likely to be the root cause?

Social networking does put a different spin on the personal connection between employee and manager. Should a manager friend an employee on Facebook? How should an employee respond to that outreach? True, this transaction is digitally mediated, but is it really any different from any other personal relationship question between supervisor and employee? Wouldn't the same rules of thumb apply in both situations? Beyond the policy issues of acceptable cyber-behavior and corporate citizenship, shouldn't "use good judgment" be the only rule managers and employees need?

Clarifying Job Roles

Once the planning is finished, there's work to be done. Decades of research have shown that challenging and gratifying work contributes significantly toward motivating employees to do the jobs required by organizations. The challenge we pose to managers is this: think of employees' jobs as malleable sets of factors, parts to be assembled to fit individual traits and simultaneously meet organizational goals.

As with work planning, managers must overcome a set of cognitive and attitudinal biases as they work with employees to design jobs. These two are particularly relevant:

- *The actor-observer bias.* Tending to attribute our own actions to situational factors and attribute the behavior of others to stable personality traits. If I feel stress before a big presentation, for example, I might ascribe it to my concern that this session will be attended by important clients, a circumstance I use to explain my sweaty palms. Conversely, if I see a colleague showing obvious nervousness before a big speech, I might put it down to his having low self-confidence. I know I'm a great presenter; I'm not so sure about him.

- *The illusion of transparency.* Overestimating our ability to understand others' personal mental states. We believe that we know others better than they know us. In a related way, people tend to think of themselves as having complex and variable personalities, while viewing others as simpler and more predictable. Don't we all think we understand the world better than the world understands us?

These biases threaten to impede managers' efforts to perceive accurately the complex needs and competencies of those around them and to use those insights to craft suitable work roles. Fortunately, managers have at their disposal some cognitive techniques that can help them succeed at their job-crafting tasks and avoid the worst effects of the actor-observer bias and the illusion of transparency.

Customize Individual Jobs

A customized role never leaps fully formed from the pages of a job description. In fact, just the opposite. Job descriptions are often works of fiction—outdated, oversimplified, sometimes wildly inaccurate snapshots of work realities. Human Resources should provide managers with the formal job specifications for the positions in the unit, but only as a point of departure. Manager and employee must look well beyond the words on the page and consider a variety of dimensions that meet at the intersection of required tasks and individual interests and abilities. At the most fundamental level, the basic elements of a job must align with the interests of the job holder. The several typologies of job components tend to agree that people's work-related interests will fall into the general categories shown in Table 5.1.

By listening to employees talk about what they like and don't like, observing how they go about their work, and perhaps running some experiments (for instance, letting people try small changes in their jobs), an astute manager can help people achieve a fit between their jobs and their work interests. With attention, most managers can figure out which employees display quantitative talent, which are conceptual thinkers, and which are most creative. The same goes for the social elements of work. Whether a person seeks or avoids social contact, displays an agreeable nature or likes to work alone, or has a calm demeanor or is prone to anxiety are all empirical questions. Careful observation and manager-employee cooperation can provide answers and help managers overcome the actor-observer and transparency biases.

In addition to these personal building blocks, managers must consider important dimensions of jobs themselves. One dimension is *job demand*, the magnitude of sustained mental or physical effort required to execute the basic job components. Job demands are high when the job holder faces frequent challenges and problems: pressure to perform, long task lists, complex role requirements, and emotional stress. Job demand is complemented by *job resources:* support from

Table 5.1: Individual Interests and What They Mean for Jobs[8]

If the Employee's Interests Lean Toward Jobs with These Elements:	She'll Get Her Kicks From:
Technical/engineering	Developing and executing systems and processes
Quantitative	Manipulating data and explaining things numerically
Conceptual	Doing research and explaining things theoretically
Creative/innovative	Inventing something new
Social/interpersonal	Connecting with others and improving their abilities and performance
Organizational control	Achieving success by overseeing others
Influencing	Affecting outcomes through communicative persuasion
Detailed analysis/execution	Flawlessly implementing existing systems and structures

teammates, problem-solving assistance from a supervisor, performance feedback (especially recognition for success), and autonomy in how they go about their work. These complement the tangible resources noted in the prior chapter's discussion of the interplay between manager and employee roles. Access to job resources helps people manage large workloads and juggle disparate assignments. They do a better job of handling emotional interactions with customers and reconciling work and home responsibilities. Said another way, job resources help to buffer the effects of work demands, reduce obstacles to performance, and bolster employee engagement in the face of stressful work requirements.[9]

Fostering autonomy requires managers to recognize and support individuals' discretion and control in deciding how to do their work. Autonomy differs in subtle but important ways from empowerment. *Empowerment* has become so common in the business lexicon that it hardly needs a definition, and so cries out for one. When people speak of empowerment, they generally refer to the transfer of power from a manager to an employee. The root words are *em* (from the Latin preposition meaning into) and *power* (from the Latin *potere*, to be able, from which we get words like potent). Empowerment refers to the transfer of a quantity of power from manager to employee. It's a zero-sum power game, where the manager's power diminishes by the amount given to the employee. Jonathan Gosling and Henry Mintzberg recommend that managers go beyond empowerment, "a word implying that the people who know the work best must somehow receive the blessing of their managers to do it."[10]

Autonomy refers to something subtly but importantly different. Essentially, it means self-rule. Its roots are the Greek words *auto* (self) and *nomy* (law). Rather than subdividing a given quantity of power, autonomy adds to the total amount of power available to do work. Self-determination is a good synonym. Think of it this way—a royal authority can empower, whereas autonomy requires self-government.

Although the results of empowering and fostering autonomy may seem similar, the dialogue that precedes them is different. The empowerment exchange between manager and employee sounds like this:

Manager: "I have power and I am transferring some of it to you."

Employee: "Thanks, boss."

The autonomy dialogue unfolds differently:

Manager: "You are competent and engaged in your work. You know the results that are expected. How do you want to do your job?"

Employee: "I'll get back to you."

Creating the conditions for autonomy to thrive requires special attention from managers. People can be empowered in small increments, but autonomy is difficult to partition. In general, people either have autonomy in how they do their work, or they don't. Effective autonomy requires the characteristics of the job to complement those of the individual. The work and work environment specifications most critical to autonomy are:

- *Ease of information access,* meaning how readily an employee can obtain the data and knowledge needed to perform his job. For autonomous work, information becomes a critically important job resource. High access means the information is easily available, with low cost of effort and time required to obtain and interpret it. Low access implies the opposite—information is difficult to get and therefore calls for a high investment of effort to acquire and make sense of it.

- *Employee expertise* indicates the degree to which the individual, by virtue of training or experience, has substantial skill and knowledge to apply to the job. In the ideal situation, the employee knows more about the job than does the supervisor. In highly technical research and development positions, for example, researchers often have greater skill and expertise in their specific disciplines than do their equally well-educated but less-specialized supervisors. If the employee doesn't possess expertise at least as great as that of the manager, autonomy will be ineffective and ultimately frustrating for both.

- *Task independence* indicates the interconnectedness among jobs. Highly independent jobs (as with a sales group in which each rep has a different product line) afford more opportunity for autonomy than jobs that function more interdependently (for instance, two programmers writing complementary code for the same program).

- *Task variability* speaks to the breadth of activity and the frequency of exceptional situations built into a job. Highly variable jobs (like those typical of lawyers and consultants) benefit from autonomy. In contrast, people whose jobs consist of relatively routine tasks that don't vary much from day to day (office receptionists, for example) gain little from autonomy.

- *Work process freedom,* referring to the degree of informality, creativity, and improvisation available in a job. Fewer rules, regulations and stipulations suggest an opportunity for autonomy. Conversely, high formalization (for example, in a position requiring rigid safety or quality procedures) limits an individual's freedom to exercise discretion on the job.[11]

In effect, autonomy serves two functions: it is a feature of a rewarding job and a reward unto itself. Although autonomy clearly has value to employees, it isn't free. It requires a cognitive investment and brings responsibility for outcomes. Conversely, it can moderate the relationship between the accountability burden that comes with self-determination and the emotional stress brought on by the weight of obligations.[12] Effectively autonomous employees also confer a benefit on the organization. They enable managers to spend less time performing and closely overseeing work and more time thinking about how to improve work processes, build networks, and craft and deliver appealing individual deals for employees. In effect, employee autonomy moves managers away from the Widget Wizard role structure and toward the People Powermeister form.

The effects of job demands and job resources will naturally vary from person to person. This is where an additional element, *individual disposition*, enters the equation. In this context, disposition refers to the tendency for people to be either proactive or passive. Proactive people believe they can control circumstances and create change in the work environment. They adopt what psychologists call a "promotion focus," meaning they exhibit persistence, motivation, flexibility in the face of challenges, and, generally, satisfaction with their work. They tend to be extroverts, seeking social contacts and looking for excitement. Managers will recognize them as the optimists who concentrate on winning and want to receive rewards for their success. Passive employees, in contrast, tend to view opportunities for change as beyond their personal scope and ability. They respond to circumstances as they occur and hope for the best. They display vigilance, risk-aversion, and loss-avoidance.[13]

So the full equation contains three factors: job demands, job resources, and personal disposition. The interaction among these three elements yields outcomes in five categories:

- *Comfort* measures the contentment that people experience at work, the absence of anxiety, tension, and worry that are beyond their ability to handle; high comfort means stress is manageable and often energizing, but not absent.

- *Learning* means the opportunity for people to acquire and use the abilities necessary to perform demanding tasks (to build human capital, in other words)

- *Confidence to execute* (which psychologists call self-efficacy) goes to the employee's belief that he or she has the knowledge and skills necessary to get a specific job done well.

- *Ownership of results* refers to the strength of an individual's sense of responsibility for the performance of the production process.

- *Engagement* means the emotional, rational, and motivational connections people have with their organizations and their work.

The chart in Exhibit 5.1 shows how these factors interact for people who have a strong inclination to influence their work environments (that is, people who exhibit high proactivity, flexibility, and motivation to succeed). Note the cluster of dark bullets in the Fulfilling Job column. For these employees, confidence in their ability to execute, ownership of outcomes, and engagement all peak when their managers take the

Exhibit 5.1: Proactive Employees Thrive with High Control and
              Challenging Work

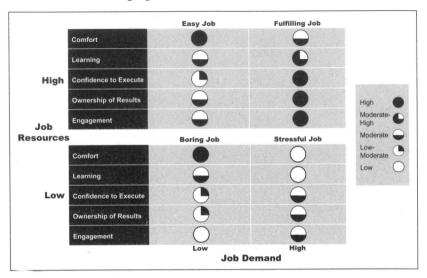

Source: Adapted from Parker, S. K., and Sprigg, C. A., "Minimizing Strain and
Maximizing Learning: The Role of Job Demands, Job Control, and Proactive
Personality," *Journal of Applied Psychology*, 1999, 84(6), 936–937.

time to ensure that competencies, roles, and resources come together to
give them high control over a challenging job. Alternatively, given low
control or less-demanding work, a naturally proactive person will generally reach lower levels of mastery, achieve lower levels of confidence in
personal effectiveness, assume less ownership of results, and feel less
engaged. Efforts to achieve self-actualization will be thwarted.

Job content also plays a role in determining how well employees
understand and respond to the link between their work and organizationally valued outcomes. For example, ensuring that people have periodic contact with the beneficiaries of their efforts can have a powerful
effect on effort and performance. In one study, researchers introduced
a group of university fundraisers (the folks who call during dinner to
ask you to contribute to your alma mater) to one of the scholarship
recipients who had benefited from their money-raising success. He told

them how much he valued their effort and how helpful the scholarship money had been to him. A month later, the research team measured the performance of the fundraisers over a week's time. They looked for differences among three groups: a group that had met with the student, one that read a letter from the student, and one that had no contact at all. They found that the fundraisers who had spent time with the student more than doubled their per-caller minutes over what they had spent before meeting him. They also secured almost three times as much money as they previously had. The researchers concluded, "Merely interacting respectfully with a beneficiary of their work enabled them to maintain their motivation, as observed in their persistence behavior and objective job performance."[14]

Exhibit 5.2 shows the same array of job factors for more passive employees, those who focus their attention on preventing downside

Exhibit 5.2: Passive Employees Seek Lower Demands—But Still Value Control

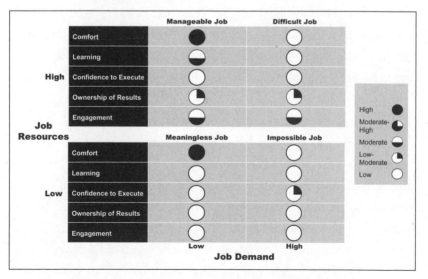

Source: Adapted from Parker, S. K., and Sprigg, C. A., "Minimizing Strain and Maximizing Learning: The Role of Job Demands, Job Control, and Proactive Personality," *Journal of Applied Psychology*, 1999, 84(6), 936–937.

events. They function best with low job demands and high control (the Manageable Job depicted in the left-hand column). Too much challenge causes discomfort and tension. Even given their relatively passive personalities, however, these employees learn more, take greater ownership of results, and exhibit higher engagement when they have direct influence over the circumstances of work.

The common factor for the most rewarding work, regardless of individual personality, is control over results. Jobs structured to incorporate this element, and the other elements depicted in the exhibits, can provide the skill development, decision input, career advancement, and work opportunities that people crave. Research in the workplace (as with one analysis conducted in the call centers of a British financial institution) confirms that this combination of factors also produces high performance.[15] Call center jobs, the research confirmed, can be stressful and unfulfilling. Astutely managed companies, however, can bolster the resource side of the equation and improve both individual performance and customer satisfaction.

For example, consider the case of Zappos, the quirky online retailer. Zappos has probably moved as far from the call-center-as-electronic-sweatshop as it's possible to go. In fact, Zappos is such an appealing place to work that it debuted at number 23 on the 2008 *Fortune* list of the best companies to work for, the highest newcomer ranking in the history of the list.

The Zappos approach shows how job design can support a customer focus strategy. The call center rep's job structure lies at the center of the company's service model. The organization begins by taking potential hires through a careful screening process that eliminates the shy, the egotistical, and the unfunny. They want people from the proactive end of the personality spectrum only. "We do our best to hire positive people and put them in an environment where the positive thinking is reinforced," says Tony Hsieh, Zappos chief executive.[16] That environment is script-free and freedom-rich. The principal job of front-line reps is not just to close a sale, but also to please the people who call in to order.

They are trained to encourage callers to order more than one size or color, because Zappos pays for shipping both ways. They refer callers to competitors when Zappos is out of stock. But most important, their jobs are constructed to let them use their creativity and their imaginations to delight customers. In one case overheard by a magazine reporter, a customer complained that her boots from Zappos had begun leaking after almost a year of use. The rep not only sent out a new pair, in spite of a policy that used shoes can't be returned, but also mailed the customer a handwritten thank-you note.[17] Rumor has it that a Zappos call center rep once spent six hours on the telephone with a single customer. This kind of initiative, combined with a job structure that affords the freedom to exercise it, captures what Zappos means by WOW: "To WOW, you must differentiate yourself, which means doing something a little unconventional and innovative. . . . We are not an average company, our service is not average, and we don't want our people to be average. We expect every employee to deliver WOW."[18]

Zappos managers are also encouraged to spend 10 to 20 percent of their time with team members outside the office. This intensive interaction enables managers to get to know their team members far better than they can in the context of work alone. CEO Hsieh says that when he confers with managers after they've taken their team members on an outing, they talk about improved communication, higher trust, and budding friendships. "Then we ask, 'How much more efficient do you think your team is now?'" Hsieh says. The answer? "Anywhere from 20 percent to 100 percent."[19]

As the Zappos example suggests, designing engaging jobs doesn't have to be limited to high-end knowledge work. Granted, research into engineering positions suggests that knowledge workers sometimes have more latitude than others to alter the boundaries of their roles by taking on unassigned tasks, teaching new skills to others, adding coworkers to their networks, and participating voluntarily on teams. But a study of hospital cleaning staff showed that, despite having a relatively prescribed set of tasks, even custodial workers can craft their jobs individually. One of the groups analyzed stayed with the standard job description, which involved little interaction with patients and other staff. They reported that they disliked cleaning in general, judged the required skill level to be low, and had little willingness to engage with others or alter job tasks. They saw their job as cleaning—nothing more. Members of a second group went out of their way to interact with patients, visitors, and others in their unit. They made an effort to add tasks and to time their work to coordinate with others. Cleaners who crafted their jobs saw themselves as playing an important role in the experience of patients.[20]

Or take the case of nurses, who can craft their jobs by creating expanded opportunities for interaction with other care providers and with patients' families. To quote the researchers from one ethnographic study, "The nurses acted as job crafters by actively managing the task boundary of the job to deliver the best possible patient care. By paying attention to the patient's world and conveying seemingly unimportant information to others on the care team, nurses re-created their job to be about patient advocacy, rather than the sole delivery of high-quality technical care."[21]

Employee and manager both have roles to play in customizing jobs. In the words of one pair of psychologists, "People are not passive receivers of information from their work environment, but rather active in interpreting their jobs, and consequently in shaping their jobs."[22] Another researcher says that "Not all employees are motivated to fulfill needs for control, positive image, and connection at work. Individuals who look to fulfill these needs at work likely will look for opportunities to craft their jobs in ways that allow them to meet their needs. Others may find that these needs are met elsewhere in their lives."[23] Only a direct manager—by empathizing with an employee's individual work needs, mediating within a work group to craft a set of personalized job demands, and ensuring that job roles support the successful execution of unit and enterprise strategy—can help an individual make the multidimensional matches reflected in Exhibits 5.1 and 5.2.

IMPROVING PERFORMANCE BY UPGRADING MANAGERS

Most companies aspire to have high-performance cultures. In our experience, only a few ever get beyond aspiration to action, and fewer still make it to achievement. One of those successful few is a company called Shutterfly, which uses its state-of-the-art manufacturing systems and innovative Web platform to make it easy for consumers to share, print, and preserve their digital photos in creative ways. From 2008 to 2009, senior management received notably higher employee survey scores for the way they articulated the organization's strategic vision, which centers on a combination of innovation and strong customer focus. Even more dramatic were better scores across the board for line manager performance. The survey respondents said the company's one hundred or so managers had improved significantly in:

- Explaining how individual work contributes to department success

- Providing employees with a range of assignments to enhance development

- Giving people regular information on their performance

- Explaining how the department contributes to overall company strategy

Through their responses, employees also gave managers the thumbs-up for crafting jobs that provide challenging and interesting work and making sure people have clearly defined performance goals and objectives.

Peter Navin, senior vice president of Human Resources at Shutterfly, explained how the organization achieved these improvements. The process began with the creation of a roadmap that

(Continued)

deliberately and clearly defined the company's path to a performance-focused culture. One element of the roadmap was a program called, "Drive a Culture of Great Leadership," which included competency models and performance management tools for all leaders across the organization. The performance management system was significantly upgraded to include a streamlined talent management review process tied to business results.

Few organizations ask managers to assess employee performance quarterly, and fewer still pay quarterly bonuses. Shutterfly does both, with bonuses dependent on the company's top-line revenue performance and achievement of goals for earnings before interest, taxes, depreciation, and amortization. "Previously," Navin said, "we paid only an annual bonus. Few employees understood our vision and strategy. Now we constantly connect a person's valuable contribution back to our overall strategy." An employee comment on the survey reinforces how well the message is hitting home: "The quarterly objective/bonus process is very helpful in driving toward a specific result and communicating the importance of a task and how that task fits in with the broader company goals. This has gone a long way toward clarifying everyone's points of focus."

The performance-enhancement process included manager training, but training didn't stop there. "We trained one hundred managers and then trained employees on the same topics the managers got. We're trying to build a culture where business objectives and leadership behaviors are part of our vernacular," Navin said.

Have Shutterfly's efforts to adopt a strategically focused performance culture paid off? Here's what Navin said: "We spent less money in marketing dollars last year and still grew revenue. We attribute that to continued innovation, supported by vision and clarity of purpose and great execution on behalf of our people."[24]

Recognize Who Can, Should, and Wants to Do What

In real life, few people sit squarely at one end or the other of the proactive–passive spectrum. As we saw in Chapter Two, most people experience some level of conflict as they choose between dominating and deferring. We want to lean far over to grab the brass ring, all the while holding tightly to the carousel horse's neck. Likewise, jobs rarely fall cleanly into either the "easy" or "impossible" categories. Managers must deal with ranges of factors for both people and their jobs. How can a manager get an accurate understanding of an individual's disposition and overcome the actor-observer and transparency biases? Research suggests that good judges of people do three things well. First, they create situations in which people manifest relevant clues to their personalities. Then, the skilled judges interpret those clues accurately and put them to use.[25] Table 5.2 summarizes how a manager might perform this sequence.

Good judges of personality have predictable traits. They tend to display:

- *Trustworthiness and fairness.* They make the people around them feel comfortable in being their authentic selves, which gives a manager access to accurate information.

- *Interpersonal awareness.* They have a heightened ability to acquire and interpret clues fully and accurately, which helps them recognize and assess the insights they obtain.

- *Sense of humor.* They have a relaxed style that puts employees at ease, an advantage in eliciting information on how people naturally behave.

- *Intelligence and intellectual complexity.* They have cognitive attributes that give them an advantage in interpreting clues and crafting jobs that accommodate individual personality.

- *Social skills.* They tend to be agreeable and extroverted, meaning they genuinely enjoy the interactions that produce personality information and have an interest in learning about the people around them.

Table 5.2: Three Steps to Understanding the Individual Personality

Step 1—Observation	Step 2—Interpretation	Step 3—Action
Manager question—How can I get information on what this person is about?	**Manager question**—What is the significance of what I've learned about this person?	**Manager question**—What actions should I take given the interpretations I've made?
Goal—Enlarge the number of relevant clues and bits of insight	**Goal**—Make sense of the information to draw correct conclusions about employee personality	**Goal**—Put the information to use for the benefit of the individual and the organization
Possible tactics:	**Possible follow-on questions:**	**Possible actions:**
Experimentation—Create situations for traits to appear. If these are true experiments, then performance failure will be treated as information, not a criterion for judgment	Do they act proactively or passively? Do they display psychological flexibility?	Job customization—craft a role that works for the person, the team, and the company
Observation—Watch how people handle their work, what energizes them, their demeanor, their interaction with others, their language, even their dress and appearance	Look for consistency—do patterns emerge? What behaviors are associated with what situations?	Place the job in the right context—individual versus team work structure, for example
Discussion—Talk to people and listen to them tell about their work. Extend observations over the long term, to improve quantity and reliability of information	Compare across team members—what similarities and differences do you see?	Support the job with the right employment deal

- *Flexibility.* They are willing to suspend premature judgment and interpretation (the application of balanced processing), which increases the probability that their ultimate judgments will be correct.

- *Self-awareness.* They understand their own personalities and so have a foundation for empathy and a frame of reference for interpreting the behaviors of others. Like balanced processing, self-awareness is an essential element of manager authenticity.

In short, they act authentically, observe astutely, and interpret accurately. Mostly, they are good listeners, and much more.

Make Teamwork Work

Sometimes, a team structure best meets the job-related needs of individuals and the strategic requirements of organizations. Structuring work in teams has become a ubiquitous artifact of organizational life. Effective team collaboration, says organizational and evolutionary psychologist Nigel Nicholson, is "widely attributed to be the single most important predictor of successful enterprise, and group breakdowns one of the most common causes of failure."[26]

Rarely do organizations dedicate themselves as thoroughly to a collaborative way of working as does high-tech icon Cisco Systems. Cisco, which makes the routers and switches that link networks and power the Internet, pursues a strategy relying on product differentiation bolstered by operational discipline. Connecting people and communities isn't just the competitive goal—it's also how the company does its work. Cisco pursues this strategy by arraying its units functionally. In the words of Randy Pond, Cisco's executive vice president of Operations, Processes, and Systems, "Cisco is the largest functionally organized company that I know of."[27] Functional organizations, which separate themselves into discrete areas like R&D, engineering, manufacturing, sales, and product development, sometimes have difficulty getting new products developed and delivered to the market. The organizational stovepipes are often so self-contained and impermeable that cooperation in the interest of a broader initiative—such as combining research expertise with product development insights—becomes next to impossible. That would be fatal for a company like Cisco, whose business relies on collaboration that drives innovation and new product introduction. So, rather than change to a fundamentally different structure (one based on lines of business, for example), the company has instituted an intricate system of committees made up of executives and managers from various functions. At the top of this structure are twelve councils, with an average of fourteen people each. Councils take charge of markets that could reach $10 billon in revenue. The small business segment, comprising companies with fewer than a hundred employees, is an example. Below the councils are some forty-seven boards, also with about a dozen members each. A board concentrates on market opportunities in the $1 billion neighborhood. Finally, working groups, small temporary teams that concentrate on individual projects, support the board and council structure.[28]

If this arrangement sounds like a matrix—point taken. Matrix structures are hardly new, and they don't come without complications. A matrix arrangement brings reporting ambiguities, as people try to figure out whether they answer mainly to their nominal manager or to a project manager for the team they've joined. It can also cause fights between managers as they duel for resources and jockey to position their projects at the head of the organizational queue. According to Nigel Nicholson, "The injection of matrix forms into traditional hierarchies typically fails because the pull of functional identity overrides the requirements of interdisciplinary collaboration."[29]

Interdisciplinary collaboration is precisely what Cisco needs to be the innovator it wants to be. So what does this all mean for managers and employees and their work? Managers must begin by deploying assets exceptionally well. The key assets under management are information and technology. Moreover, given a matrix structure, managers must do their asset deployment, as well as their coordinating and cultivating, in a focused but infrequent way. You might call it *punctuated management*—intense and vital contact between managers and employees, in an episodic form.

In another sense, the Cisco structure calls for a redefinition of *line* management. In this way of working, project managers oversee the execution of tasks by paying attention to:

- *Outlines.* Negotiated agreements between employees and managers, governing how work will get done
- *Time lines.* Agreed-upon calendars for the production of results
- *Deadlines.* Clear understanding of the final goal and its due date
- *Telephone lines.* Technology support to connect individuals and groups

This approach to configuring work calls for an extraordinary level of trust among managers and between managers and employees. Managers must have confidence that employees who are out of sight (except in a teleconference) are nevertheless working to their productive maximums. In effect, managers must fight against the illusion of control, since there's no way they can closely direct people who have many bosses. Employees, in turn, must trust their managers to perform a conscientious and comprehensive assessment of their work results, because those results will often be delivered to someone other than an employee's formal supervisor. Managers who share resources, including the human capital of employees in common, must negotiate for the use of those resources in good faith, with the greater good of the organization always forefront in their minds. As Cisco CEO John Chambers says, leading only the people reporting directly to them is not how Cisco managers should behave: "That's not what cross-functional leadership is about.... Whoever serves on each of these councils and boards and working groups, from each functional group, has to be able to speak for the whole group. Not go back and ask permission, but has to be able to speak for the group."[30]

Cisco would probably admit that the roles of supervisors and managers in its technology turbocharged matrix are still under construction. After all, laying a matrix on top of a functionally oriented pyramid calls for substantial focus and energy. For this reason, the council and board structure has taken from 2001 to 2009 to become fully effective. No doubt managers still struggle with player-coach responsibilities, and spans of control probably need to be worked out for various managerial positions. But one thing is clear: Cisco has decided that the collaborative, punctuated leadership and management encouraged (in fact, required) by its matrix structure are critical to acquiring and defending a differentiated product position. The competition is no pushover— companies like Hewlett-Packard and IBM aren't likely to let Cisco win without a fight. An innovative organizational architecture, with all it implies for leaders and managers at all levels, represents a key weapon in Cisco's competitive arsenal.

Carefully Catalyze Self-Managing Teams

Many organizations want to foster team-based collaboration without the complexities of a matrix approach. Some choose instead to institute self-managing teams. Like matrix configurations, self-managing teams are not new. And, like organizational matrices, they are easy to get wrong. Especially in organizations with cultures that encourage heavy manager direction or the opposite, unfettered individual initiative, autonomous teams can prove more frustrating than effective. The paradox of managing effectively from the sidelines has its quintessence in how supervisors build and work with self-managing teams.

A study done in the customer services division of Xerox Corporation explored the kind of manager behaviors that enhance or hinder the performance of self-managing work groups. Like Cisco, the modern incarnation of Xerox has chosen to pursue an innovation-intensive focus on product differentiation. Anne Mulcahy, former Xerox CEO, ensured that research and development would remain a continuing priority of the company. She is on record as emphasizing that Xerox is also dedicated to delivering a great customer experience. She came by her customer focus naturally, having started with Xerox as a sales representative in 1976.[31] If anything, her successor, Ursula Burns, is working to accelerate the company's progress toward higher revenue through tighter customer ties and more profitable products and services.[32]

At the time of the study, the Xerox service organization was divided into nine geographical areas that were in turn subdivided into districts and subdistricts. A manager headed up each subdistrict, which had twenty to thirty technicians apiece. Technicians worked in teams of between three and nine members. Their jobs were to respond to customer calls about machine breakdowns and visit customer sites to perform preventive maintenance. The study looked specifically at two forms of manager involvement with the teams: team design and manager coaching.

Thoughtfully designing a self-managing team involves a broad array of dimensions. The Xerox research team, headed by Dartmouth professor Ruth Wageman, looked at such design elements as:

- *Clarity of purpose.* The team knows what it is supposed to accomplish.
- *Stability of team membership.* The team has a consistent membership of between four and seven members who bring diverse task-relevant skills to the job.
- *Task interdependence.* The team's work requires a cooperative effort in order to be successful; work better done by individuals is excluded from the team's charter.
- *Meaningful goals.* The team has objective performance targets that are challenging but achievable.
- *Process agreement.* Team members agree about how they should work together, how much collaboration they need, how they should seek advice from other teams, and how much experimentation they should do with work procedures.

- *Supportive reward system.* Managers reward success, and 80 percent or more of the available rewards are contingent on team rather than individual performance.

- *Resource availability.* The team has access to plenty of information (such as trends in customer feedback and machine performance), training, and physical assets (tools and materials, for example).[33]

Different styles of manager coaching encompassed such elements as:

- *Informal rewards and cues.* Rewarding the group for problem solving and signaling, by spending time with the group rather than with individuals, clarifying that the team has responsibility for managing itself

- *Problem-solving consultation.* Broadening the group's repertoire of solution skills through teaching and facilitating troubleshooting sessions

- *Assistance with team process.* Surfacing and helping the team deal with intrateam disagreements and conflicts and reinforcing that specific individuals, or the manager herself, are mainly responsible for overseeing the team's work

- *Intervening in tasks.* Dealing directly with customers without involving the team

- *Identifying team problems.* Pointing out concerns or shortcomings in team performance[34]

The research team classified the first two forms of manager coaching—providing autonomy-reinforcing rewards and building the group's toolkit of skills—as "positive coaching." Conversely, two other elements—intervening in tasks and pointing out the team's problems—tended to reduce the team's sense of collective responsibility. The researchers labeled these "negative coaching."[35]

The Dartmouth group assessed team performance by looking at such factors as customer satisfaction with service; parts expense; time to respond to customer calls and complete repairs; and machine reliability. The team came to a conclusion that at first seems surprising but makes sense on further reflection: no form of manager coaching improved team performance. The coaching elements that the researchers called positive coaching were associated with overall levels of successful team self-management and quality of group process. But they had no significant correlation with achievement of objective performance standards. In contrast, teams that were designed well (had a clear statement of purpose, consistently worked interdependently on tasks, executed a strategy of sharing successful practices, and benefited from a team-oriented reward system) *did* perform better.[36] The takeaway for managers: create the architecture for self-managing teams carefully and then honor the concept of self-management. Be a good manager by providing information and material resources. Be a good leader by providing direction, establishing clear and challenging goals, helping when the team needs to get over process hurdles, and rewarding the team when it succeeds— but only as a group. Otherwise stay out of the way.

Monitoring Progress

Monitoring work progress and results, the third dimension of the manager's task-execution responsibilities, should directly reflect the logic established in work planning and job role clarification. In a product-differentiation strategy, for example, innovation matters. Therefore, the manager of the R&D unit will pay special attention to metrics indicating successful new product commercialization. Individual and team work flows will be structured to focus attention on product development, and customized jobs will provide for the free-flowing creativity necessary to inspire innovation. With a customer-focused retailing strategy, buyer satisfaction and repeat purchasing drive success; measures of these factors will rise to the top of the manager's scorecard. Store schedules will put the best salespeople on the floor during peak periods of customer flow. Sales jobs will be streamlined so people can pay close attention to buyer

needs without other distractions, thereby increasing the customer satisfaction and sales-per-customer measures. If low-cost product and service
delivery define an organization's strategic intent, managers will pay
attention to measures that indicate productivity and minimization of
waste. Managers will ensure that job demands and resources are balanced
to make high-output work sustainable.

Monitoring work results brings the risk of falling victim to a
particular measurement fallacy. We call it the lost-keys-under-the-
streetlight fallacy—the tendency to measure what's easy to quantify,
rather than what matters, like the man searching under a bright light
for the keys he dropped three blocks away. When it comes to remaining
vigilant about the streetlight measurement tendency, few organizations
face greater challenges than do call centers. They typically monitor a
dizzying array of numbers, from call waiting time to call resolution
time to customer attitudes, with variations and permutations of
many metrics. Some yield insights, while others are merely easy to
capture.

For the most part, measures fall into one of two categories: call
handling efficiency and customer satisfaction. In a study by the
International Customer Management Institute (ICMI), respondents
said that the most common service measure is percentage of calls handled
within twenty seconds. The goal is typically 80 percent.[37] Only about
40 percent of call centers measure first-contact resolution (FCR), a more
important indicator of customer service performance. FCR has links
with enhanced customer satisfaction, greater agent satisfaction, increased
revenue generation, and (surprise) lower operating costs.[38]

The Philippines-based call center organization eTelecare has taken
measurement beyond call handling time and even beyond FCR.
Managers pay especially close attention to cost per resolution. This
measure incorporates the cost of call center operations required to handle
a call (including subsequent calls to take care of the same problem) as
well as the expense associated with dispatching the call for further resolution steps. In handling technical support for a major U.S. electronics

manufacturer, the company reduced cost per resolution to 40 percent less than the client company had achieved in its own U.S. call center. eTelecare delivered a cost per resolution 30 percent below U.S. call center outsourcers and 16 percent less than the electronics company's call center operation in India.[39]

The company's success demonstrates what can happen when an organization achieves clarity about its strategy, measures what matters to clients, and then supports the strategy with a supervisor role that makes human capital a competitive advantage. Supervisors at eTelecare invest an hour a week coaching each employee, on top of the time they spend monitoring employee performance. They also put at least 10 percent of their time each week into developing process improvements.[40]

eTelecare has garnered a long string of awards that attest to the high-quality service its CSRs provide. The organization won a 2009 customer relationship management award from *Customer Interaction Solutions* magazine. The company has also received multiple Best Outsourcer awards at the International Call Center Management Conference. As founder Derek Holley says, "Our clients don't just come to us because of our cost advantage relative to their in-house U.S. operations, they want to be sure that we will deliver superior service to their customers. They stay with us because they simply can't replicate our service levels in their own operations."[41]

SUMMARY: MANAGER AS ETHNOGRAPHER

What seem like the most pedestrian of manager responsibilities—planning work and getting it executed—turn out to comprise a complex set of intellectual and psychological requirements. Performing this role calls for managers to be insightful observers of human personality and behavior—to be field researchers in their own tribes, so to speak. Using the information they gather from living with their work groups, high-performing managers will:

- Not just use planning tools effectively, but also challenge the intellectual biases and perceptual shortcomings that undercut sound use of those tools

- Not just ensure fair workload distribution, but also involve individuals in crafting their jobs and deciding how their work can best be accomplished to achieve strategic goals

- Not just treat all employees equally well, but also go beyond equity to individual focus, understanding and responding to the subtle differences in what drives different people's work involvement and engagement

- Use metrics that take the focus away from effort and instead emphasize results that matter to business success

- Not empower employees, but instead create the circumstances for them to exercise effective autonomy

- Start the week by asking, "How can I do less hands-on work and spend more time helping the team perform better?"—rather than beginning with a to-do list laden with direct output tasks

The work planning, execution, and monitoring concepts described here reinforce the notion that an effective manager does his work offstage. Certainly that's true at Cisco, where managers occupy the nodes in a complex web of collaborative activities. The workings of the Cisco matrix emphasize the importance of extra-unit outreach, described in the manager role discussion of Chapter Four. The success of eTelecare reminds us that managers whose roles let them spend the majority of their time and attention building employee skills and enhancing work processes can significantly accelerate organizational performance. They can succeed in doing so, however, only when their spans of control are circumscribed and their responsibility for direct production is significantly limited.

Effective offstage managers must become comfortable in ceding to others significant authority over the planning and execution of work.

They lead in ways that reflect the demands of our evolutionary roots: they equip us to do our work well, and then leave us alone to do it. This requires them to build a strong foundation of mutual trust with employees and to display authentic humility in challenging their own planning and control biases. The payoff of these approaches to planning work, defining jobs, and monitoring results is competitive advantage. Done right, they also make employee self-actualization a likely outcome, rather than a fortunate accident.

CHAPTER OUTLINE

Acting as a Human Capital Treasurer

Help Employees Formulate Career Plans and Choose
the Best Learning Modes

Create a Constellation of Learning Contacts

Help People Travel Multidirectional Career Paths

Providing Direct Development

Coach Effectively

Believe in People's Ability to Develop

Goal Setting and Performance Feedback

Build Self-Efficacy Through FAMIC Goal Setting

Reinforce FAMIC Goals with FITEMA Performance
Feedback

6

Developing People

In a televised speech on April 18, 1977, U.S. president Jimmy Carter delivered what he called "an unpleasant talk" about the energy crisis that he said threatened the country. He urged American citizens to view the effort required to overcome the problem as "the moral equivalent of war."[1] In so doing, the president was using a metaphor to dramatize the problem, convince Americans of its gravity, and galvanize them to action. Metaphors like this draw their power from the object of comparison. By referring to war, the president evoked images of sacrifice, hardship, effort, solidarity, and, ultimately, victory. These entailments enrich metaphors and make them coherent within the context of our knowledge and experience.[2]

Drawing on these same principles, we suggest that *human capital treasurer* is an apt metaphor for the role managers play in employee development. It brings a broad and instructive array of entailments. Like financial treasury, human capital treasury focuses on a valuable asset (not money, but rather employee knowledge, skills, talents, and behaviors). Like a corporate treasurer, a human capital treasurer has responsibility for custodianship and growth of those assets, not through cash and investment management but instead through insightful, individualized learning strategies. Most important, like a company treasurer, a manager grows and guides the investment of an asset he does not own, much as a company's treasurer husbands financial assets that belong to the organization's shareholders.

We frequently hear how, in these turbulent times, organizations expect their people to define and pursue their own human capital growth strategies. The tagline: employee self-development. The translation: don't expect our help in building your competencies. Employees have gotten the message. Almost three-quarters of the respondents to our 2010 global workforce study said that they, not their employers, hold the primary responsibility for career management. But only 55 percent said they feel comfortable taking on this responsibility. Moreover, employees consistently confirm that career development is a key driver of engagement and of the decision to remain with an organization over the long term.[3] The importance employees place on learning and development, coupled with inconsistent support and investment from organizations, creates an importance/performance gap. This breach yields an opportunity—a necessity, we would say—for managers to step in and play a key role in employee growth.

Indeed, we expect the manager's responsibility for employee development not to atrophy under the weight of economic pressure or corporate indifference, but rather to grow deeper and broader. We pose this challenge to managers: make growth of human capital assets a core part of your responsibility and an essential element of every employee's job. If learning isn't woven into the fabric of each employee's work experience, then that experience is incomplete.

Acting as a Human Capital Treasurer

Randy MacDonald, senior vice president of Human Resources at IBM, takes issue with the notion that organizations should adopt a laissez-faire attitude toward employee development. "I heard an HR person once say, 'your career is your responsibility.' Let me tell you something, the CFO, when he gives one of our line guys $3 billion to go build a new plant, he doesn't say, 'Go build the plant and do what you want with it.' No, that CFO and that line person are going to manage that asset."[4] We agree with McDonald's notion that, like the financial assets of a company, human capital deserves significant attention from managers and organizations.

To define the exemplary manager, and to determine where employee development should fall among that manager's priorities, salesforce.com, a leading cloud computing company, put this question on an employee survey: "If you were to imagine your ideal manager, in what areas would you want that manager to be most capable?" From a list of seventeen factors, employees chose "Help with career advancement" as the most important item on the ideal manager's to-do list. The second most important factor was "Giving you regular feedback on your performance." "Coaching you in ways that help you do your job better" and "Giving you autonomy to decide how best to do your work" were fourth and fifth on the list. Yes, employees said, they want the organization to invest more in learning and development programs. But they also said that they expect managers to work with them directly to help them advance on the strength of their competencies and their ability to function independently.[5]

Let's first consider how managers work at the contextual level, helping people find and exploit the organization's learning and career development resources.

Help Employees Formulate Career Plans and Choose the Best Learning Modes

Like a good treasurer, a manager must have a plan for asset growth. Looking ahead to the employee's next opportunities, identifying the learning required to take those steps, and suggesting the path forward—these form the core of manager responsibility for human capital development planning. Of course, all ways of learning are not created equal; some learning modes work better than others for certain purposes. To avoid misguided investments and wasted effort, managers must help employees match the mode with the type of learning needed. For instance, they need to know that:

- Mentoring works well when people need to grasp the nuances of organizational culture, brainstorm career direction, or navigate internal politics. A mentor has less to offer, however, when the employee needs to acquire a specific skill rather than a bit of more general organizational wisdom.

- Coaching can help with skill improvement, insofar as a coach can give targeted advice to help improve a particular aspect of performance.

- Classroom training works well for picking up aspects of knowledge that don't require same-day application and for topics that call for little one-on-one contact between teacher and learner.

- Just-in-time training, especially delivered electronically, can provide an efficient dose of knowledge on a specific topic.

- On-the-job training (OJT) works in cases where hands-on application can accelerate learning and where the targeted skill can be acquired and used quickly. However, OJT requires supervisors and peers who have the time, inclination, and skill to pass on what they know.

- Using projects for learning has a dual benefit—the project effort produces results and the individual gains practical skills and knowledge in the process. Employee and manager must jointly assess the individual's learning need, find a suitable project, set goals for learning and project output, monitor progress, and retrospectively assess the acquisition of skills and knowledge. They must also choose the next project with all this in mind.

- As we saw in Chapter Five, work that combines abundant job resources with challenging expectations for performance promotes the growth of human capital. Managers can do a lot to ensure that jobs like these provide the maximum opportunity for employees to expand their skills and knowledge. Managers can also encourage contact with other workers who have useful information or solutions to problems. This informal transfer of insights works well when employees need to know about the short cuts, rules of thumb, inside sources of information, and common-sense applications that make things work. People can get it precisely when it's most valuable, from peers and managers they trust, through the learning style they prefer, and in the quantity they need and can absorb.[6]

- Transfer to other functions—a special kind of on-the-job learning— requires that both employee and manager have the right goals in mind when contemplating the move. Spending time in another part of the organization can help people learn new techniques, enlarge their technical vocabularies, understand issues from other units' perspectives, and build personal networks. But the time spent traveling through the organization may also detract from a deeper focus on learning about one's primary functional area.

- Communities of practice, the informal, emergent groups that tend to coalesce spontaneously around disciplines and areas of common interest, are great ways for people to confer, collaborate, share information, and teach each other. The price of admission is intellectual contribution; the payoff is the knowledge and insight available from a network of colleagues. Social media offer a way to accelerate community connections, with some users contributing to and becoming part of the content, and other users consuming it.

Counseling employees about how to select from this portfolio of options is becoming a needed-to-play competency for managers who aspire to act as effective human capital treasurers. Indeed, there is a relationship between employee engagement and preferred information sources for career advice. Table 6.1 shows those sources for a broad population of U.S. workers.

Highly engaged people turn to their supervisors for career planning help, and they look elsewhere almost as frequently, including to the

Table 6.1: Highly Engaged Employees Seek Career Advice from People, not Tools

Source of Career Advice	High Engagement (%)	Low Engagement (%)
Immediate supervisor	23	8
Network of contacts within the company	20	8
Employee's research on the Internet or other sources	19	44
External network of contacts	14	21
Company-provided resources or tools	13	4
People in the employee's work group	11	14

Source: *Driving Business Results Through Continuous Engagement: 2008/2009 WorkUSA Survey Report*, Watson Wyatt Worldwide, 15.

network of contacts we discuss shortly. People who say their engagement is low will spend far more time searching the Internet or seeking career counsel from contacts outside the organization (perhaps because they know that's where they will soon find themselves).

Good managers, like good treasurers, will call on many sources to help with asset management and development. Working offstage, however, an effective manager need not always be the central player in delivering day-to-day development experiences.

Create a Constellation of Learning Contacts

The more we study how learning takes place in organizations, the more we understand that employees benefit from having access to multiple sources of advice, counsel, and knowledge. It's helpful from time to time to seek out a confidant, a peer, or a manager (other than the direct boss) to get off-the-record advice or have the occasional *mea culpa* conversation. A growing body of research suggests that having a constellation of developmental relationships benefits people far more than relying on a single source for coaching and mentoring. In a study of attorneys at prestigious New York law firms, researchers Monica Higgins and David Thomas from the Harvard Business School found that having an array of developmental contacts within the organization did more for young lawyers striving for partnership than did having a single, even senior and effective, mentoring contact. They concluded, "Our results show that while the quality of an individual's primary developmental relationship does affect short-term career outcomes such as work satisfaction and intentions to remain [with the firm], it is the composition of one's entire constellation of developers that accounts for longer term career outcomes such as organizational retention and career advancement."[7]

The research also made a point about the particular importance of a network of contacts in the current work environment: "In an era of organizational restructuring and globalization, it will become increasingly difficult for individuals to develop and maintain single sources of mentoring support. Both mentors' as well as protégés' careers are likely to be in flux.... Individuals will need to search for alternative sources of help as they navigate their careers."[8]

We can think of the constellation of development sources as a network of relationships with the primary manager as the central point (the pole star, if you will). The manager, in turn, helps create the constellation by making his contacts available to trusted employees. In the words of two researchers who have studied workplace networks, "The outcomes of this process for members [of managers' networks]... are positive... they are able to establish relationships similar to their leaders', resulting in the trust and respect of important contacts in the organization."[9] The social capital represented by these relationships constitutes an important class of job resources. We know from the job structure model in Chapter Four that such resources help people cope with a variety of job-related stresses that could affect an individual's work attitudes, performance, and career progress.

Help People Travel Multidirectional Career Paths

The late lamented vertical career path has gone the way of the dinosaur, the dodo, and the dollar cup of coffee. Some organizations still offer an upward, linear career path, but many of those have flattened the organizational hierarchy so much that career ladders have far fewer rungs than they once did. In place of the ladder, we have the multidirectional career configuration. Whereas the phrase "at a crossroads" once meant a potentially troubling career crisis, it's now a commonplace event in the lives of people for whom positive career movement can be up, sideways, or (temporarily) down. Managers stand at the intersections of those pathways, like cops directing traffic and helping employees choose the right direction.

If you're Cisco Systems, your matrix structure must influence how you envision individual development and career progression. Why would a networked company in the network business not view individual learning and career movement as an interconnected set of lattices and ladders? As far back as 2001, Cisco was putting in place the early forms of the matrix that now channels development energy for company products and individual careers alike. In that year's soft economy, the organization focused relentlessly on taking advantage of the downward trend in technology markets to exercise what John Chambers called a "breakaway strategy." The committees and cross-functional teams necessary to connect centralized functional units began to take shape.[10] But the organization also knew that engineers with customer familiarity and multiproduct engineering know-how would represent the most powerful coordinating mechanism the organization could have. Given the company's strategy, increasing the speed and effectiveness of internal employee movement took on a high strategic priority. It was not just a nice thing to do to appease restless people.

Nearly a decade later, the company has expanded its structural matrix, as we saw in Chapter Five. Organizational architectures like this lend themselves to a complementary career matrix. A multidirectional career approach is intended to build an organization's human capital by giving people flexibility in how they construct their long-term working lives. Employees map and pursue individualized learning experiences and career options along four dimensions:

- *Pace.* How quickly an employee progresses to increasing levels of responsibility and authority

- *Workload.* How much work is expected of an employee, typically measured in hours or days per week, month, or even year

- *Location and schedule.* Where work gets done and when

- *Role.* What capacity encompasses the individual's work, from individual contributor to senior leader[11]

As described by Cathleen Benko and Anne Weisberg, authors of *Mass Career Customization*, the how-to manual for constructing lattice-and-ladder career paths, "Employees and their managers partner to customize careers by selecting the option along each of the four dimensions that most closely matches the employee's career objectives, keeping in mind their life circumstances and the needs of the business at any given point in time."[12] Benko and Weisberg say that "MCC [mass career customization] requires a significant amount of time on the part of both managers and employees to engage in meaningful career conversations. MCC provides the structure, but managers need to buy into the business case and be appropriately recognized by leadership for taking the time required to execute MCC effectively. Trust is equally important in this process."[13]

Besides carving out time and building trust, helping an employee navigate a lattice-and-ladder career structure requires managers to:

- *Display sophisticated understanding of the production function and project/unit contribution to strategy.* They must apply systems thinking to their project management, understanding how inputs and outputs interact. They must hold projects and processes together as people cycle onto and off of project work and into and out of career phases.

- *Span boundaries and establish their own networks in the organization.* Managers must be able to navigate the organization, locating development resources and helping each employee find the right next opportunity.

- *Be creative in helping people craft individualized career strategies.* Managers must be a direct source of development for employees, and also know when to focus development locally and when to guide them in looking elsewhere.

- *Show sensitivity to fairness across employees in the unit.* With people crafting customized careers, managers must ensure that job and career elements fit the person and are equitable (though not necessarily identical) across the group.

- *Develop a command of organizational tools.* Managers must be able to guide people to advanced organizational tools that help employees plot career paths. Genentech, for example, has created a catalogue of scientific disciplines, from antibody engineering to structural biology, and put it on the company Web site. Readers can peruse the biographies of researchers in each discipline at Genentech, learn about what they are currently working on and understand what inspires them, and find out what kind of people they are looking to recruit.

Evolving internal transfer approaches to teamwork, job mobility, and career movement have two goals: to make human capital growth an organization-wide effort, not a unit-specific one; and to afford employees the opportunity to have diverse, multicontact experiences that accelerate learning. Even in organizations that don't have matrix structures, such approaches can give employees a degree of career self-determination that is often absent in more conventional (and increasingly rare) vertical approaches to career progression. Cisco's Susan Monaghan, vice president of employee engagement, describes the organization's philosophy of career progression:

> We want managers to think of our employees as Cisco talent, not their talent. Managers need to be willing to let good people move on in order to expand their careers and grow their skills. This will require us to see people beyond who they are in their current job and recognize them for past experiences and unique towering strengths. People are a sum total of all of this, and an individual's personal vision should not be bound by the current job description. The manager's job is to translate and connect what's good for the person with what's good for the company. Playing this role will require managers to step back from today's job and think about how to build sustainable talent for Cisco.[14]

Back in 2001, a Cisco career services manager described an incident that captured perfectly the desired manager behavior. "This week, a manager e-mailed the new manager about a person who was considering a transfer. He said, 'This guy is my absolute number one employee—his performance ratings have been consistently stellar. He can truly make a contribution to your team. I don't want to lose him, but I know this move is in his best interest, so call me if you have any questions.' When every manager in our company acts that way, then I know we'll be providing end-to-end career support."[15]

Providing Direct Development

In a world where organizational focus on employee development has been compromised and learning investments threatened, managers' direct efforts to help people build their human capital take on increased urgency. An astute manager has a wide array of approaches at his disposal for engaging in direct human capital-building efforts with employees. These include:

- *Coaching.* Providing hands-on skills-improvement advice and instruction by putting learning and action close together; encouraging performance, nurturing, and reinforcing success

- *Teaching.* Imparting knowledge; learning and action may be separated by time and space

- *Informing.* Providing information on specific job functions and broader organizational and strategic context

- *Mentoring.* Giving the employee career guidance, general development counseling and advice, sponsorship, and support

- *Exemplifying.* Displaying the desired attitudes and actions[16]

Managers may engage in any or all of these actions more or less constantly and without clear delineation of when one form of direct development stops and another begins. We will focus chiefly on coaching, the term we hear most often from our colleagues in Human Resources.

Coach Effectively

Plenty has been written about how managers should act as employee coaches. Indeed, when asked about the roles of managers, Human Resources people most often say that they expect their company's managers to coach employees. Participants in the Randstad *World of Work* survey chose "Being able to share my knowledge with others" as the number one reason for considering a managerial role.[17]

Social scientists who observe hunter-gatherer groups know that group leaders achieve and hold positions of power partly because they help individuals, and the group at large, to become more successful. They develop others' ability to find the best water hole rather than just leading people to it. Modern organizations expect the same from their managers. They call it coaching or training but rarely define what it means. Still, it's a rich idea, one that goes back to how learning occurs in environments where the next generation's ability to learn what the last generation knows is critical to the survival of the band.

We can imagine, for example, how the skilled leader of a hunting party might develop the knowledge and skills of less-experienced companions. To begin with, the learning would take place in the camp, as novices listen to hours of stories about foraging activities, and on the job, as they join hunts and learn from the coaching of experienced hunters and from their own mistakes.[18] Development would focus on critical skills: identifying animal prints; finding game; pursuing animals; shooting arrows or throwing spears; and making the kill. The manager-coach would:

- Explain the importance of a successful hunt, providing basic information about the band's need for protein

- Create practice opportunities, perhaps through spear-throwing or arrow-shooting contests, giving young hunters a chance to hone their skills before it really counted

- Use the moment of performance to offer immediate advice (demonstrating the right way to throw a spear)

- Give the novice hunter some autonomy in choosing how to go about the hunt, thereby improving decision making as well as motivation

- Assess performance immediately, constantly, and objectively through a continuous dialogue about strategies, techniques, and results

- Reinforce success through specific praise, commenting favorably on a good throw, even though the thrower might not have hit the target

- Offer a near-term opportunity to improve (urging the hunter to find and pursue another antelope, after missing the last one)

- Make the rewards for good performance and the downside of poor performance equally clear (bringing down the antelope provides dinner, not to mention praise and glory for the successful hunter; missing it means everyone goes hungry)

Our continuing theme of managing with a light touch pertains as well to these coaching elements. Employees want the ability to determine the moment of coaching, the amount they will receive, and the approaches used. Intrusive or heavy-handed efforts to compel learning produce more resentment than results.

Many managers say they don't have time to spend working with individuals and teams in this highly focused, attention-demanding process. For them, the kind of role restructuring discussed in Chapter Four could reshuffle the elements of the manager's job (for instance, permitting a larger allocation of time to people focus, perhaps supported by a reduced span of control) and provide the hours needed for effective direct (and indirect) employee development.

Believe in People's Ability to Develop

Such factors as inadequate time or insufficient ability certainly detract from the manager's capacity to coach effectively. But there may also be a simpler, more insidious obstacle: manager attitude. Some managers believe that it's possible to develop fundamental individual abilities, whereas others don't. Stanford psychology Professor Carol Dweck, who has studied the beliefs people hold about the changeability of personal characteristics, labels the two opposite attitudes *entity*, or fixed ability theory, and *incremental*, or malleable ability theory. Those who hold an entity theory believe that employees' most basic attributes are hardwired and largely resistant to change. Those who subscribe to the notion of malleability have a different attitude. They consider even basic qualities to be amenable to improvement.[19] In essence, Dweck says, between the immutable elements of an individual's portfolio of attributes (physical characteristics like color blindness, for instance) and the highly flexible ones (for example, the widespread ability to learn to ride a bicycle) lie what she calls "the levels in between."[20] These in-between attributes, which include a wide range of abilities and even personality character-istics, represent the disputed territory for holders of entity and incre-mental beliefs.

The differences play out in how managers evaluate employee performance and decide how and whether to invest effort in coaching. Studies by a team of researchers from Southern Methodist University (SMU) and the University of Toronto showed, for example, that managers who subscribe to the fixed-ability theory tend to resist adjusting their opinions about employees over time. They hold tight to their beliefs that employee ability is enduring and static, even if the individuals' actual performance improves or declines noticeably. In other words, their first impressions of people are "sticky." Because they don't really think people can change, they tend to ignore or discount evidence of performance adjustments.[21] In contrast, managers who believe in the efficacy of development show a much higher inclination to acknowledge performance changes. Beliefs about the probability of real change affect managers' willingness to invest effort in coaching employees. The stronger the belief in the plasticity and malleability of individual skills and attributes, the stronger the manager's inclination to put time and energy into building employees' skills and knowledge.[22]

So then, a key question: when managers believe their efforts will provide a meaningful boost to employee performance, what kind of coaching do they provide? Research and observation by Carol Dweck and others indicate that they tend to:

- Observe employee work closely, and praise process, strategy, and effort first, results second, and talent not at all

- Both challenge and nurture; they don't reassure people that they are "fine as they are," but instead dare them to do better

- Tell people the truth about their performance and then give them the means to improve

- Give people autonomy in how they want to develop their abilities[23]

Not only do these behaviors pay off in terms of performance, but they also tend to turn employees themselves into incremental theorists. In Dweck's words, referring to experiments with students, "When students are praised for their intelligence, they move toward a fixed theory. Far from raising self-esteem, this praise makes them challenge-avoidant and vulnerable, such that when they hit obstacles their confidence, enjoyment, and performance decline. When students are praised for their effort or strategies (their *process*) [italics in original]], they instead take on a more malleable theory—they are eager to learn and highly resilient in the face of difficulty. Thus self-theories play an important (and causal) role in challenge seeking, self-regulation, and resilience, and changing self-theories appears to result in important real-word changes in how people function."[24]

Building people's belief in their ability to grow and adapt can have impressive results. One experiment, designed to test ways of increasing the resilience and self-confidence of minority college students, used a set of simple but powerful techniques. First, the students were taught that doubts about fitting in at college are common at first, but short-lived. They were presented with survey statistics and personal testimonies from upperclassmen to reinforce this idea. They wrote a speech, which they videotaped, explaining why people's perceptions of acceptance might change over time. Compared with a control group, African American students in the experimental group took more challenging courses, retained their motivation in the face of adversity, reached out to faculty members three times as often, and spent significantly more time studying each day. Students in the experimental group improved their grades in the semester following the intervention, whereas students in the control group saw their grades fall.[25]

Belief in the ability of individuals to learn and grow—or skepticism about that ability—can become a deeply embedded trait of organizational culture. Few organizations, however, have made development, especially the forms delivered by first-line managers, as critical a pivot point of organizational culture as has Yum! Brands. Yum! is the corporate umbrella for some of the most recognizable quick-service restaurant chains on earth. The company's operations include KFC, Pizza Hut, Taco Bell, and Long John Silver's. If you haven't eaten at one of these restaurants lately, then perhaps you haven't been to the mall recently. Or maybe you don't have teenage children.

In 1997, when the company launched itself following its spin-off from PepsiCo, it set about to change some of the cultural elements that had characterized the PepsiCo mother ship. Among other changes, Yum! inverted the organizational power pyramid. At PepsiCo, business took place in the restaurants, but true influence resided at the corporate headquarters. At the newly launched company, however, the RGM (Restaurant General Manager) was touted as "our #1 Leader … not senior management." Corporate headquarters was rechristened the "Restaurant Support Center," to signify that the restaurants represented the operating center of the organization. Most significantly, the entire above-restaurant management team underwent title changes. Area managers became "area coaches," operations directors became "market coaches," and division vice presidents morphed into "head coaches."[26]

Changing titles was a nice symbolic step, but it would have meant little without operational backup. At Yum!, the process part began with a boot camp for the entire operations group. Managers went through a training regimen during which they relearned the basics of making and selling their food products. They had to pass a test and have their competence certified. While this was taking place, the company's organization development team created job maps and descriptions of the roles, responsibilities, behaviors, and expected outcomes of coaching actions. Finally, the company developed a simple model for coaching employees in a fast-paced, high-turnover business. It had three basic components: Exploring (observe what's going on, ask questions, and listen to the answers); Analyzing (look at the facts, figure out whether problems are isolated or systemic, find the root causes); and Responding (provide feedback, teach new skills, offer support, and gain commitment).[27]

Change efforts like these don't succeed without the energetic support of company executives. David Novak, chairman, president, and CEO of Yum! Brands, falls into that passionate supporter category. To begin with, he equates great leadership with great coaching. Second, he subscribes to an incrementalist development philosophy: "What I think a great leader does, a great coach does, is understand what kind of talent you have and then you help people leverage that talent so that people can achieve what they never thought they were capable of." Novak also believes in focusing development efforts on one person at a time: "The best leaders I've known really take an active interest in a person. And once that person demonstrates they have skill and capability, they try to help them achieve their potential. That's always been my thinking about management. If you have someone who's smart, talented, aggressive, and wants to learn, then your job is to help them become all they can be." He also seems to know that past performance is relevant chiefly as a springboard to future success: "I hate Monday-morning quarterbacks. So I try to focus my meetings on building and sharing know-how that will help us win going forward. I focus my meetings on beating last year."[28]

At Yum!, coaching by managers—all managers—has taken on a central role in the organization's quest for a competitive edge. Granted, operations like Yum! Brands restaurants succeed or fail for a variety of reasons. At Pizza Hut, for example, sales are heavily influenced by new product launches. But ultimately, efficient, cost-controlled operations and consistent product quality will carry the day in a crowded competitive field. And, though corporate operating manuals and policy guidelines can help a restaurant run efficiently, the most important determinant of performance will be the way a restaurant manager works with her staff to minimize waste, maintain product consistency, and keep customers happy.

For Yum!, the local focus seems to be working. During the first four years following the culture change effort, Pizza Hut experienced record results in same-store sales and historic lows in restaurant manager turnover.[29] In fiscal 2009, Yum! announced its eighth consecutive year of annual earnings-per-share growth of at least 10 percent.[30]

Goal Setting and Performance Feedback

Among the many processes that managers implement and oversee, few produce as much frustration as goal setting and performance evaluation. Organizations lump these processes under the heading of "performance management." They speak of "managing" performance as if it involved following a simple recipe: start with a pinch of goal setting, add a splash of performance ratings, throw in a dash of rewards, don't forget just a soupçon of training, and voilà, a high-performing person. But people aren't cakes, and human performance is far too complex to be approached with a formula. Although setting goals and providing performance feedback build the foundation for development strategies and tactics, organizations continue to think of them as mechanical programs chiefly consisting of forms, schedules, rating schemes, and computerized systems. Among the participants in our Reward Challenges and Changes (RCC) survey, 43 percent said that their approaches to performance management are only somewhat effective or not at all effective. When asked about the principal challenges to effective performance assessment and improvement, survey respondents said that managers represent the most significant obstacle to success. Figure 6.1 shows that three of the top frustrations fall on the shoulders of managers.

The echoes of the manager role structure discussion of Chapter Four come through loud and clear. Managers don't have, or aren't willing to take, sufficient time to dispassionately assess employee performance, in part because they have too many other diverse tasks to perform and oversee. Sometimes, they also lack the human capital management abilities required to coach effectively. And notice the ninth factor in Figure 6.1—the familiar span of control bugaboo. More than 60 percent of the respondents to the RCC survey said having too many employees to evaluate is at least somewhat of a challenge for managers.

Employees also express frustration about managers' and companies' performance assessment and improvement efforts. In Towers Perrin's 2007 global workforce study, only half of the employee respondents

Figure 6.1: Why Performance Management Systems Fall Short—
Look to the Manager

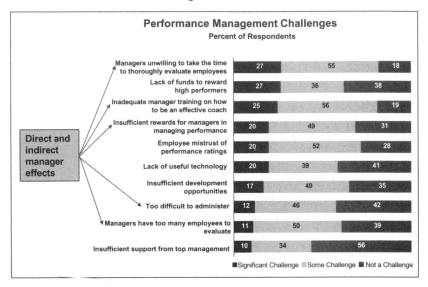

Source: *Reward Challenges and Changes—Top Line Results*, Towers Perrin, 2007, 41.

said their managers provide performance goals that are challenging but achievable. Employees consistently tell us they want to have a continuous, informal dialogue about performance with their managers. Yet few organizations approach performance assessment this way. Among the RCC respondents, only 5 percent said their managers provide ongoing performance feedback. More than half make performance assessment an annual event.[31]

Further complicating the assessment and improvement process is the asymmetry of emotion to which people are prone. We experience negative emotions far more strongly than we experience positive ones. As a result, negative feedback, however constructive or well intended, produces an emotional reaction that interferes with the hoped-for self-improvement response. Emotional asymmetry thus works against one of the assumptions most fundamental to the performance management construct: that pointing out unmet goals should increase motivation and effort to close the gap between goals and performance. In the words of psychologist Nigel Nicholson, "The rationality of performance management systems means in practice a cool emphasis on areas of deviation from standard. The ideal of learning from failure is seldom achieved, not least because of the asymmetry of emotional reactions to positive and negative stimuli—the power of aversion is much greater than the power of reinforcement."[32]

Real performance improvement occurs only when managers undertake a performance assessment and improvement process that links past performance, self-efficacy, goal setting, and future performance. The keystone in this performance architecture is self-efficacy.

THE ASYMMETRY OF EMOTION

Psychologists have identified a wide range of phenomena that underscore how negative events, feelings, and impressions overpower positive ones. One team of psychologists who studied emotions expresses it succinctly: "Bad is stronger than good."[33] Threats and losses (plummeting investments, abandonment by friends, failure to win the club golf championship) have greater impact on the human psyche than gains and victories (beating the market, making friends, winning the championship trophy). Psychologists call this the *positive-negative asymmetry effect*. By one estimate, for a marriage to succeed, favorable interactions must outnumber unfavorable ones by at least five to one.[34] That's why mental alarm bells should ring when a wife asks, "Do these pants make me look fat?" or a husband says, "My hairline hasn't receded much since college, has it?" The wrong response carries a high emotional price for both parties.

In the workplace, emotional asymmetry manifests itself in the way downdrafts (events that engender negative emotions) seem to
(Continued)

outnumber uplifts (workplace positives that improve employees' emotional states). Employee participants in one study gave positive ratings to 80 percent of their interactions with their supervisors. However, the effects of the negative interactions on employee mood were about five times as strong as the positive effects. Hence, even though most employee-supervisor encounters are positive, the overall net effect tends to the negative side because of the asymmetry of emotion.[35] Marriage and management—two emotionally laden relationships.

The process of setting goals and assessing performance can tip the emotional balance either way. When those experiences contribute to building self-efficacy, the net emotional effect may well be positive. When they also form part of a manager's engaging but light-handed style—stimulating employees intellectually and attending to each person's individual needs—the result can be "broad, deep, and long-lasting effects on the individual employees and the organization as a whole."[36] But when the performance management process turns sour, emotional asymmetry magnifies the negative effect.

Build Self-Efficacy Through FAMIC Goal Setting

Think of self-efficacy as self-confidence with a thermonuclear boost. Stanford psychologist Albert Bandura defines self-efficacy this way: "Perceived self-efficacy refers to beliefs in one's capabilities to organize and execute the courses of action required to produce given attainments."[37] As to the importance of this cognitive construct, Bandura lays it out plainly: "Those who have a high sense of efficacy view situations as presenting realizable opportunities. They visualize success scenarios that provide positive guides for performance.... A high sense of efficacy fosters cognitive constructions of effective courses of action, and cognitive enactments of efficacious actions, in turn, strengthen efficacy beliefs."[38] We saw this effect with jobs that provide challenges and support resources, leading to success that increases confidence to execute and ownership of results.

The mutual reinforcement of performance and self-efficacy gives it much of its power and makes it relevant in the context of performance assessment and planning. The process works like this:

- Effective performance—that is, achievement of personally meaningful goals—boosts self-efficacy to accomplish specific tasks.

- Higher self-efficacy influences the next stage of goal setting, raising the targets, and sharpening the identification of future performance strategies.

- These strategies produce even better future performance, sending self-efficacy still higher, further raising goals and enhancing performance strategies, which increases accomplishment by yet another increment.

The linkage of positive performance and self-efficacy creates a powerful force for individual, team, and organizational achievement. It puts a pinpoint focus on the manager's responsibility: use the goal-setting and evaluation process to put power behind self-efficacy.

The critical first element in this chain reaction is the setting of initial performance goals. Substantial evidence, both academic and practical, suggests that explicit, challenging goals enhance individual motivation. The higher a person's expectation that a certain behavior will achieve desired outcomes, the greater the motivation to perform the activity.[39] Conversely, goals that seem out of reach have little motivating power. Organizations often use "stretch" goals as a way to motivate people to accelerate their effort and therefore their achievement. Stretch goals seem like a handy shortcut, a way to get people to jump several performance levels at once. Their success depends on two underlying notions: first, that challenging objectives motivate; and second, that even if people fall short of achieving the goal, they will still feel a sense of accomplishment at having come close. The first premise is correct; the second, more dubious. In fact, motivation can't last without what Bandura calls "affirming accomplishments." Negative feedback, when it works at all, engenders performance motivation only when the discrepancy between past goals and past performance is relatively small. Supervisors and organizations alike should take the longer view, letting the combination of challenging but achievable goals and self-efficacy work to increase performance incrementally and steadily.

Many organizations train managers and employees to establish goals that follow the acronym SMART: specific, measurable, agreed-on (or attainable), realistic, and time-bound. These elements are fine as far as they go, but several other important criteria are missing. To make the most of the not inconsiderable energy that does, or should, go into setting goals and assessing progress, other criteria come into play. Effective goals—that is, goals that move both individual and organization up the ladder of improved performance—must not only be SMART but also FAMIC:

- *Few in number and focused.* Too many goals produce confusion and contradiction. It's better to focus attention on a few important objectives than to dilute effort across many elements.

- *Aligned internally and organizationally.* Goals shouldn't contradict each other or force employees to make impossible and conflicting choices. Many goal-setting exercises contain an unstated assumption: any goal that supports the organization's best interest must *ipso facto* confer a benefit on the individual. But is this always the case? An approach called empathy box analysis can help identify misalignment between organization and individual benefit and suggest how to establish a mutually advantageous target. Table 6.2 shows an example.

  In this situation, the organization derives a clear benefit from increased sales volume and the greater revenue it produces. The organization assumes that the resulting higher commission for the sales representative will bring individual and company interests into alignment (cell 1). By the same token, a sales representative who sells less

Table 6.2: Individual and Organizational Goals Don't Automatically
Align

Goal	Outcome for the Organization	Possible Outcomes for the Individual	
		1	**2**
Sell more	Positive—higher revenue	Higher commission Feel rewarded	Increased sales quota Reduction of territory or reassignment to another territory Feel unappreciated, stressed
		3	**4**
Sell less	Negative—lower revenue	Lower commission Feel pressure to work harder, more effectively	Status quo (if the sales shortfall isn't too great) Feel relieved

Source: Adapted from Heslin, P. A., Carson, J. B., and VandeWalle, D., *Practical Applications of Goal-Setting Theory to Performance Management,* pheslin.cox.smu.edu, 93–95. Forthcoming in J. W. Smither (Ed.), *Performance Management: Putting Research into Practice,* San Francisco: Jossey-Bass.

than her target will earn a lower commission, perceive herself out of sync with the organization's goals, and work hard to correct the shortfall (cell 3). But look at cells 2 and 4. In cell 2, selling more produces a clear downside for the individual. The company may shrink a lucrative territory or raise sales quotas. Either change would make it harder for the sales rep to hit future sales goals. And, as cell 4 suggests, selling less isn't entirely negative, at least in the short run. Quotas presumably remain the same, or may even drop, and the familiar sales territory will likely remain intact. The message of all this is: aligning individual and organizational benefits is both important and more difficult than it sometimes seems. To establish mutually reinforcing goals, managers must pay close attention to the subliminal twists and turns of employee interests.

- *Mastery building.* Gaining mastery over a craft is one of life's greatest sources of engagement and self-actualization. Goal setting contributes to mastery when tasks and the related expectations are broken down into incremental steps that become progressively more challenging. According to Albert Bandura, "People gain their satisfaction from progressive mastery of an activity rather than suspending any sense of success in their endeavors until the superordinate goal is attained."[40] Especially early in an individual's learning process, goals should be expressed in terms of skill development and knowledge acquisition ("learn to do x, become expert in y") rather than performance alone. As expertise improves and performance gets better along with it, challenging, high-expectation performance goals become appropriate. When fulfilling jobs incorporate mastery building, autonomy and competence can work like riders on a tandem bicycle, together powering intrinsic motivation.

- *Incremental.* Taking maximum advantage of an individual's self-efficacy to raise aspirations and performance requires a manager to work with employees to set challenging but feasible goals. Goals should be expressed in workable increments and reviewed frequently. Small wins build big momentum. It's also easier for employees and managers alike to respond to minor setbacks before they become big ones.

- *Controllable.* In a complex organizational environment, achievement of goals will often depend on an array of factors, some within an individual's control, some at least partly outside the range of personal influence. Exhibit 6.1 shows how goal achievement (the vertical axis) and perceived control over achievement (the horizontal axis) interact to influence self-efficacy.

     Self-efficacy reaches its highest level (the upper right-hand box) when an individual achieves his goals *and* perceives that those goals were largely under his individual control. Achievement of goals subject

**Exhibit 6.1: Goal Achievement and Individual Control Build
            Self-Efficacy**

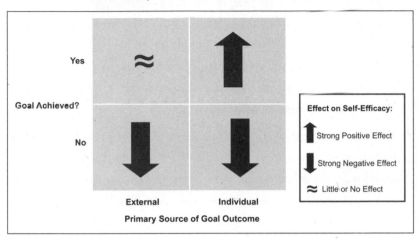

Source: Data from Tolli, A. P., and Schmidt, A. M., "The Role of Feedback, Causal
Attributions, and Self-Efficacy in Goal Revision," *Journal of Applied Psychology*, 2008,
93(3), 697.

to substantial external influence (a strong economic environment, a
competitor's failure, a lucky break) has little effect on individual self-
efficacy. Failure to achieve the agreed-on goals, whether attributable
to personal shortcomings or to external factors ("The sun got in my
eyes, coach. That's why I dropped the ball.") tends to reduce self-
efficacy. The upper right-hand quadrant is also where an individual
is most likely to respond to a manager's performance feedback by
increasing future goals and performance intentions.

Reinforce FAMIC Goals with FITEMA Performance Feedback

Once goals are set, of course, they have little meaning without skillfully
given feedback. As with goal setting, effective feedback requires adherence to a few key provisos. To reinforce self-efficacy and overcome the
negative emotional reaction that bad news and perceived criticism often
provoke, manager feedback on goal performance must be FITEMA:

- *Fairly determined.* People must understand performance standards and have an opportunity to influence their determination. Employees must have confidence that the manager has knowledge of the employee's work, understands work-related goals, and knows why they were set where they were. Moreover, people must believe that the same performance standards apply to all employees in the group, receive a thorough explanation of evaluation results, and have a mechanism for challenging conclusions with which they disagree.

- *Individual, not comparative.* People react best when they receive feedback framed against their individual performance in the context of goals, past achievements, or rate of improvement. Comparing one person to another elicits an ego-protection impulse that interferes with attention to improvement strategies.

- *Task-focused, not person-focused.* Feedback carries the greatest cognitive power, and the lowest emotional drag, when concentrated on job performance and outcomes achieved, not on the character or the personality of the employee.

- *Error-tolerant.* It is axiomatic that people can learn from their mistakes, but only when managers treat mistakes as opportunities to improve and not as signs of personal flaws. Our research shows that supervisors in high-performing organizations encourage people to learn from their shortfalls. This attitude is particularly important when novices are learning new skills. Managers can minimize harm to the organization by focusing employee efforts on incremental goals, so that errors are small and easily corrected in the next performance period.

- *Matched with the cadence of work.* Feedback should come at the completion of a discrete unit of work: a week's production, a project completed, a month's worth of sales, or a year's output of new product research. This isn't to say that a good manager shouldn't monitor work constantly and engage in a continuous dialogue with employees. But a manager must tread a fine line between overobserving (second cousin to micromanagement) and remaining too distant. Employees working autonomously want to be left alone to do their jobs. Matching feedback with the rhythm of work gives the individual a chance to produce an output undistracted by over-the-shoulder oversight. By the same token, assessment of work products as those products are completed means that feedback comes with a proximate opportunity to put improvement advice to use in the next production cycle.

- *Action-oriented.* Feedback has little meaning without plans for improvement. Pointing the feedback discussion toward concrete actions enhances goal achievement. Focusing on future improvement also gives the discussion a positive spin. This increases the likelihood an employee will walk out of the feedback session with a sense of optimism and a renewed energy to get it done the next time.[41]

Goal setting and results assessment that follow these principles give managers a platform for handling what many believe is their toughest challenge—dealing with poor performers. With specific, unambiguous, controllable goals, manager and employee should be able to agree on the causes of any performance shortfall. They can proceed to determine whether the issue lies with actual performance or with goals that, despite everyone's best efforts, were somehow unrealistic. With consistent dialogue and a focus on performance discrepancies as they arise, it should be possible to determine what needs to be addressed—employee competence, job demands and resources, external factors—to rectify performance concerns. This is not to suggest, however, that even an objective, fact-based assessment of performance deficiency will permit managers to avoid entirely the effects of emotional asymmetry. People simply react too strongly to bad news for that to be practical. However, by following the FAMIC and FITEMA precepts, managers give themselves and their employees the best possible chance to minimize the negative emotional effect.

We admit it—FAMIC and FITEMA may seem like a lot to handle. Still, we think it's worth the effort for managers to set goals and assess performance according to these guidelines. If this serving of acronym soup seems a bit too rich, then just keep in mind the words of psychologist Mihaly Csikszentmihalyi. He says that maximum focused engagement in achieving goals (a state he calls "flow") "tends to occur when a person's skills [are] fully involved in overcoming a challenge that is just about manageable."[42] The message to managers, then, is this: spend the time to develop employees' skills, set goals that are within the individual's grasp but not too easy, increase them over time in manageable increments, and make sure that people control the resources and circumstances to achieve what they've agreed to do. Coordinating these efforts with development strategies and career path mapping yields a powerful and integrated process for building high-performance people and competitively strong organizations.

SUMMARY: BUILDING TOMORROW'S ASSETS

Brook Manville, consultant and former chief learning officer and customer evangelist of Saba Software, sees two main schools of thought on what managers can do to build human capital: "The first is a sort of engineering approach, the idea that managers can put in place tools, systems, processes, and infrastructure that can move the organization to predictable and measurable goals. The second is a sort of gardening approach, the idea that managers at most are creating context, environment, and nourishment for people to do the right thing, but that the outcomes are much less predictable and can only be influenced so far by managers." He thinks the evolution of the manager's role as human capital treasurer will take us to a point between the extremes: "As always, I think the next truth will lie somewhere in the middle. We will increasingly see both managerial intervention—new tools, new infrastructure, new systems—and at the same time a greater embrace within those new contexts of self-organizing, individual-empowering, culture- and values-driven approaches.... We will see an ongoing synthesis between engineering and gardening."[43]

Manville's manager-as-gardener image captures the dichotomy of caring and support without total control. A gardener weeds, fertilizes, and protects the plants from pests, but the plant ultimately grows on its own. Likewise, a manager helps an employee assess his or her needs, introduces learning sources, and nurtures the development of each individual's particular talents, skills, and knowledge. To evoke a less elegant metaphor, we can say the manager functions as an individual's developmental GPS, suggesting a direction, plotting a development course through the organization's geography, and guiding but not compelling a particular route to human capital growth.

The manager's development responsibilities take on different shadings depending on an organization's competitive focus. In a product-and-service differentiation strategy, managers must ensure that competency growth is fast and nimble, to keep up with a shifting competitive world. If operating efficiently forms the centerpiece of strategy, learning will often take place close to the job and emphasize finding better ways to do things. When customer attention dominates an organization's competitive intent, learning must help employees interpret and respond to customer requirements. Regardless of which strategy an organization pursues, however, our data indicate that a strong contribution by managers to employee development is a hallmark of high-performing companies (that is, organizations scoring in the top ranks of our global survey database for both financial performance and employee engagement). Among high-performing companies that have a differentiation strategy, 70 percent or more of employees agree or agree strongly with this statement: "My supervisor develops people's ability." By contrast, lower-performing companies get manager scores in the 50–60 percent range for this item. We see similar results among the groups that emphasize operating efficiency and customer focus, with scores approaching 80 percent for managers' development efforts among high-performing organizations, and scores 10 to 25 percent points lower for their poorer-performing competitors.[44]

Making employee growth and development into a contributor to competitive strategy requires managers to go beyond the typical definitions of coaching and advising. Strongly performing managers whose development efforts make a difference to competitive success will:

- Not assume people's skills and attributes are largely fixed, but rather adopt the perspective that some dimensions of growth are feasible for most employees

- Not merely show people how to do their jobs better or connect them with training courses, but instead work with employees to form imaginative development plans and create a wide network of internal and external learning contacts

- Help people discover and travel diverse career paths, rather than merely discouraging them by saying that upward-sloping career vectors are unavailable

- Not just coach people to improve skills, but rather coach in a way that reinforces autonomy and self-efficacy

- Create an environment that nurtures human capital, rather than trying to engineer its growth

- Not stop at SMART goals or manipulate with stretch objectives, but instead make sure that employees have FAMIC goals and receive FITEMA feedback with incrementally challenging performance targets

Perhaps more than any other role change, increasing a manager's allocation of time and energy to building employees' human capital alters not only the structure but also the main intent of the manager's job. The shift of attention to human capital treasury reinforces the emphasis on employee and team output and reduces the primacy of individual managerial production. Elevating the focus on building employees' intangible assets also lifts the manager's eyes from a myopic focus on today's performance and requires her to think as well about future production—because today's human capital is the intellectual foundation for tomorrow's competitive success. Here is how Cisco's Susan Monaghan expresses this idea, reflecting the employee perspective:

"Managers should coach people to determine what's possible in the future, not just in how to do today's job. Managers must help people dream. We don't just want managers to help people go from point A to point B. We want managers to act almost as life coaches. This requires a one-to-one relationship with every employee and a one-to-one view. A career should be like a mini-tapestry, with threads running in multiple directions but creating an overall pattern."[45]

CHAPTER OUTLINE

Transforming the Extrinsic into the Intrinsic

Individualizing Rewards

Boosting Engagement Through Recognition

Inclusiveness Creates the Opportunity

Communication Defines the Context and Sets the Ground Rules

Trust Provides the Emotional Foundation

7

Delivering the Deal

What do a diamond, a Rachmaninoff rhapsody, and a hummingbird's wings have in common? All three represent variations on simpler themes. By combining a set of triangles, you can make the geometric figure of a diamond. Rachmaninoff took the basic harmonic progressions expressed by Niccolo Paganini in his violin *capricci* and created *Rhapsody on a Theme by Paganini* for piano and orchestra. And hummingbirds, like all birds, have wings. The hummingbird's wings pivot, however, a variation that allows them to hover the way no other bird can.

The relationship of people with organizations provides many examples of contemporary variations on long-established themes. Few elements of working life, however, have exhibited as many permutations in the last two decades as has the social contract between employees and organizations. Our research shows that, more than ever before, employees believe they must be self-reliant when it comes to ensuring that their deal with the organization yields value to them commensurate with their human capital investment. When we asked who has primary responsibility for career management and other key elements of their deal with the organization, respondents to our 2010 global workforce study responded overwhelmingly, "I do." Our survey results showed that:

- Seventy-five percent say they, not their companies, have primary responsibility for their financial future.

- Fifty-seven percent say they must provide for their own retirement income.

- Fifty-one percent agree that they have the principal responsibility for addressing their health care needs.

- Seventy-six percent agree that they have the main responsibility for ensuring their individual health and well-being.[1]

What is more, people expect that the weight of these responsibilities will fall on their shoulders with equal or greater impact five years from now. Coupled with employees' growing sense of self-reliance is an abiding concern about their ability to formulate and execute the plans needed to ensure their security. Generally, less than half of the respondents to our workforce study survey said that they feel comfortable with their ability to manage each of these areas. And they don't expect much help from their companies. Only about half said that job security and stability are achievable within their current organizations; less than one-third said that significantly higher compensation is a feasible goal.[2]

Given this uncertain landscape, what is the manager's role in supporting the exchange of value between individual and organization? In our view, it hinges on reciprocal return on investment. Employers want people to willingly, fully, and enthusiastically invest human capital in their jobs and their organizations. Employees want a return on that investment. Managers can do much to broker the exchange. On the one hand, they can deliver rewards in a way that maximizes their value to employees. On the other, they can help ensure that reward distribution supports employee engagement and ensures companies derive maximum worth from the value they provide to people. The key, we believe, is personalization.

Transforming the Extrinsic into the Intrinsic

The concept of individual customization, established in our discussion of job structure and revisited in the consideration of people development, emerges with full force in the delivery of the deal. To the manager falls the responsibility for helping employees navigate the organizational reward environment, to help them find personal motivation within the context of the organization's deal. Psychologist Mihaly Csikszentmihalyi describes the desired state like this: "Individuals must become independent of the social environment to the degree that they no longer respond exclusively in terms of its rewards and punishments. To achieve such autonomy, a person has to learn to provide rewards to herself."[3] For managers, this means delivering extrinsic rewards in a way that touches each employee's individual need for intrinsic fulfillment.

When considering rewards, most people think first about the formal financial programs on which organizations place so much emphasis. But decades of research have reinforced that intrinsic rewards like challenging and fulfilling work and growth opportunities drive employee engagement and satisfaction much more strongly than do pay and financial benefits. Intrinsically satisfying elements are a variation on the rewards theme, an opportunity for managers to customize and improvise how they ensure a return on each individual's contribution of human capital. To succeed in this, managers must remain vigilant about how tasks and organizational reward programs are positioned in the minds of employees. The framing of job requirements, and the reward outcomes they produce, can make a profound difference in their effect on intrinsic motivation.

Consider, for example, the examples in Table 7.1. They represent a continuum of motivational vignettes.

In the first two examples, coercive and external motivation, the pressure to perform is clearly externally imposed. These forms of motivation rarely produce anything more than grudging compliance. We hope few managers operate at these levels (though we know that some do). The next example, introjected motivation (when a person adopts external interest as her own, especially to avoid guilt or maintain feelings of self-worth), begins to show a glimmer of intrinsic motivation power. But

Table 7.1: The Continuum of Intrinsic and Extrinsic Motivation

Type of Motivation	Manager Says:	Employee Responds:
Coercive	"This is an order. Do it—or else."	"I'll either avoid doing it if I can or just go through the motions."
External	"Do this (probably unpleasant) thing and you'll get a reward."	"If the reward is enough to outweigh the unpleasantness, I'll do it. If not, I'll shirk."
Introjected	"Your team is counting on you to do this."	"This feels like a guilt trip, but I want to be a team player, so I guess I owe it to the group to do what's asked."
Integrated*	"This task has high strategic importance to our organization. There's a big bonus for you if you succeed."	"I'll do it because I identify with my organization, accept our mission, and want to help us succeed. The bonus tells me what the organization wants and reinforces the importance of the job."
Intrinsic	"What would you like to do and how?"	"I'll choose to do this because I get great pleasure and satisfaction from the work. I love getting better at it and being able to do it my way."

*Combines what Ryan and Deci call identified and integrated motivation.
Source: Adapted from Ryan, R. M., and Deci, E. L., "Self-Determination Theory and the Facilitation of Intrinsic Motivation, Social Development, and Well-Being," *American Psychologist*, 2000, 55(1), 72.

the motivation will have limited force and be short-lived. In the next case, integrated motivation, what is essentially extrinsic becomes largely intrinsic. This is the target scenario for most managers—to connect people with the collective interest and help them integrate it into their own view of the organization. It's also where financial rewards for performing successfully in implementing organizational strategy may help to increase feelings of intrinsic motivation and fulfillment. The last example, fully intrinsic motivation, has the strongest links with self-generated energy. The elements of individual autonomy and competence growth are clear.

We would advise managers who want to elicit intrinsic motivation in a reward environment rich with extrinsic reward tools to review the goal-setting and feedback discussion. We believe that setting energizing FAMIC goals provides a good start. Follow those with efficacy-enhancing FITEMA feedback. Connecting organizational reward programs with achievement of these goals, guided by this kind of feedback, gives managers a way to generate intrinsic motivation even when the reward environment is heavy with transactional financial elements.

Individualizing Rewards

We've seen how proactive and reactive people take different views of their jobs and their opportunities for autonomy at work. Managers must recognize and respond to these variations. To deliver a customized deal effectively, managers must start by accepting this truth: employee perceptions of reward system clarity, consistency, and motivational power depend on highly personal differences. Consequently, having uniform reward programs across an enterprise won't make everyone in the organization feel equally well compensated or engaged in their work. The beauty of the reward is in the eye of the receiver.[4]

For example, consider the central tenet of the deal between individual and organization—the expectation of reciprocity. People who receive something of value usually feel an impulse to give something in return.[5] However, the worth of the elements exchanged remains subject to each party's subjective valuations and beliefs about what constitutes an acceptable bargain. Organization researchers have discovered that people differ not only in how they value various rewards but also in the strength of their dedication to a rigorous exchange-based relationship. Some employees have a strong sense of what social scientists call exchange ideology. The effort they invest in work depends directly on their perception of how the organization has treated them. If they experience a decline in reward value—a reduction in bonus payments, for instance, or a cutback in learning opportunities—their high exchange ideology will lead to reduced feelings of obligation and commitment. In contrast, other employees view the give-and-take between individual and enterprise in broader terms. For them, a solid work ethic overrides the short-term focus on the details of exchange.[6]

Ultimately, individual traits like these affect a person's perspectives on every part of the deal, and on the concept of the deal itself. How is a manager to discover and comprehend these nuances? Here are some ways:

- Talk with employees about their work experiences. Find out how prior deals, both fulfilling and disappointing, have conditioned the individual's attitudes about rewards and reciprocity.

- Expect employees to show individual variations not only in the strength of their exchange ideology, but also in how they view the chronological connection between performance and rewards. People who consider themselves fast trackers, for example, may expect a bonus, a promotion, or a cool new project after every successful effort. In contrast, people with a long-term career focus and high organizational commitment may show more patience with time lags between human capital investment and reward. It's OK with them if accounts balance over the long term.

- Understand that employees view the manager herself as a representative of the organization. As researchers Robert Eisenberger and his team express it, "Beliefs in organizational support or malevolence may be fostered by employees' anthropomorphic ascription of dispositional traits to the organization.... Employees personify the organization, viewing actions by agents of the organization as actions of the organization itself."[7] Employees with strong exchange ideology pay particular attention to their managers' actions. Delivery of valued rewards heightens their trust. The opposite occurs when people don't receive rewards that conform to their personal needs or reflect their idiosyncratic definitions of an acceptable exchange.

These factors make up the human context within which managers must craft person-specific deals that reach employees' intrinsic motivations. Armed with insights about what drives intrinsic motivation for employees with different attitudes about rewards and exchange, managers can proceed to craft customized reward arrangements. Research into the effects of customized deals shows that they increase the sense of obligation people feel toward the company and nourish the commitment to reciprocity.[8] These strengthened bonds constitute the payoff for the extensive time and effort managers must invest in discovering and acting on the deal requirements of every employee in the unit.

Table 7.2 shows how a manager might construct different individualized deals for two people in a work unit. We've referred to them here as the Star Contributor and the Future Executive.

Both deals afford substantial opportunities for autonomy and competence building, but they're aimed at the particular needs and aspirations of the individuals. The manager who designed the two deals would have paid close attention to the exchange ideologies of the two employees. The Star Contributor, for example, might require a rapid succession of high-profile projects as a reward for performance. The Future Executive, in contrast, might be willing to accept a longer-term *quid pro quo* for his contribution. When we survey managers, we find that the most astute among them are aware of the power of customizing these reward areas. One participant in a manager survey put it this

Table 7.2: How Two Individualized Deals Might Look

Elements of the Deal	Star Contributor	Future Executive
Work design elements	Stimulating projects to work on	Growing responsibility for team or project leadership
	Membership on teams with smart people	Challenges reflecting both team relationships and project operations
	Challenges reflecting technical issues and questions	Ownership of results emphasizing project completion and performance
	Ownership of results emphasizing technical or functional elegance	Access to the latest project management tools and approaches
	Access to the latest, most sophisticated tools	
Growth opportunities	Career development plan focused on achievement of high technical contributor status	Career development plan focused on achieving executive rank
	Contact with network of senior experts in the discipline	Leadership responsibility for increasingly larger and more important projects over time
	Mobility around the organization	Leadership training
	Attendance at technical conferences	Technical training sufficient to keep skills current and credible
	Ongoing education to enable continuing innovation	
Recognition	Technical contributions acknowledged	Project success acknowledged, leadership potential reinforced
	Opportunity to present to external technical conferences	Opportunity to teach leadership as part of organization's learning and development curriculum
Compensation	Base salary reflecting market levels	Base salary reflecting market levels
	Goals and incentives emphasizing intellectual capital development and commercializable contributions	Goals and incentives emphasizing team effectiveness and project success
Benefits	Standard health and welfare and retirement benefits	Standard health and welfare and retirement benefits
	Flexible schedule and work location	Cubicle (eventually office) with a window

way: "I have no ability to provide pay incentives for most things, so I must take advantage of learning and job enhancement opportunities, which has worked out very well—I would argue better than financial incentives."

Employees' inclination to lobby for a customized deal—and to focus that arrangement on either relational (intrinsic) or transactional (extrinsic) elements—will reflect enduring personality traits. People who take a proactive approach to their work, for example, are more likely to ask for a customized work arrangement than those more passive and introverted. Moreover, research suggests that people who are wary of reciprocation and highly attuned to the perceived equity of rewards will tend to emphasize transactional elements such as pay and benefits. Conversely, employees who have less suspicion about reciprocation and worry less about the immediate exchange will focus more attention on intrinsic, relational factors. They are in it for the long haul and don't insist on a short-term value-for-value deal. The same is true for people who exhibit high conscientiousness. These dependable, strong achievers also tend to view their human capital investments as a long-term play. They are willing to delay gratification and not press for a near-term transactional exchange.[9]

Although individualized deals are usually heavy on intrinsic reward elements, customization can also extend into traditionally inflexible areas, like pay. Take, for example, the compensation structure at San Francisco-based Skyline Construction. Skyline was named by *The Wall Street Journal* as one of the fifteen top small workplaces in America in 2009. All of the company's stock is owned by employees, including unionized workers. What's interesting about Skyline, however, is that they give a group of management employees the ability to choose how they will divide their total compensation between base pay and bonus. One manager, with a wife, two children, and a home in an upscale suburb, says he prefers the security of a higher salary and lower incentive: "I can bank on that, and I don't have to take the risk." Others who are less risk-averse can opt for a lower base but higher earnings potential from a bigger bonus opportunity. Bonus factors include such nonfinancial measures as customer satisfaction and timely project completion. Skyline pays no bonuses if the company doesn't generate an operating profit. Plus, the company supports the flexible pay plan with an additional critical element: open-book management. All of these mechanisms reinforce individual flexibility and support a culture of involvement. It's also a culture of success—the company doubled its revenue between 2004 and 2007.[10]

In crafting and delivering customized deals, managers balance the interests of the employee with those of the organization. But there's another constituency with a horse in the race: other employees in the unit. Individualized deals are constructed to deliver a win-win outcome for individual and organization. But they also need to produce a third win—or at least a no-lose—for the individual's coworkers. Research by Lei Lai of Tulane University, Denise Rousseau of Carnegie Mellon, and Klarissa Chang of the National University of Singapore identifies the conditions under which coworkers feel most at ease with other people's individualized deals:

- *Personal friendship.* People more willingly tolerate individualized deals enjoyed by those whom they consider friends.

- *Social exchange.* People who view the relationship with their employer as a social exchange based on mutual respect and reciprocity have a positive attitude toward individualized deals; those who perceive their relationship to be entirely economic express a more negative opinion.

- *Comparable opportunity.* People who believe they too have the opportunity to forge a customized deal have higher acceptance of other workers' individualized arrangements.[11]

In the long run, it does the organization little good to gratify the needs of one or a few individuals but make other employees feel unfairly treated. Not everyone wants or needs a customized deal, but all employees must believe they have equal opportunity to create one.

Boosting Engagement Through Recognition

A successful business is like a powerful sports car: it moves quickly, turns nimbly, and handles curves without losing momentum. And sometimes a business, like a car, will hit a speed bump, go into a ditch, or run out of gas. Regardless of the driving conditions, both perform best when they have strong engines. For a Ferrari, the power comes from a 500-horsepower, V-12 power plant. In a corporation, the engine is employee engagement.

Like sports-car drivers, managers are constantly looking for ways to generate more power. One of the best ways to boost a car's output is to turbocharge it. Adding a turbocharger, which pumps heated air into the cylinders, can increase horsepower by 30 to 40 percent. How can a company achieve a similar power boost? Joint research we conducted with O.C. Tanner Co., a major provider of appreciation awards, training, and consulting, showed that manager-delivered recognition of employee performance boosts engagement the way a turbocharger cranks up a sports car's horsepower. Figure 7.1 illustrates this effect.

The right-hand pair of bars depicts organizations that have an unfavorable engagement environment (low scores in such areas as development opportunity and senior executive concern for employee well-being). Even in those low-engagement workplaces, recognition from immediate supervisors and managers has a dramatic effect. In these environments, strong manager performance in recognizing employee performance increases engagement by almost 60 percent, from 33 percent of employees giving a favorable engagement score to 52 percent. In organizations with a culture more strongly supporting employee engagement (represented by the left-hand bars), the effect of manager recognition is less striking, but nevertheless significant—a gain in favorable engagement scores from 77 to 91 percent, an increase of almost 20 percent.

Figure 7.1: Recognition from the Manager Boosts Employee
             Engagement

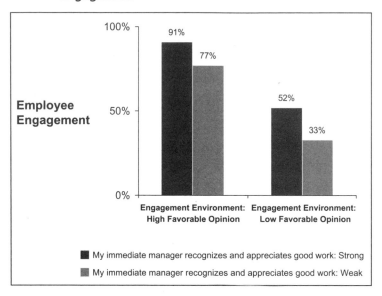

Source: O.C. Tanner 2008 Global Recognition Study.

Our research reinforced that recognition from managers has another important effect on engagement. We asked the survey respondents to specify the organizational context in which they had received their most fulfilling recognition. The majority said that their best experience had occurred within their teams or work groups (35 percent of the respondents) or at the department level (37 percent).[12] Departments and work groups are the supervisor's and manager's home turf, the place where he has the greatest impact as a leader and as a source of appreciation. These are the venues where a pat on the back, a word of praise in front of the team, or the public presentation of a commendation has great power to increase employee engagement, not to mention intrinsic fulfillment and motivation.

The research told us that effective recognition from managers encompasses three basic requirements: inclusiveness, communication, and trust. These factors are shown in Exhibit 7.1.

Exhibit 7.1: Three Requirements for Effective Manager Recognition

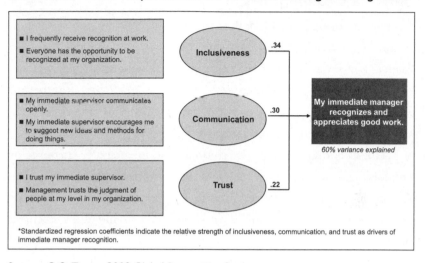

*Standardized regression coefficients indicate the relative strength of inclusiveness, communication, and trust as drivers of immediate manager recognition.

Source: O.C. Tanner 2008 Global Recognition Study.

These three main drivers of effective recognition seem like basic requirements for good management. However, each factor has specific aspects that can power up or power down the effect of recognition on employee engagement.

Inclusiveness Creates the Opportunity

Inclusiveness begins with frequent recognition opportunities. Can you imagine a sports announcer who asks the crowd to hold its applause until the end of the game? Of course not—fans want to clap and cheer at every opportunity, and the athletes want to hear their appreciation. The same notion—at lower decibels—pertains at work. Frequent recognition is like applause—it rewards the accomplishment in real time. To be inclusive in their appreciation of employees, managers need to ensure wide availability of recognition opportunities. This means not only that everyone must have the opportunity to excel and be appreciated, but also that the criteria and rules, formal and informal, must be clear and fairly applied to all employees.

Communication Defines the Context and Sets the Ground Rules

Communication means more than just keeping information flowing. It means being unambiguous about the connections among goals, performance, and rewards. For recognition to act as an effective engagement driver, managers must confer with employees to define clear performance expectations and, with equal clarity, convey to employees what shape the rewards for performance will take.

The second element in the communication category, encouraging employee efforts to develop new and better ways of doing work, takes the manager-employee conversation to a higher level. We already know about the power of autonomy. It frees employees to find and implement better ways to work and enables them to define the activities they perform and the mechanisms by which they can do well. Control over the elements of performance, in turn, confers greater responsibility for results, enhances the opportunity for skill development, and makes recognition for achievements that much richer.

Trust Provides the Emotional Foundation

Our research showed that reciprocal trust establishes the emotional basis for effective recognition. As we know from Chapter Three, trust is part of the foundation of the manager performance model. In the context of recognition, trusting a manager means having confidence that the manager will keep the employee's well-being at heart and recognize performance whenever (but only when) recognition is earned.

On the flip side, perceiving reciprocal trust from management confirms that the organization was right to foster employee autonomy. To put it bluntly, managers won't support self-determination for people they don't trust. A manager's confidence in employees, in turn, comes from the belief that employee decision making will pay off for the organization as well as for the workforce. Believing in management's trust heightens the sense that recognition for accomplishments is deserved and therefore makes it all the more powerful.

THE PSYCHOLOGY OF RECOGNITION

As social scientists and neuroscientists study the behaviors and attitudes of people at work, they have uncovered some of the psychological and physiological mechanisms that underlie the power of recognition from managers. It turns out that recognition, engagement, and performance form a self-reinforcing system, shown in Figure 7.2.

Figure 7.2: The Circle of Recognition and Engagement

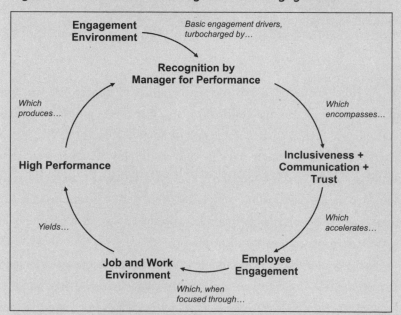

Source: O.C. Tanner 2008 Global Recognition Study.

Recognition sparks feelings of engagement as well as the belief that performance will yield reward. Reward and recognition, and the events that signal them, trigger the release of the neurotransmitter dopamine from several sites in the brain. Research shows that

(Continued)

the effects of dopamine are particularly strong when a positive event is unexpected—an unanticipated award, for example, or impromptu praise for success on a risky project. When an employee has met the defined criteria for recognition, the moment of recognition is expected—appreciated but not unpredictable. But when a manager surprises an employee with unanticipated recognition, the emotional power increases significantly. Dopamine, and the positive mood it creates, contributes to innovative thinking and creative problem solving, both important contributors to high performance. High performance, in turn, produces the next round of reward and recognition, which gives rise to engagement and innovative solutions to problems, and the circle continues.[13]

As organizations look for ways to build and sustain marketplace momentum, they must capitalize on the power of recognition. It represents one of management's most potent tools for focusing employees on what matters to the enterprise and reinforcing the behaviors that contribute most directly to strategic success. Managers who work tenaciously to improve inclusion, communication, and trust can provide the extra edge that yields a competitive advantage, the power surge that pushes one organization ahead of the others.

Smart organizations realize that, even (or especially) in a challenging economic environment, they need to continue investing in employee recognition. At United Airlines, for example, recognition isn't just nice to do—it's a critical element of the deal with employees, intended to directly support the business strategy. Despite revenue and cost pressure, United has more than doubled its funding for employee recognition, from a per-employee average of $20 to about $50. To reward success in just one key area—achieving on-time performance—United has set aside $30 million. "We've put a big focus on recognition," says Cynthia Starz, United's Managing Director of Leadership & Organizational

Development. "We want to create a more personal connection between employees and the company."[14]

United's summary of its competitive strategy is "Focus on 5 Safely." The phrase refers to major imperatives that constitute United's belief about what it takes to run a good airline. The five are:

- Score high on basic Department of Transportation service measures in areas like on-time performance and baggage handling.

- Deliver a clean, workable product—that is, make the aircraft environment part of the service package.

- Achieve industry-leading revenue by getting the most out of both ticket sales and incremental items like extra baggage charges and onboard food sales.

- Carefully manage and, where possible, reduce operating cost.

- Ensure customer contact personnel are courteous, caring, and respectful, with customer and employee satisfaction as the ultimate measures.

All United managers have a recognition tool kit with ideas and rewards associated with each of the five imperatives. The organization also provides an online tool that enables managers to recognize employee performance in specific Focus on 5 Safely imperatives. Using the tool, a manager can either obtain a token of recognition (for example, a plaque) or print a certificate for an employee. United management will be able to track how frequently and consistently specific managers use the tool for recognizing employee performance. In addition, managers have received training focused on leading their teams. A key component includes tips and tools for effective recognition.

The focus on the power of manager recognition is part of a broader set of leadership expectations at United. The airline has implemented a system for measuring how well leaders at all levels use recognition and other tools to keep employees engaged in serving customers and operating efficiently. United has also studied employee and customer survey data, along with operational and financial metrics, to define the link between employees' workplace experience and the desired business results. Knowing that successful companies leverage leadership to drive results, United has created a Leadership Effectiveness (LE) index.

United's LE index is designed to measure leader alignment, employee enablement, performance management, high performer retention, and employee development. "The leadership index covers everyone from the chairman on down to anyone who has at least one direct report. We're trying to make sure that people at all levels are focused on leadership, that we reinforce their understanding of the impact they have as leaders and signal-senders," Starz says.

The description in Table 7.3 expands on the components of the LE index.

For 2010, United set a goal of 7 percent improvement from the 2008 LE baseline figure. Each of the top 250 leaders of the company has an individual 2010 objective, with a weight of 10 percent, exclusively focused on improving his or her division's LE scores. Senior leaders also have a portion of their performance pay tied to LE.

SUMMARY: MANAGERIAL ALCHEMY

It is difficult to overestimate the motivational power many executives and most organizations ascribe to financial rewards. "Pay for performance" has become a largely unchallenged, albeit aspirational, foundation for reward strategies. Among respondents to our Reward Challenges and Changes survey, only 18 percent say their organizations have no formal program for differentiating performance and steering comparatively higher levels of financial rewards to people designated as high performers.[15] Stanford Professor Jeffrey Pfeffer goes to the heart of the matter when he says, "The big push for incentive pay stems from a belief that if employees were just compensated appropri-

Table 7.3: United Airlines Leadership Effectiveness Index Structure

Leadership Effectiveness	
Perceptual Measures of Leadership Effectiveness 50% Weight	*Observable Measures of Leadership Effectiveness 50% Weight*
Leader alignment Measures leader's understanding of and support and accountability for enterprise business objectives	**Internal leader promotion rate** Captures movements into leadership positions
Employee enablement Gauges employees' perception of having the tools, skills, information, and manager support to do their jobs effectively	**High-performer retention rate** Reflects ability to keep higher-performing employees in the organization
Performance management Reflects employee assessment of their managers' ability to provide timely, helpful, and clear performance feedback and recognition	**Quality of performance management** Assesses value of performance reviews using random sample of review write-ups

ately, virtually every organizational and management problem could be solved."[16]

And how well do the programs actually work? Not very well, if you ask employees. Across our database of survey responses, less than two-thirds of employees of U.S. firms say they understand how their performance bonuses are calculated. When asked to consider their total compensation, 67 percent say they are fairly paid for the work they do. But only 43 percent believe their organizations do a good job of matching pay to performance.[17]

We don't mean to suggest that incentive plans have no place in the deal between individual and enterprise. Intelligently defined and judiciously used, they have great power to signal to employees the behaviors and results the organization values most. That's how Shutterfly uses its quarterly bonuses (see the sidebar in Chapter Five). Incentives can also play an important part in a manager's efforts to gather her team and recognize contribution—as long as the recognition encompasses more than just financial rewards. Consider this description of a reward-allocation philosophy, a paraphrase by Pfeffer of the thoughts of George Zimmer, founder of clothing retailer Men's Wearhouse: "You want incentives to be just large enough but not too large.... You want rewards to be large enough to be noticed, and you want to use them to provide an occasion for celebration and recognition, to let the group come together and share successes and enjoy each other's companionship. But you certainly don't want to make the incentives so large that they begin to drive and thereby distort behavior."[18]

Managers who hope to use the reward tools afforded by organizations to deliver an engaging and energizing deal to employees must:

- Not just administer the organization's reward systems, but also perform a kind of alchemy, transforming extrinsic financial incentives into sources of intrinsic fulfillment

- Not deliver the same reward portfolio to everyone, but instead create individualized deals for each employee; managers must understand that, although those deals may not differ greatly across the employee population, it's important that each person feel as though his deal is custom-tailored for him

- Not just execute the recognition programs provided by the company, but rather create a recognition-rich environment in which formal and informal, predictable and unanticipated recognition turbocharge employee engagement

Ultimately, an employee's work and the deal that rewards him for the quality and quantity of that work are inextricably bound. Managers must recognize that, in a sense, work and reward are one and the same. They can be guided by the words of American civil rights activist and author W.E.B. DuBois: "The return from your work must be the satisfaction which that work brings you and the world's need of that work. With this, life is heaven, or as near heaven as you can get. Without this—with work which you despise, which bores you, and which the world does not need—this life is hell."[19]

CHAPTER OUTLINE

Coping with Imposed Change
Embrace Positive Change
Handle Adverse Change

Choosing to Change
Enhance Individual Creativity
Build Adaptable Teams

Sustaining Engagement
Foster Well-Being
Ensure Performance Support

8

Energizing Change

Reinhold Niebuhr, American theologian and social critic, offered his serenity prayer as a way to think about circumstances and our power to change them. His words have become familiar: "God, give us grace to accept with serenity the things that cannot be changed, courage to change the things which should be changed, and the wisdom to distinguish the one from the other."[1] Useful as this guidance is, however, it doesn't cover every form of change we face. It ignores the imposed alterations, modifications, and deviations—some pleasant, many not—that take place because of factors outside organizations' control.

Figure 8.1 shows the paths of change, beginning with the two different change forms:

- Imposed change, in response to circumstances largely beyond the control of people and companies

- Chosen change, the kind pursued by innovative organizations, especially those in fast-moving markets and rapidly evolving industries

Chosen change, we assume for this discussion, will have a positive intent. However, it may also require employees to adapt in some way. Imposed change typically brings stress and challenge, requiring people to adapt if events produce positive effects, and to exhibit resilience if the transition is more difficult. By *adapt* we mean to modify actions and attitudes to make the most of new circumstances. If those circumstances are harmful—positions eliminated, support resources reduced,

Figure 8.1: Energizing Change—Adaptability and Resilience Are
the Keys

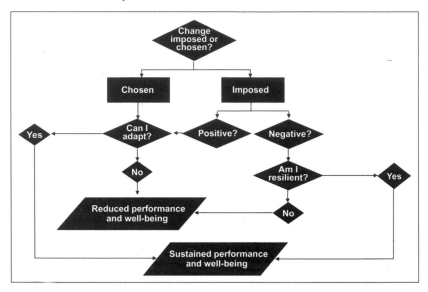

workloads increased—then adaptability is not enough. Under those conditions, employees must be *resilient*. They must withstand the shock of change, adjust to new realities, and rebound from the experience to perform as strongly as before, or even more strongly. Whether change is imposed or actively pursed, positive or negative in its ultimate effects, employees will inevitably need to respond in some way. For the outcomes of change to include sustained well-being and continued or improved performance, managers must take steps to build the organization's change capability. They do this by helping to build each employee's change readiness and capacity to withstand uncertainty and turmoil.

Coping with Imposed Change

Economic pressures, new competitors, other companies' novel product and service offerings, technologies that promise efficiency improvements

—these outside forces and many more can force executives to conclude that something about business strategy, production processes, or resource allocation must change. As Figure 8.1 suggests, how people respond to the challenges of externally imposed change will depend largely on whether their adaptability or their resilience is called upon, and on how they respond to that call.

Embrace Positive Change

When organizations respond to external forces by resolving to change, they need to carve out specific roles for line managers. By doing so, they improve their chances that employees will not just accept, but also embrace, the new ways of working. One study, conducted by a team of researchers at Troy University and Auburn University, looked at how health care workers adapted to the introduction of new record-keeping technology. The team studied how nurses and other workers responded to the transition from using laptop computers for patient care documentation to using hand-held devices. Nurses also had to move from printed patient care plans to automated clinical planning software. The nurses hadn't sought these changes. From their standpoint, the new ways of working were imposed by the organization. From the organization's standpoint, the potential benefits were clear. Nurses would become more efficient, improving the continuity of patient care and reducing the expense associated with copying and pushing paper.

The researchers found that individual adaptability in response to new work-altering technology depends on the degree to which managers:

- *Ensure that technology provides work support and improves performance.* When a job becomes more interesting and its mastery more fulfilling, individual performance improves. Work process changes that add to job enrichment and mastery therefore contribute to performance. Managers needed to make sure that the new devices made jobs easier, not harder, and workers more productive, not less so. Change that brings out what is essential and important about the job contributes to success. New ways of working that distract workers from what seems most interesting and involving about their work does the opposite. We know from our discussion of job content that challenging and demanding work, if properly supported, produces a host of positive effects. New, efficiency-enhancing technology can provide such job support. Conversely, if technology reduces job complexity and challenge to the point where work becomes simplistic, laden with minutiae, or devoid of challenge, employee engagement may be eroded. No nurse wants his or her work to become more about pushing buttons than serving patients.

- *Involve workers in the introduction of new technologies.* Involvement means giving the affected populations some say about when and how technology would be introduced. It requires managers to seek employees' advice on how employees, patients, and customers might respond to new ways of doing things. Control, in turn, increases the likelihood that workers will accept modifications in how they do their work. Also, involving workers who have direct influence over production and service delivery will build their confidence that new technology will enhance (and not degrade) their ability to serve patients and customers effectively. The goal is to give people substantial control over their workplace destinies. Doing so increases feelings of autonomy, self-efficacy, and mastery.

  Following a circular path, self-efficacy itself promotes the adoption of technological innovation. According to Albert Bandura, "Early adopters of beneficial technologies not only increase their productivity but can gain influence in ways that change the structural patterns of organizations.... Beliefs of personal efficacy to master computers were predictive of early adoption of the computerized system. Early adopters gained more influence and centrality within the organization over time than did later adopters."[2] The engagement path progresses like this: involvement in change efforts boosts control and engagement, which increase self-efficacy, which fosters rapid adoption of job-

enhancing technology, which increases engagement-driving connections with the organization. A virtuous circle, if there ever was one.

- *Clarify individual roles within the affected organizations before new technology comes on the scene.* Role clarity goes to the heart of rational engagement. It forms an essential connection between individual work and organizational success. Ambiguity about roles and lack of clarity about contribution to unit and enterprise success provoke negative reactions to technological changes. Conversely, workers who have a better line of sight between their jobs and the success of the organization show more inclination to embrace changes of all kinds. Their comfort with change becomes all that much stronger when their managers help them envision a positive effect on product and service outcomes.[3]

Findings like these have been replicated in other circumstances where organizations responded to external conditions by introducing change intended to improve work processes. For instance, researchers from the University of Queensland in Australia conducted a two-year study of organizational changes in the Queensland Public Service (QPS) depart-ment. QPS undertook the organizational restructuring in response to recommendations from an independent external review body. The goal of the changes: to increase program efficiency while maintaining high-quality service for external clients. The QPS experience provides a good example of change that originated externally but had a prospectively positive result. Over the course of the two-year analysis, the researchers found that employees with high self-efficacy experienced greater job satisfaction over the period of change in spite of increases in three sources of change-related stress: role ambiguity; higher workloads; and what the academics called "change-related difficulties" (disruptions to workflow, loss of personnel, and concerns about long-term career prospects). They said, "Change-related self-efficacy was an important buffer of three change-related stressors in the prediction of employee adjustment, 2 years after the organizational change process was initiated."[4]

The consistent pattern across these examples is the effort that companies made, in part through supervisors and managers, to increase employee adaptability. Involvement in change efforts gives employees an element of control, which makes change seem less threatening and makes accommodating it less daunting. Managers can increase employees' sense of security and stability by keeping them informed of progress and helping to preserve clarity about their roles and contributions. Perhaps most important, managers can build employees' self-efficacy by the way they recognize and reinforce strong performance during periods of uncertainty. The secret to adaptability is preserving whatever shouldn't be changed—successful techniques, strong inter-employee relationships, team structures that work—while making the changes that will produce genuine improvement. On this point we agree with Jonathan Gosling and Henry Mintzberg: "Change cannot be managed without continuity. Accordingly, the trick...is to mobilize energy around those things that need changing, while being careful to maintain the rest."[5] Sounds like something Reinhold Niebuhr might say.

Handle Adverse Change

Anyone who has lived through a downsizing knows that external factors can sometimes lead companies to make painful changes. This kind of change is represented by the imposed negative change/resilience path shown in Figure 8.1. Organizational and clinical psychologists have had ample opportunity to study the impact of downsizing and other adverse changes and stressful events over the last forty years. Building on the initial work on grieving by Elisabeth Kübler-Ross, researchers have plotted the journey that employees take through the coping process. In the work context, the stages of adjustment begin with shock/surprise and progress to denial/anger, depression, acceptance/experimentation, and closure/moving on. Individual feelings of self-worth cycle up and down during the process, as Exhibit 8.1 shows.

For employees to feel a commitment to the organization during times of adverse change, they must understand the context and business

Exhibit 8.1: Coping with Adverse Change—How the Manager Can Help

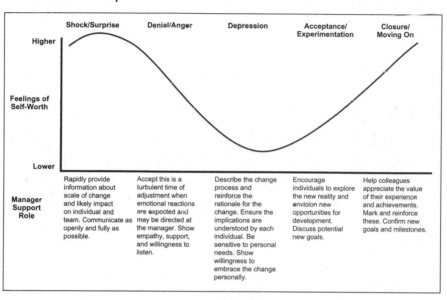

	Shock/Surprise	Denial/Anger	Depression	Acceptance/ Experimentation	Closure/ Moving On
Manager Support Role	Rapidly provide information about scale of change and likely impact on individual and team. Communicate as openly and fully as possible.	Accept this is a turbulent time of adjustment when emotional reactions are expected and may be directed at the manager. Show empathy, support, and willingness to listen.	Describe the change process and reinforce the rationale for the change. Ensure the implications are understood by each individual. Be sensitive to personal needs. Show willingness to embrace the change personally.	Encourage individuals to explore the new reality and envision new opportunities for development. Discuss potential new goals.	Help colleagues appreciate the value of their experience and achievements. Mark and reinforce these. Confirm new goals and milestones.

Source: Adapted from Kübler-Ross, E., *On Death and Dying*, New York: Macmillan, 1969; and Cameron, E., and Green, M., *Making Sense of Change Management*, 2nd Edition, London: Kogan Page, 2009.

case for change. The case needs to be made at two levels. From those at the top of the enterprise, employees typically expect to hear about the rationale for a major business change, the external pressures that have led to the change, and the consequences associated with not changing. However, they prefer to learn from their managers how the change is likely to affect them personally. They want to hear from, and be heard by, someone who knows them and is familiar with their day-to-day work lives.

The manager support roles outlined in Exhibit 8.1 provide a roadmap for guiding people through the process of difficult change. But employees need something more to deal with trauma in a way that minimizes its emotional and cognitive effects and preserves performance. That additional element is resilience. Resilient employees emerge from traumatic experiences with at least as much vitality as they had before the bad times occurred. Resilience incorporates adaptability, but goes further. Adaptability enables people to change as circumstances require. Resilience provides the capacity to handle more profound, more disruptive change and to emerge from the experience with strengthened resolve and greater performance capacity.

CAN RESILIENCE BE TRAINED?

Some jobs require constant adjustment and flexibility. Combat troops, for example, cope with unpredictable hazards and fast-moving situations every day. Resilience equips them to bounce back from the unpredictability, confusion, and trauma that inevitably accompany combat. The ability to modify plans, change strategies, absorb losses, and persevere are essential to battlefield success. Even the best battle plans don't eliminate the need for flexibility.

The U.S. Army has begun piloting the use of resilience training among soldiers, their families, and army civilians. Resilience training is the latest in a series of programs designed to address worries about post-traumatic stress disorder, a debilitating condition with both psychological and physical symptoms. The Army sees the training as a part of a multifaceted soldier fitness effort designed to bring mental fitness up to the same level as physical fitness. As one participant said, "Resilience training encourages a person to take a mental note of their past behavior and present situation and promotes alternative ways to view the occurrence." Phase 2 of the program will involve establishing a school to train leaders, including squad leaders and platoon sergeants, on how to impart resilience training to their troops. Phase 3 will extend this on a voluntary basis to family members and Army civilians.[6]

Psychologists at the University of Pennsylvania Positive Psychology Center will conduct the training with first-line sergeants who interact directly with new recruits. "The time to train is not immediately before you are deployed," says Brig. Gen. Rhonda Cornum, who heads the Comprehensive Soldier Fitness Program, which includes the resiliency training program. "Drill sergeants are the key to this; they have a huge impact on new soldiers."[7]

As with virtually all psychological traits, resilience has a dispositional component. People who display resilience have what one team of researchers called "a dynamic psychological capacity of adaptation and coping with adversity."[8] Proactive people, those who seek challenges rather than avoiding them (we met them back in Chapter Five), tend to deal relatively effectively with a variety of occupational stressors, including change. Resilience also has both personal and environmental aspects that managers can influence. We have identified three actions that managers can take to increase employee resilience. Our recommendations come in part from analyzing data from the Towers Watson global database of high-performing companies. Figure 8.2 shows the areas in which high-performing companies improved in 2009 over the 2008 high-performance scores, in spite of the economic recession.

Minimize Risk to the Deal

Managers can reduce the impact of adverse change by reinforcing the organization's commitment to honoring its deal with employees. As a stable basis for exchange, the deal must remain the solid, predictable core of the relationship between employee and organization. When change threatens the deal, people become distracted and distrustful. Note in Figure 8.2 that continuing to offer long-term opportunities to employees is a distinguishing factor of high-performing companies. In effect, these organizations have said to people, "We know times are tough, but we value you and what you bring to our organization. We intend to preserve that relationship."

Figure 8.2: High-Performing Companies Improved in Difficult Times

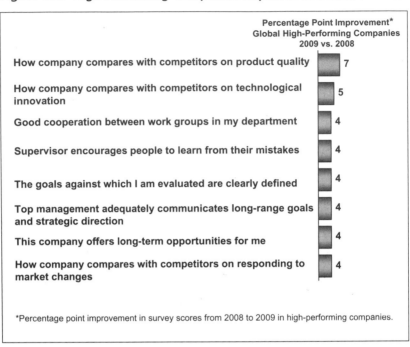

	Percentage Point Improvement* Global High-Performing Companies 2009 vs. 2008
How company compares with competitors on product quality	7
How company compares with competitors on technological innovation	5
Good cooperation between work groups in my department	4
Supervisor encourages people to learn from their mistakes	4
The goals against which I am evaluated are clearly defined	4
Top management adequately communicates long-range goals and strategic direction	4
This company offers long-term opportunities for me	4
How company compares with competitors on responding to market changes	4

*Percentage point improvement in survey scores from 2008 to 2009 in high-performing companies.

Source: Towers Watson analysis.

In some cases, of course, organizations believe they have no choice but to alter the deal, usually to reduce cost in the face of economic pressure. Smart companies minimize the shock by avoiding layoffs where possible and aiming the biggest economic hits at the populations that can most afford them. In early 2009, for example, Hewlett-Packard (HP) CEO Mark Hurd announced that, in spite of continued economic pressure, the company would resist further staff reductions. Instead, HP would apply salary reductions across the employee population. But the pain was apportioned according to level in the organization. The pay of executive council members was trimmed by 15 percent. Other executives got 10 percent reductions. The base salaries of exempt employees went down by 5 percent, and nonexempt employees experienced cuts of 2.5 percent. Hurd took a 20 percent reduction. "We have to do something because the numbers just don't add up," he said. But he also told employees, "My goal is to keep the muscle of this organization intact." And he was prepared to take heat from Wall Street: "I'll be asked by investors, 'Where's the job action, where are you taking out this roughly 20,000 positions?' Well, I don't want to do that. When I look at HP, I don't see a structural problem of that magnitude."[9]

Widescale change like this affects not only how people perceive the integrity and effectiveness of executives, but also how they judge the fairness and trustworthiness of their immediate managers. People assess most forms of change, even those that have economy-wide causes and organization-wide effects, through the filter of their relationship with their direct supervisors. Like politics, all change is local. Employees will wonder to themselves whether and how their managers could have buffered the effects of change and whether they should have done something to make things better, or at least not as bad. The storehouse of trust shared by employee and manager will affect how an individual resolves these concerns. Consequently, every manager needs to ensure that any modifications to the employee deal scrupulously follow the criteria we define in the next chapter: fair process, fair outcome, fair individual treatment, and fair explanation. Note that in high-performing organizations, managers also make sure that employees have clearly defined performance goals. An environment of change is no time for ambiguity about what organizations expect employees to deliver or how they will be rewarded for their performance.

Build Human Capital to Support Change

In many organizations, the first response to economic pressure and the perceived need to cut cost is a reduction in funding for training. Of the respondents to a Towers Perrin survey of cost cutting in 2008 and 2009, 45 percent said they had cut training programs or planned do to so within the next year and a half. Almost all of these cuts were expected to be applied organizationwide.[10] Witnessing this kind of action, employees must ask themselves, "Of all the assets this company could stop maintaining during times of economic pressure and change, why would they choose human capital, the one asset that will contribute most to our eventual recovery?" Good question—we often ask it ourselves.

Fortunately for line managers, the power of low-cost informal learning makes it a feasible strategy for continuing to build employee human capital, even, or perhaps especially, in times of cost cuts and organizational restructuring. In some cases, managers may be able to take advantage of reduced workloads to give people the development projects that didn't made the list when work flows were heavier. For the same reason, cross training may become more feasible. Firsthand experience with other jobs in the unit has several benefits: it expands employees' understanding of the group's strategic contribution; improves their ability to be effective team members; and increases the versatility that makes them valuable employees during lean times.

We've previously discussed how manager-directed learning can help employees build self-efficacy and mastery. But it can also do more. Research by a team from the Georgia Institute of Technology and the University of South Carolina–Upstate on how people respond to traumatic change suggested that individuals' beliefs about their abilities may buffer the effects of stressful job conditions. When people feel competent and confident in their ability to do their work well, uncertainty about the future decreases, fear of failure declines, and perceived loss of control diminishes. Job-related self-efficacy thus leads to change-specific self-efficacy. Self-efficacy in dealing with change, in turn, boosts resilience. Their analysis showed that high self-efficacy correlated with people's willingness to support change. After studying change experiences in a wide variety of organizations, the researchers concluded, "Individuals who feel more confident about their ability to handle change (i.e., have high change self-efficacy) should be less negatively affected by the demands placed on them by workplace changes and thus more willing or committed to support such changes than those with low change self-efficacy."[11] In high-performing companies, supervisors also take pains to make it clear to people that, even when everyone feels the urgency to adapt and perform well, it's OK to learn from things that go wrong. This sends two messages to employees: it's still important to grow human capital; and mistakes aren't fatal, even when the pressure's on.

Sharpen the Strategic Focus of Work

Employees in high-performing organizations have confidence that their companies are beating the competition in product quality, innovation, and market flexibility. In other words, tough as times may be, these people believe that their organizations have maintained a focus on competitive leadership. Moreover, they express faith that executive leaders have a plan for preserving and extending that advantage in the future. What better way to build employee resilience than to reinforce their confidence in the company's future, and underscore their role in contributing to it? Belief in competitive superiority is a powerful tonic for the ills of economic trauma.

Managers contribute in part by ensuring effective cooperation among the unit's work groups. This not only brings the strategic focus down to the local level, but also reinforces the social contribution to individual resilience. Psychologists know that supportive relationships heighten resilience to stress.[12] Employees get a double benefit when they also perceive that the manager has focused team and individual efforts on strategically important goals aimed at achieving success in spite of marketplace challenges.

Resilience is like the tree in the Chinese proverb. The best time to build resilience, or plant a tree, was in the past. The second-best time is today. Everything a capable manager does every day contributes to employees' ability to function in any environment, including one full of turmoil and uncertainty. Farsighted organizations, the ones that know that hard changes are sometimes unavoidable, can support managers by providing employee training to increase resilience. Truly resilient employees emerge from change having grown and gained insight, so their future performance may improve because of the experience.

Less-resilient people may simply revert back to their prior comfort zones—not a bad outcome of change, but not the best possible one. Employees who fall even further down the resilience scale may recover from change but never overcome the perception of loss and harm. Their motivation and engagement will continue to suffer. For some employees, the response to change may take dysfunctional or even pathological forms, leading to destructive behaviors.[13] Clearly, the stakes are high.

DESTRUCTIVE RESILIENCE

The bankruptcy of Lehman Brothers, a Wall Street stalwart with 150 years of history, was one of the most dramatic failures of the 2008 financial crisis. Ironically, according to one insider, a culture of resilience helped bring about the organization's demise.

Hope Greenfield, the firm's former chief talent officer, says Lehman had a long history of "edging up to the brink of disaster and then pulling off a miracle."[14] Lehman survived the difficult economic times of the early 1970s, then reestablished itself as an independent organization after being acquired and then spun off by Shearson. In the 1990s, the firm weathered foreign currency crises that should have sunk the company for good. Lehman was the only investment bank to lose almost all of its office in New York in the attacks of September 11, 2001. The company's ability to keep functioning by creating a new trading floor in New Jersey just a few days later was, in the words of Greenfield, "an incredible feat of sheer determination by thousands of employees."[15]

And that's the problem. With a history of consistently bouncing back from near-fatal disaster, the firm's culture had absorbed the belief that the company could survive anything. Heroic resilience became embedded in the organization's self-definition. Why not— miraculous nick-of-time rescues had become almost routine. But this success had its roots not in a systematically created and mind-fully nurtured employee capacity for resilience. Instead, resilience in the Lehman culture took on a do-what-it-takes, work-around-the-clock, ultimately unsustainable form. The company survived on Hail Mary luck and willpower, with a bit of hubris thrown in. This is not a formula for dealing successfully with serial change.

Resilience doesn't just happen. It consists of more than just a willingness to make supreme sacrifices in the face of traumatic experience. An organization is resilient only if its people are, and they are resilient only if their managers build the capacity employee by employee. Clearly, Lehman's people had strength and intelligence—the firm couldn't have survived and prospered for a century and a half otherwise. But they should have heeded this thought (which echoes the ideas of Charles Darwin): "It is not the strongest of the species that survives, nor the most intelligent, but the one most responsive to change."[16]

Choosing to Change

For an example of change with a strategic intent and presumed positive outcome, witness the evolution of Google since its incorporation in 1998. The company began life as a search engine provider, but its revenue model quickly evolved as the organization found a way to put advertising alongside search results. Later, Google introduced its Gmail service, which links advertising with the content of incoming messages. With this early form of artificial intelligence in its hip pocket, the company moved on to create or acquire Web features like Google Docs, Google Spreadsheets, Blogger, and the now ubiquitous YouTube. Nicholas Carr, former editor of the *Harvard Business Review* and author of *The Big Switch*, believes these Web applications signal a fundamental change in Google's business model. The next step involves continued moves into cloud computing, the data processing and management model that puts computing power into large centralized stations (in essence, computing utilities) that in turn sell this capacity to users. Says Carr, "Google is already a central computing utility. Up to now, it's supplied a limited number of computing services, mostly search. But what it wants to eventually become is the computer that people use instead of their PC or their company's data center." Think about that— Google as the world's computer, a far cry from its origins as a simple search provider.[17] The organization's business model no doubt will continue to evolve, especially if it succeeds in realizing its aspirations to expand the use of artificial intelligence and to deepen its ability to predict and act on the wishes and intentions of its users. Perhaps some day, a Google device (possibly a ninth-generation Nexus One phone) will whisper in your ear the answer to a question you merely thought.

What might this continued change mean for Google employees? Will they remain a bunch of technogeeks free to pursue their passions, or will the weight of corporate bureaucracy ultimately stifle their creativity? Google now employs some twenty thousand people. That's about the size that Microsoft and Cisco had reached when they began to struggle with the yin and yang of preserving an agile culture while toeing the line for a growing community of customers and investors. Will Google remain, like Xerox Parc or the old Bell Labs, a place for great minds to apply unfettered inventiveness? Will developers continue to have the freedom to spend 20 percent of their time working on pet projects, or will the next business model bring a more corporate (that is, restrictive) feel? Will the company's most imaginative employees be able to adapt to the next business model, or will they leave, disgruntled, to start their own businesses farther south on Highway 101? How must managers at Google (and other organizations with a strategic emphasis on innovation) energize change so that employees adapt and prosper? We have some ideas.

Enhance Individual Creativity

Pygmalion was a sculptor from Greek mythology. He fell in love with a female statue he had carved. The Pygmalion effect is the term psychologists now use to refer to the influence expectation has on performance. The greater the expectation placed upon people, the better they do, to a point. Remember the discussion of goal setting from Chapter Six, where we said that goals that are just about manageable have the greatest power to produce mastery and self-efficacy. In a work setting, managers set expectations for employee behavior, including creativity, by virtue of what they say (for example, by stating explicit performance expectations) and by how they behave. By providing resources, facilitating teamwork, and recognizing successful creative efforts, managers convey the expectation that employees should be creative. Properly calibrated, these actions not only build creative capability, but also increase employees' sense of self-efficacy.

In the words of Pamela Tierney and Steven Farmer, who studied the Pygmalion effect in an R&D setting, "Those employees for whom supervisors held higher creative expectations reported that their supervisors rewarded and recognized their creative efforts, provided more resources, encouraged the sharing of information, collaboration, and creative goal setting, and modeled creativity in their own work."[18] Tierney and Farmer point out the practical consequences for manager behavior: "Although other factors may come into play, our findings indicate that it is possible for supervisors to either stimulate or stifle employees' creative efforts by their beliefs and associated actions. This fact may become particularly relevant among members of the workforce who do not naturally view themselves as creative. Our finding that an employee's sense of mastery for creative tasks is linked to that employee's interpretations of the supervisor's actions highlights the importance of supervisors clearly communicating high expectations for employees' creative potential."[19]

The manager does not act alone. Her supportive actions must be bolstered by an organizational willingness to accept and accommodate new ideas. The sociopolitical context of organizations can at times militate against creative change, which entails, after all, a disruption to the status quo. Onne Janssen from the Netherlands looked at the relationship between manager support for innovative behavior and the perceived influence that individuals felt they had in the workplace—their belief that their actions would indeed achieve the desired effect. His research produced clear results: "Employees' sense of influence needs to be augmented by perceptions that their supervisors are likely to support their innovation.... Employees feel that their supervisors are the key actors who have the power to grant or deny them the support necessary for the further development, protection, and application of their ideas."[20]

The manager thus plays a dual role: fostering an environment that encourages and expects creative behavior, and providing the support necessary to ensure that such behavior is accepted and assimilated within the organization. We will return later in the chapter to the manager's role in providing performance support.

Build Adaptable Teams

Team adaptation denotes the ability of group members to respond to emergent circumstances, using their resources either individually or collectively to meet expected or unexpected demands and to incorporate these into their repertoire of behaviors. A team headed by Shawn Burke of the University of Central Florida has advanced a model of team adaptation. The model posits that, "Adaptation lies at the heart of team effectiveness.... Team adaptation is manifested in the innovation of new or modification of existing structures, capacities, and/or behavioral or cognitive goal-directed actions."[21] Adaptation shares some features with team innovation, but also goes beyond it. Innovation may produce desirable ideas and novel products and services, but innovation as an activity may not change how the team functions. Team adaptation catalyzes that transformation.

Burke outlines four phases in the adaptive cycle within a team: *situation assessment, plan formulation, plan execution,* and *team learning.* Table 8.1 describes them and suggests ways in which managers can foster team adaptability.

Table 8.1: Developing Adaptable Teams

Phase	Features	Manager's Role
Situation assessment	One or more team members scanning the environment for cues likely to affect the team's mission. The new cues stimulate the creation of new mental models, leading to revised team situation awareness.	Help the team recognize the value of new cues that may disrupt habitual work routines. Suggest milestones, such as project halfway points or appraisal times, as a trigger to adapt or clarify and redefine purpose. Help team assimilate and share understanding of new schemata.
Plan formulation	Agreeing on a course of action, creating and revising goals and priorities for the task, within the context of evolving environmental circumstances and constraints.	Encourage the group to review and possibly revise members' roles and accountabilities, as well as overall performance targets for the task. Ensure that the team feels safe to challenge and speak up and that information is adequately shared. As the plan is developed, offer counsel on which environmental factors are relevant to the task and which are not.
Plan execution	Working toward the goal through individual or team actions, accompanied by mutual assistance by team members who monitor and give feedback, provide backup support, and communicate updates on progress.	Connect with external sources, provide judicious team and member coaching, ensure adequate resource availability, facilitate team problem solving, agree with team on how and when to review progress and revise procedures.
Team learning and review	Developing team knowledge through ongoing reflection of activities and results, and incorporating those insights as a guide for future behavior. Using appropriate measurement and reward tools to ensure activities and results are evidence-based.	Encourage learning, which requires open discussion of mistakes and unexpected outcomes as well as successes, to foster an open climate of exchange within the team. Adaptation is continuous, so learning should be seen the same way, with sufficient time allocated to learning reviews. Ensure that measures are rigorously applied and analyzed and that team-based rewards link with performance.

Source: Adapted from Burke, C. S., and others, "Understanding Team Adaptation: A Conceptual Analysis and Model," *Journal of Applied Psychology*, 2006, 91(6), 1189–1207.

Burke and team extend the relevance of team adaptation to organizational performance as a whole: "Fostering team adaptation remains important to the effective functioning and thereby viability of organizations. In fact, the implications of the advanced model of team adaptation cross a wide spectrum of organizational functioning to extend to system design, information technology design, job design, assessment for selection, socialization efforts, individual development, team development, and more broadly, the facilitation of change at multiple levels."[22]

To be sure, the slings and arrows of outrageous fortune will at times so disrupt events that there is no choice but to decommission a team and start again with a new group. More often, we believe, teams can adapt their approaches, goals, and even membership to respond to redirection. The manager's success at promoting team-level adaptability will depend in part on how well she stimulates and supports flexibility without interfering in team functioning.

Sustaining Engagement

Whether imposed or chosen, major workplace change almost always brings stress. Stress, in turn, can undermine employees' rational and emotional engagement. Sustaining engagement through periods of stressful change is therefore a critical part of the manager's role. Engaged employees strongly connect with their organizations and consistently demonstrate willingness to go beyond minimum performance requirements. That willingness is never more important than when organizations are working their way through difficult transitions.

Why do some employees continue contributing to their companies in spite of turmoil while others become frustrated and burn out? Why do some keep on working productively as others struggle and fall short, distracted and enervated by the chaos around them? Why are some employees always at work and ready to contribute while others respond to strain by either staying home or showing up but underperforming?

Individual attributes certainly play a role, but organizations and managers have a significant effect on how and how well employees cope with the consequences of change.

Our recent research on these questions has identified two factors required to sustain employee engagement through challenging periods:

- An organizational climate that promotes employees' physical, psychological, and social health (we call this *well-being*)

- A work environment that enables productivity (we've named this *performance support*)

Managers play a critical role in ensuring that the organization delivers in both areas.

Foster Well-Being

Within the organizational context, well-being comprises three related aspects of individual wellness:

- *Physical Health.* Overall bodily wellness, encompassing general health as well as specific medical conditions. From the company's perspective, physical health manifests itself in factors like low absenteeism, low presenteeism,[23] strong productivity, and high levels of stamina and energy on the job.

- *Psychological Health.* Optimism, confidence, and perceptions of satisfaction and accomplishment, balancing factors such as stress, anxiety, and feelings of frustration. Psychologically healthy people typically express happiness, positive attitude, and enthusiasm for work.

- *Social Health.* Quality of relationships with supervisor and colleagues. People who experience high social health say that they get along well with fellow employees, feel treated with respect, and are able to balance their work and personal lives.

Well-being helps sustain engagement by providing employees a shield against the stresses associated with workplace change.

The work environment created by first-line supervisors and managers has a direct effect on employee well-being. A growing body of studies shows, for example, that supervisor and manager behavior affects individuals' blood pressure and risk of heart disease. To test this relationship, researchers from the Karolinska Institute and Stockholm University in Sweden tracked the cardiovascular health of male employees aged nineteen to seventy, over nearly a decade. Those who deemed their managers to be the least competent had a 25 percent higher risk of a serious heart problem. In a British study published in 2005, the researchers found that men who described their supervisors as fair and just had reduced stress and a 30 percent lower risk of coronary heart disease than those who said they were treated unfairly at work.[24]

A related Swedish study produced a specific list of manager behaviors that contribute to employee well-being in a dramatic way—by reducing ischemic heart disease.[25] The analysis was intended to assess the factors underlying a recent finding that there is an average excess cardiovascular risk of 50 percent in employees who are exposed to an adverse social and psychological work environment. The team of Swedish doctors and academics set about to determine precisely what kind of manager performance elements contribute most to employees' avoidance of cardiovascular problems. They identified four manager behaviors strongly associated with lower incidence of ischemic heart disease:

- Providing the information people need to do their work

- Effectively pushing through and carrying out changes

- Explaining goals and subgoals for work so that people understand what they mean for their particular parts of the task

- Ensuring that employees have sufficient power in relation to their responsibilities[26]

These themes aren't surprising—they reflect key elements of the task execution and employee development components of our manager performance model. What may be more surprising is the effect these factors produce not only on the psychological and social aspects of employee well-being, but also on the physical aspects. These three forms of well-being influence each other, of course, and so a manager's effect on any one will likely manifest itself in the others as well. As the researchers observed, "Psychosocial stress has been shown to increase the progression of coronary atherosclerosis. One could speculate that a present and active manager, providing structure, information and support, counteracts destructive processes in work groups, thereby promoting regenerative rather than stress-related physiological processes in employees."[27]

Employee well-being is important for reasons that extend beyond sustaining engagement and providing regenerative power in the face of organizational change. The well-being of the workforce also has major implications for organizations' health care costs. By one calculation, American employers spend $13,000 annually per employee in total direct and indirect health-related costs.[28] Moreover, for every dollar expended on medical services and pharmaceuticals, companies spend another $2.30 on health-related productivity costs—the expenses associated with absenteeism and presenteeism.

Depression is the single most expensive health condition, carrying an annual total cost of more than $350 per full-time employee. Of that total, more than three-quarters comes from lost productivity because employees don't come to work or are relatively unproductive when they do show up.[29] In this context, consider how managers who perform in ways described by the Swedish research team—being present and active, providing information and support, reducing workplace stress—can yield significant health care cost reductions for their organizations. By reducing the care requirements associated with depression and anxiety alone, managers can make a major financial contribution to their companies. Add to that the competitive advantages that accrue to companies whose employees not only require significantly lower health care support, but also continue to innovate and produce efficiently in spite of traumatic change that threatens to cripple the competition. There lies a multifaceted marketplace edge ready for the taking, an advantage to which managers can make a material contribution.

The most forward-thinking organizations have introduced well-being programs that incorporate manager involvement into broader initiatives aimed at creating a healthy work environment. This is the approach taken by WorkSafe Victoria (WSV), an Australian state authority with responsibility for ensuring adherence to health and safety laws and providing care and insurance protection for workers and employers in Victoria. According to Dale Nissen, the WSV well-being program manager: "We were already supporting some health initiatives but decided to pull these together into a well-being program in 2007, with strong support from the top and mutual commitment with employees." The program, called "Feeling Good@Work," includes an online site where employees can learn about available activities as well as complete self-assessments and review and update their own records. Says Nissen, "We created some big events to get the momentum going, such as our Global Corporate Challenge, a team-based walking challenge which involved walking round the globe over the Internet. After 12 months of exercise programs, people now are used to doing exercise at work, using the facilities we provide."[30]

The WSV program incorporates involvement from managers at all levels of the organization. Says Geraldine Coy, WSV's head of HR, "We've worked on a leadership development program to ensure that we are bringing the various threads of well-being, career, learning, and development into a set of congruent messages for our people. Every year we run a forum for our people managers. The last two have put emphasis on the well-being program to ensure managers are up to date with our progress and given the opportunity to act as role models themselves."[31]

Ensure Performance Support

Managers provide unit-specific support for performance by making sure employees have the wherewithal to execute their jobs effectively. Providing support means ensuring that workplace strain isn't exacerbated by inadequate tools, insufficient resources, taxing work, or organizational barriers. Managers get high scores when employees perceive that:

- Physical work conditions are comfortable and conducive to high productivity

- All the resources required to do their jobs (physical, financial, informational) are readily available

- The necessary equipment and tools have been provided

- Safety on the job is never compromised, even at the expense of output

- Unit staffing is sufficient to ensure that the workload is manageable and fairly spread

This list may seem familiar—we included these kinds of factors in our definition of job resources in Chapter Five. Much as they help make challenging work fulfilling, they also help sustain employee engagement. When managers deliver these requirements, as Figure 8.3 shows, they also boost the effect of employee engagement on company profit.

High performance support adds to the profit margins of both low-engagement and high-engagement organizations. In both engagement categories, performance support contributes about five percentage points to profit results. Among the worldwide respondents to our 2010 global workforce study, 74 percent of those who gave their managers high ratings for effectiveness also agreed that their managers succeed at removing obstacles to doing their jobs well. In contrast, only 12 percent of those who scored their managers as ineffective overall gave a positive rating for clearing obstacles.

Figure 8.3: High Performance Support Correlates with Increased
Profit Margin

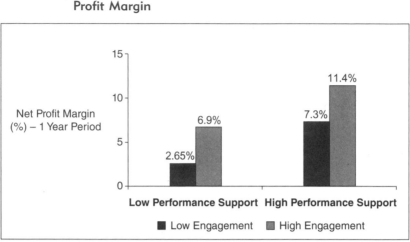

Source: Towers Watson analysis.

Together, well-being and performance support have a complementary effect on the sustainability of engagement. Neither factor by itself
is sufficient, but together they produce a powerful result for individuals
and organizations. Exhibit 8.2 shows the results of various combinations
of high and low engagement, well-being and local performance support.

Remember, these factors act not as *drivers* of engagement, but rather
as *sustaining* elements. We see many companies, including some going
through rapid transitions, that record high engagement scores, particularly
if their change efforts involve sexy new business strategies or appealing
innovation efforts. However, these companies are often too distracted by
their redirection or restructuring activities to worry about employee well-
being or the details of unit-level support. Consequently, they find that
their engagement scores drop and their ability to preserve the momentum
of change diminishes. Neither well-being nor performance support alone
can preserve high engagement. But together, they can help an organization emerge from the trauma of change with an employee population still
committed to the organization and willing to work hard on its behalf.

Exhibit 8.2: Engagement Becomes Sustainable with Employee Well-Being and Local Performance Support

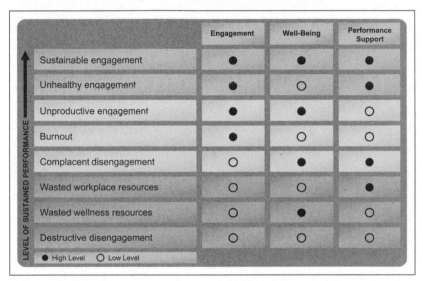

	Engagement	Well-Being	Performance Support
Sustainable engagement	●	●	●
Unhealthy engagement	●	○	●
Unproductive engagement	●	●	○
Burnout	●	○	○
Complacent disengagement	○	●	●
Wasted workplace resources	○	○	●
Wasted wellness resources	○	●	○
Destructive disengagement	○	○	○

LEVEL OF SUSTAINED PERFORMANCE

● High Level   ○ Low Level

Source: Towers Watson analysis.

SUMMARY: MANAGING CHANGE

Creating change in organizations is often seen as a job for the CEO and his team of senior executives. Certainly, in large-scale change programs, their involvement is essential. Alternatively, organizations that see senior leaders as the primary instigators and drivers of change may pay insufficient attention to how effective change actually happens.

In the context of change, much of what we expect of managers falls into the leadership category. The requirements we've laid out, with a focus on creating the circumstances in which people willingly—or at least cooperatively—move toward the future, belong squarely under the definition of strong leadership. At the same time, change at the individual and unit levels also calls for effective management. Procuring the resources for local performance support is an example. Failures of leadership can leave employees with insufficient direction, whereas failures of management may mean employees have to do too much work with too little support. The former brings chaos; the latter brings burnout.

Whether leading or managing, supervisors must redouble their attention to the people-focused part of their jobs. We might even suggest that successful change requires managers to move a bit toward the center of the stage, to reduce the distance we have recommended they otherwise maintain from the work of their autonomously performing employees. Adaptability, resilience, and well-being result from the manager's specific attention to individual employees. This is no time for a manager to be closeted in his office revising budgets or writing reports. Instead, managers need to be with their employees, not interfering with their work, but ensuring that everything they do contributes to individuals' ability to survive and thrive in spite of workplace disruption.

Regardless of the sources of change or the kind of employee response required, the manager nevertheless carries a heavy burden. The attention required of managers touches all parts of the manager performance model described in Chapter Three. In seeing to the execution of tasks, managers must know that the uncertainty brought by change means the focus on strategically critical work is more important than ever. People need to be confident that, in an unpredictable world, their work helps to create the organization's future. Involvement, autonomy, self-efficacy, and mastery become more important in times of change than in stable periods. They build employees' confidence in their ability to maintain their valued and valuable positions with the enterprise. For the same reason, continuing to provide learning opportunities not only enhances the shared human capital asset but also gives employees hope for a future where their skills will be necessary for organization success. Preserving the deal between individual and enterprise reinforces the organization's determination to continue rewarding the fruitful investment of human capital. Recognizing those who perform well sends the message that, especially when the ground is shifting, high performers stand out; their contributions deserve special acknowledgment.

Organizations that navigate change successfully have managers who make the case for change, who explain why things need to be different, and who never fail to provide full, honest, and timely information. These actions lie at the core of authenticity. They reaffirm that employees can trust their managers, even if the news isn't always good or the immediate future not entirely rosy. At the same time, managers need to encourage realistic hope in employees, give them reason to be optimistic about the future, and increase their confidence that the organization knows how to survive and will ultimately thrive.

To help employees handle the stresses and make the most of the opportunities associated with major change, effective managers will:

- Carefully consider the magnitude and sources of change and help each person respond with the appropriate levels of adaptability and resilience

- Do everything in their power to preserve the deal between employees and the organization, knowing that trust for both company leaders and unit managers is at stake

- Not just keep people focused on their work, but also help them raise their sights and draw energy from the opportunity to leapfrog weakened competitors

- Convey high expectations for innovation, and back these up with encouragement, support, and resources

- Help teams navigate change, but do so with respect for team competence and therefore a suitably light touch

- Not just help employees survive the emotional toll exacted by uncertainty and tension, but also invest in preserving their well-being and in keeping them healthy physically, psychologically, and socially

Much of what we've recommended in this chapter will sound familiar. An environment of change doesn't modify the requirements for strong manager performance. Rather, it intensifies the importance and heightens the need.

CHAPTER OUTLINE

Connecting Authenticity and Trust

Building Trust Through Authenticity
> Maintain Openness
> Clarify and Focus Work
> Display Scrupulous Fairness

Implications for Manager Performance
> Executing Tasks
> Developing People
> Delivering the Deal
> Energizing Change

9

Authenticity and Trust

Everything **in the** universe is interconnected. We know this because Douglas Adams, author of books about how to find your way around the universe, said so. Or more precisely, Dirk Gently, the main character in Adams's book *Dirk Gently's Holistic Detective Agency*, said so. Dirk is a private detective who uses telekinesis, quantum mechanics, and trips to the Bahamas to solve cases and, in the process, save the human race from extinction. His understanding of what he calls "the fundamental interconnectedness of all things" makes his detection approach holistic in the largest possible way.[1]

We too have a sense of interconnectedness, and we didn't need to go to the Bahamas to get it. Take authenticity and trust, for example. Integrity is a main pillar of authenticity. Integrity means adhering consistently to a code of high moral ethics and behavior. Consistency, in turn, forms a core element of trust. We think of authenticity and trust as sequential and complementary elements that add power to our manager performance model. In the architecture of our model, they form the foundation, the basis for strength and stability.

Connecting Authenticity and Trust

Trust is defined as the willingness of one individual to make himself or herself vulnerable to another. The acceptance of vulnerability must be grounded in the expectation that the trustee will act in a predictable way that benefits, or at least doesn't harm, the person granting trust. People are willing to trust one another when they have confidence in what the individual *can do* (ability to confer a benefit on the trustor) and what the individual *will do* (predictable inclination to exercise that ability).[2] Trust thus has both a cognitive aspect (experience tells me that I can predict how this person will act) and an emotional aspect (our relationship provides a foundation for the beneficial behavior I expect to receive).[3] But trust is also paradoxical. Belief in another's trustworthiness precedes trust, but trustworthiness can't be proven unless trust is first given.

Of all the elements in our manager performance model, none has a more dramatic effect on a manager's ability to work effectively offstage than reciprocal trust. If employees don't trust the people with whom they transact their business, then transactions will be few, meager, and unfulfilling. Conversely, managers who foster trust, and who do all the other things we've described to make individuals and groups effective, create the environment for individual and group success. Peter Drucker put it this way: "The leaders who work most effectively, it seems to me, never say 'I.' And that's not because they have trained themselves not to say 'I.' They don't think 'I.' They think 'we'; they think 'team.' They understand their job to be to make the team function. They accept responsibility and don't sidestep it, but 'we' gets the credit.... This is what creates trust, what enables you to get the task done."[4]

By behaving authentically, managers establish the groundwork for trust. Authenticity is a relatively new concept in the lexicon of leadership, although the idea dates back at least to the classical Greeks. An inscription at the Delphic oracle, attributed to the Seven Sages, says "Know thyself." In Shakespeare's *Hamlet*, Polonius counsels his son, "This above all: to thine own self be true." Interest in authenticity and its application to business has been fueled by concerns about how unethical behavior can produce large-scale economic failures (Enron, WorldCom, Barings Bank, and Parmalat, to name a few examples). In response, many organizations have developed codes of conduct or values statements that include references to ethical behavior. External pressure to behave ethically might produce some positive effect, but our conception of authenticity draws on a different source. As we mean it, authenticity originates from within the individual. It implies a drive to behave with integrity even when no outside force demands compliance.

Authentic behavior is not a unitary, either-you-have-it-or-you-don't concept. Rather, it comprises a set of attributes that any individual may display to a greater or lesser extent. A research team led by Arizona State University's Fred Walumbwa studied populations as diverse as Chinese, Kenyans, and North Americans. They found supporting evidence for four components of authenticity:

- *Self-awareness.* Mindfulness about how one experiences and makes sense of the world. Self-awareness denotes an accurate understanding of personal strengths and weaknesses, and insight into how one's behavior is perceived by, and affects, other people.

- *Relational transparency.* Being consistent and genuine in interactions with others and presenting one's true and honest self to the world, without pretense, manipulation, or intentional distortion. That value of transparency applies to close associates as well as to oneself; a manager strong in relational transparency helps others identify both positive and negative aspects of their behavior.

- *Balanced processing.* Willingness to evaluate all relevant information, including data that are challenging or uncomfortable, before reaching a decision. Authentic leaders are less likely than others to ignore or distort information they may not want to hear, to deny the relevance of messages about their personal shortcomings, or to punish the bearers of those messages.

- *Internalized moral perspective.* Guiding one's behavior and decisions by personal ethical standards rather than by external pressures from a group, organization, or society. As Walumbwa and his colleagues explain it, a person's moral perspective is guided by deeply held values that enable the individual to avoid acting merely to please others or to attain rewards or avoid punishments."[5]

A group of researchers from the University of Nebraska has studied and elaborated on authentic leadership. They summarize the relationship between authenticity and trust this way: "Authentic leaders act in accordance with deep personal values and convictions, to build credibility and win the respect and trust of followers by encouraging diverse viewpoints and building networks of collaborative relationships with followers."[6]

Building Trust Through Authenticity

Our research suggests that three primary factors influence trust between managers and employees. Trusted managers, we've found, communicate openly, focus work on what matters to the unit, and handle performance management processes with objectivity and fairness. These elements appear in Exhibit 9.1. Authenticity, as we will explain, adds power to each factor.

Exhibit 9.1: Three Factors Drive Employee Trust

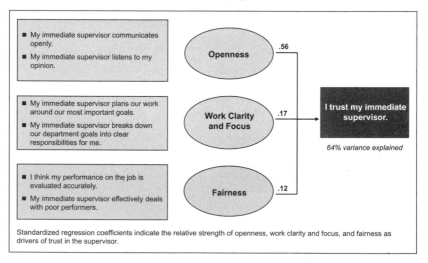

Source: O.C. Tanner 2008 Global Recognition Study.

Maintain Openness

Paul Zak, professor of neuroeconomics at Claremont Graduate University, has studied both the economics and the neuropsychology of trust. Zak says sunlight nurtures trust and darkness destroys it.[7] Openness that fosters trust lets sunlight in. This means frequent, honest, personal chats on topics like performance, department and company success requirements, and status updates. Supervisors, in turn, must listen to the opinions and concerns of employees, whenever employees have something to say. Electronic media provide no substitute for personal contact when it comes to building trust. In the 2009 Edelman Trust Barometer,[8] 40 percent of a sample of people across eighteen countries said that personal conversations—with friends, peers, others in the organization—were a credible, trusted source of information about companies. Only about half that number said social media, blogs, and Web sites provided trustworthy information. A meta-analysis by Kurt Dirks of Washington University in St. Louis and Donald Ferrin (then of the State University of New York at Buffalo, now with the Lee Kong Chian School of Business, Singapore Management University) showed that employee participation in decision making is critical to developing trust.[9] Employee involvement in key decisions signals that the manager has confidence in, as well as concern and respect for, the contributions of employees.

Openness draws on the self-awareness and relational transparency elements of authenticity. Self-aware managers understand their personal strengths and weaknesses; they have what we think of as internal honesty. They also have insight into how their expressions of leadership will be received and interpreted by others, given the context in which their words are spoken and their actions taken. Words and deeds associated with a crisis have particular power to reinforce or undercut the appearance of self-awareness. U.S. President George W. Bush discovered this in the aftermath of Hurricane Katrina.

In the last few days of August 2005, the sixth largest hurricane ever recorded, and the third strongest ever to make landfall in the United

States, caused more than 1,800 fatalities and an estimated \$75 billion in physical damage.[10] The tragedy created a leadership moment for President Bush, an occasion for him to express his empathy with the victims of the storm and to give them confidence that he understood and knew how to alleviate their suffering. By all accounts, he failed to seize this opportunity. Most famously, he expressed support, in a typically informal way, for Federal Emergency Management Agency chief Michael Brown: "Brownie, you're doing a heckuva job." Brownie, it turns out, had not been doing a heckuva job. Just ten days after Bush's tossed-off endorsement, Brown resigned amid public outrage over his scant qualifications and the administration's failure to provide prompt and effective aid to New Orleans and the rest of the region. Bush clearly did not understand how his misplaced loyalty to a subordinate, and his vernacular, almost nonchalant way of conveying that support, would offend hurricane victims. Self-awareness calls for reflection, mindfulness, and caution in expression. President Bush failed on all three counts.

Open communication between manager and employee also depends on a transparent relationship between them. Transparency connotes clarity and absence of obstruction in the mutual expression of each party's true motives and needs. In a transparent relationship, each person presents his or her true self—a genuine individual brand, so to speak. By brand, we don't mean an artifact of self-promotion or a self-serving depiction of admirable features only. Instead, we define a personal brand as the behavioral promises that each of us makes and keeps. By staying consistent in what she says and does, a manager gives others confidence that they can understand and predict how she will react in any situation. A brand thus becomes an efficient bundle of impressions people can store cognitively and refer to when they need to know who we are and how we will respond to circumstances at work.

Personal brands are familiar to all of us. Celebrities routinely create them as a way to make their images stick in the minds of the public. Sometimes their brands stand out for their consistency and genuineness.

Actor Paul Newman, for example, was known as a skilled actor, devoted family man, generous philanthropist, and successful businessman. His behavior reinforced these impressions. He won an Academy Award in 1987 for *The Color of Money* and also received eight other nominations during his career. All proceeds, after taxes, from his Newman's Own food products go to charity. He was married to actress Joanne Woodward for fifty years. When asked about infidelity, he said, "Why go out for hamburger when you have steak at home?" Newman's brand reflected competence in his craft and a truthful and steadfast devotion to his values.

In contrast, consider what has happened to the personal brand associated with golfer Tiger Woods. Thanks in part to his connections with companies like Nike and Accenture, Woods reinforced his reputation as the best golfer of his generation—and perhaps of all time—by presenting a set of admirable personal traits: focus, skill, competitiveness, tenacity, discipline, analytical insight. He wasn't just good at hitting golf balls—his brand reflected the ultimate in talent and success. He came up a little short on integrity, however, as the world discovered when his numerous sexual transgressions became public. He had frequently been seen in public with his beautiful wife and children, adding doting father and attentive husband to his collection of admirable features. His peccadilloes therefore became all the more damaging to the brand image that he and his sponsors had created and cultivated.

We hasten to say again that our definition of brand relies on truth. If the brand and the person beneath it are inconsistent, then relational transparency is absent. Tiger's cautionary tale reminds us that integrity—firm adherence to a code of behavior under all circumstances—is crucial to relational transparency. If self-awareness is internal honesty, then relational transparency is external honesty. The two reinforce each other. When they come together, an individual (manager or not) will:

- Have a clear sense of his personal traits (the brand elements)
- Enact them consistently under all circumstances (deliver the brand promise at all times)

- Admit mistakes and deviations from expectations (everyone makes them; honest admission is necessary and cover-ups always work out badly)

- Not take himself too seriously—This is Rule Number 6 from Roz and Ben Zander's *The Art of Possibility*. Rule Number 6 (there are no other rules) urges people not to get too caught up in personal brand creation. It happens naturally, organically, as we simply behave reliably according to personal standards. Humility and sense of humor are important; too much effort seems strained and insincere. Conveying a genuine personal brand encourages others to do the same. The Zanders say that, "When one person peels away layers of opinion, entitlement, pride, and inflated self-description, others instantly feel the connection. As one person has the grace to practice the secret of Rule Number 6, others often follow."[11]

Clarify and Focus Work

Employees must believe that managers can guide employees' efforts toward the work that matters most to the success of the unit and of the broader organization. It's difficult, in practical terms, to place every element of every job clearly into the bigger picture. That's where trust comes in. When employees trust managers to understand the organization's direction and link work to those higher-level intentions, employee confidence in the significance of their tasks increases. Initiative and performance both go up as well. Improved performance, in turn, underpins increased trust.

Kurt Dirks studied the trust → performance → trust cycle in U.S. men's college basketball. He found that trust in the coach works both as a determinant of team performance and a product of it.[12] After analyzing the win-loss records of thirty teams and interviewing many players and coaches, he concluded that trust strongly influences the relationship between past performance and future performance. The two teams reporting the highest trust in their coach early in the season produced impressive success. One team was ranked number one before being upset in the national championship tournament; the other played in the championship game. Comments from one player capture the underlying trust-performance link: "Once we developed trust in Coach _____, the progress we made increased tremendously because we were no longer asking questions or were apprehensive. Instead, we were buying in and believing that if we worked our hardest, we were going to get there."[13]

Making a tight connection between unit goals and the actions necessary to achieve them requires thorough, unbiased information collection combined with objective assessment—the balanced processing component of authentic leadership. We know from our discussions in earlier chapters, however, that cognitive biases (framing effect, illusion of control, planning fallacy) often confound managers' analytical efforts. These biases can sidetrack even the best attempts to achieve accuracy and arrive at well-supported conclusions. Balanced processing can help by forcing managers to look beyond the unchallenged beliefs and unexamined attitudes that threaten to distort their reasoning.

In deciding how to pursue the war in Afghanistan, President Barack Obama employed an exhaustive process of information collection and evaluation, in the hope of developing a logical, philosophically defensible strategy. His approach demonstrated balanced processing by:

- Taking into account extensive information from various, often competing sources. The strategy formulation process required some three months to unfold. During that time, the president reviewed three dozen intelligence reports and received information and advice from military leaders, cabinet heads, members of congress, and diplomats.

- Ensuring that the analysis was framed not only in a military context (through a critical look at comparisons with the Vietnam conflict) but also an economic one (as revealed by a private budget memo estimating a $1 trillion cost for expanded military presence, roughly the same amount as Obama's health care plan).

- Considering elements under U.S. control (troop deployment numbers, for example) as well as factors less subject to American influence (corruption in the Afghan government and Taliban entrenchment in Afghan society, for instance).

- Mapping alternatives to clarify actions and consequences. Central to the president's thinking about strategy was a graph plotting troop numbers over the period of build-up and draw-down. Obama challenged his advisers to move the curve to the left—that is, augment troop numbers quickly, achieve military goals, and then withdraw the forces swiftly.

- Encouraging debate and disagreement. He not only invited competing voices to propose options, but also withstood pointed criticism of the final plan and even threats from leading members of Congress to withhold financing for the war.[14]

By placing information and analysis in several contexts, identifying both controllable and noncontrollable elements, and looking at scenarios from many perspectives, the president's planning process enabled his team to confront cognitive biases associated with problem framing, illusory control, and overconfidence in planning.

In the context of trust, balanced processing represents intellectual honesty in the interest of aligning effort and resource investment with group goals. It requires dedication to objective and impartial reasoning, even when taxing or personally uncomfortable. Sometimes, listening to opposing points of view will test a manager's dedication to remaining away from center stage. Astute managers know that participating in the debate and controlling the discussion are different things.

Taken to its extreme, balanced processing appears to suggest indecision and temporizing. Competitive environments rarely afford the luxury of extended time to formulate and carry out strategic plans. Managers must therefore weigh the need for a balanced and comprehensive analytical approach against the inevitable pressure to move quickly and decisively.

Display Scrupulous Fairness

In the workplace context, fairness takes four distinct forms:

- *Procedural fairness (fair process).* The perceived consistency and equity of the processes by which performance is assessed, rewards are allocated, or other organizational decisions are made. People believe processes are procedurally fair when they have the ability to voice their views and exercise influence over the outcome. Managers support procedural fairness when they answer such questions as, "How will this work?" and "What's the intention?"

- *Distributive fairness (fair outcome).* The degree to which an outcome conforms to the individual's personal sense of worth or deserving. Distributive fairness is heightened when people see the connection between results and performance ratings, between performance and rewards, between contribution and outcomes. Managers increase employees' confidence in distributive fairness when they deliver a just and equitable (if not necessarily equal) outcome—in effect, the individual manifestation of a fair procedure through fair distribution.

- *Interpersonal fairness (fair treatment).* The consideration, respect, and sensitivity that people receive when decisions are made and enacted. Interpersonal fairness reflects how people experience the emotional context of reward delivery and other organizational events. Managers heighten the sense of interpersonal fairness when they listen to their employees' concerns one-on-one, act on them whenever possible, and pass them on for an organizational response only when necessary.

- *Informational fairness (fair explanation).* The clarity of explanation that accompanies events like performance discussions and reward distribution. The criteria for informational fairness include reasonableness, candidness, thoroughness, and timeliness. No varnishing the truth or holding back information, however unpleasant it may be.[15]

Employees pay special attention to how their managers handle the distributive, interpersonal, and informational elements of perceived fairness. Trust increases when people believe their performance has received a fair assessment and when supervisors ensure that others are held to similar standards. Tolerance of low performance reduces perceptions of fairness and, consequently, of trust in the manager.

People tend to look to organizational policies in forming judgments about procedural fairness. But attitudes toward managers dominate the overall trust calculus. Research shows that perceived managerial trustworthiness influences people's view of the trustworthiness of the organizational entity as a whole, whereas the opposite does not seem to be true. A study by Jaepil Choi of the Hong Kong University of Science and Technology surveyed 265 supervisor-employee pairs in four companies in the northeastern United States. The analysis confirmed that employees look to their managers for distributive, interpersonal, and informational justice. But Choi also observed that "the manager's behavior did seem to play a significant role in determining employees' reactions both to the manager and to the organization. A supervisor's behavior has an immediate impact on various aspects of subordinates' organizational life, so it is not surprising that perceptions of the supervisor's fairness would have great implications for employees' reactions."[16]

Uncompromising fairness, reflected in performance assessment and myriad other ways, requires an unerring ethical compass. In the authenticity framework, this quality emerges as internalized moral perspective. It is the most fundamental form of honesty, the element of character that underlies internal, external, and intellectual honesty.

The most dramatic examples of fairness and internally anchored morality are often negative, cases where the absence of internalized moral perspective brought low an individual or an entire corporation. The first decade of the twenty-first century produced many examples of moral compasses that failed to point true north. The downfall of New York governor Eliot Spitzer is one. Spitzer rose to power as a fierce crusader for ethics in business. As attorney general of New York, the position he held for eight years before winning the governorship, he aggressively pursued Wall Street fraud, among other targets. He went after such high profile firms as Merrill Lynch, which he attacked for distorting its stock analysis to punish companies that weren't Merrill customers. The resulting settlement cost Merrill Lynch $100 million and helped make Spitzer *Time* Magazine's "Crusader of the Year" in 2002.[17] Over time he added investment banks, insurance companies, and environmental polluters to his target list. Spitzer seldom missed an opportunity to chide his perceived adversaries, as he did in a piece he wrote for *The Wall Street Journal Online* in April 2005. In that article he scolded the *Journal* and business lobby groups for not condemning corporate wrongdoers more vehemently. He wrote, "Why wouldn't the *Journal* and business lobby groups denounce such improper conduct? Why wouldn't they advocate the highest standards and urge prosecutors to root out the corruption and restore the integrity of the markets?" He went on to lay much of the blame at the feet of immoral executives: "A key lesson from the recent scandals is that the checks on the system simply have not worked. The honor code among CEOs didn't work."[18]

Spitzer showed the flaws in his own honor code just three years later when he resigned the governor's office after revealing his involvement with high-priced prostitutes. It turns out that, just to complete the irony, Spitzer had prosecuted at least two prostitution rings as head of the state's organized crime task force. In a press conference he held a few days before giving up the governorship, Spitzer said, "I have acted in a way that violates my obligation to my family and violates my or any sense of right or wrong. I apologize first and most importantly to my family. I apologize to the public to whom I promised better."[19] He evidently grasped the concept of an internally anchored code of moral behavior. His simply did not guide him in the right direction.

Enron, the corporate icon of failed moral standards, shows what happens when an organization's culture deviates from a central code of ethical behavior. Enron's major transgressions are well documented. Improper accounting, questionable insider transactions, and cutthroat treatment of customers and partners made the company a paradigm of corporate dishonesty. Even in little ways, the behavior of Enron's leaders demonstrated the damage that can come from ignoring moral values. To be sure, Enron had a stated set of values: respect, integrity, communication, and excellence. But, says Sherron Watkins, former vice president for corporate development and the most famous Enron whistleblower, "Enron executives did not demonstrate that they valued integrity; it was way down the list." For example, executive travelers were directed to use the travel agency owned by Sharon Lay, sister of Enron Chairman and CEO Ken Lay. "Forcing the employees to use his sister's agency told everyone that once you get to the executive suite, it's okay to take assets for you and your family," says Watkins.[20]

The absence of internalized moral perspective among Enron executives contributed to a dearth of trust at all levels of the company. Enron prided itself on being full of brainy people. The company reinforced its smartest-guy-in-the-room culture through a performance evaluation process that came to be called "rank and yank." Employees and managers spent about two weeks each year ranking fellow employees' contributions to the company, giving scores from 1 down to 5. The process included a forced distribution, so that each division was required to put 20 percent of its employees into the bottom category. That bottom fifth was supposed to be shoved out the door.[21] Enron was not a place where performance assessment created a platform for improvement. Either you were bright enough to make it or you weren't. It's hardly surprising, therefore, that people had every incentive to act in untrustworthy ways by giving their peers low ratings, even if not deserved, and thereby making themselves look better by comparison. They had little incentive to look at the honest facts, particularly if the facts told an inconvenient story. Moreover, when you play a zero-sum game, where somebody must lose for others to win, pressure to make the numbers becomes pressure to make up the numbers.[22]

This kind of performance evaluation process falls far short of meeting the criteria for engendering trust. Instead, it makes competition turn vicious, trust and authenticity disappear, organizations fail, and cheating to become institutionalized. As the University of Nebraska research team expressed it, "Cultures that reflect a preoccupation with short term performance results at the expense of ethical considerations will not facilitate the development of authenticity, in part because honesty, integrity, and high moral standards are not distinctive and/or prototypical values."[23] Enron's people may have been the smartest in the room, but their success was ultimately limited to what they could accomplish by taking from each other and from their external partners. No amount of brain power could expand their success beyond the limited boundaries of their sparse trust and impoverished authenticity.

The world of corporate ethics is full of gray areas, situations where the right choices can be unclear as well as difficult. Sherron Watkins suggests a simple test that anyone—executive, manager, or employee—can use to choose the path to take. When faced with a morally ambiguous decision, she advises, tap into your internal moral perspective and then ask yourself three questions:

- Would you be comfortable explaining your decision to a respected manager?

- Would you be satisfied with how your decision could be treated by the media?

- After explaining your rationale, would you be at peace with the reaction you got from your mother?

If the answer to any of the 3M (manager, media, mother) questions is no, then the decision doesn't measure up on your internal moral yardstick. And if that's the case, Watkins has this warning: "If your own personal value system is not validated or if you are uncomfortable when your value system gets violated, leave that organization. Trouble will hit at some point." She should know.[24]

Maintaining openness, structuring work for maximum clarity and importance, and acting with fairness all seem like good practices to embrace under any circumstances. Why do they have any special power to increase trust? Because each factor, in its way, makes less daunting the leap of faith that trust requires. When it comes right down to it, none of us can predict with complete accuracy how anyone will act in a given set of circumstances. Hence, trust requires faith—the belief that things will turn out all right even in the absence of perfectly predictive information. Anything that closes the faith gap builds comfort and certainty. Candid discourse, for example, helps people comprehend the risks required and the rewards available in their work. Focusing effort on what really matters and translating goals into relevant personal actions provides a roadmap to performance—fewer mysteries, less ambiguity, a clear destination, and a reason to drive toward it. Fair and accurate performance evaluation and real consequences for high and low performance let people know where they stand against the agreed-on criteria for reward and recognition. The ultimate payoff closes the circle: performance produces results, outcomes justify trust, and recognition of performance elevates engagement.

Implications for Manager Performance

Authenticity and trust influence how managers enact all other elements of the manager performance model, beginning with task execution.

Executing Tasks

In the context of job design, trust produces two important benefits. The first is psychic and has to do with stress management. As we discussed in Chapter Five, the most productive jobs combine high but achievable performance demands with abundant support resources, including the manager's trust. Conversely, as Exhibits 5.1 and 5.2 illustrate, high demand coupled with low support produces jobs that are stressful or impossible to perform. A downward spiral takes hold: lack of trust reduces autonomy, which increases stress and diminishes individual well-being. Stress hormone production goes up and trust drops further.

THE NEUROPSYCHOLOGY OF TRUST

Observers of people and society have differed about the advisability of trusting our fellow *homo sapiens*. On the positive side of the ledger, La Rochefoucauld said, "It is more shameful to mistrust one's friends than to be deceived by them." But others sound a cautionary note. The always-prudent Benjamin Franklin, for example, said, "Distrust and caution are the parents of security."

In a general sense, though, modern life seems remarkable for the prevalence of trust in our most common interpersonal transactions. We frequently line up with strangers to take money from an ATM, trusting that we won't be mugged. We drive at homicidal speeds on two-lane roads, trusting that the person coming in the other direction will stay on his side of the center line. We buy food from restaurants trusting that we won't get sick, and medicine from pharmacies assuming that we won't be poisoned. In the large percentage of cases, our trust is gratified. Dissembling may be common in Shakespeare comedies, but most of the people we encounter are who they appear to be.

Like other evolved human behaviors, trust has a biological side. Studies by anthropologists, scientists, and psychologists paint a picture of how brain chemistry determines trust and related elements of human interaction. Paul Zak's research has confirmed that the neuroactive hormone oxytocin has a strong influence on individuals' inclination to trust. Oxytocin is produced by the hypothalamus and secreted into the blood by the pituitary gland. Numerous studies of mammals have shown that oxytocin facilitates attachment with offspring and promotes prosocial behaviors, such as trust, among unrelated members of the group. Oxytocin is a physiologic signature

(Continued)

of empathy, the ability to create a psychological representation of what another is feeling. Oxytocin influences trust by inducing dopamine release in the brain regions associated with reward, thereby reinforcing generosity. In other words, it feels good to trust.[25]

Oxytocin release can be enhanced in a variety of ways, including touching, providing a safe environment and, of course, receiving a signal of trust from another, as between a manager and an employee.[26] Conversely, feelings of distrust stimulate the production of testosterone, which in turn provokes aggressive responses that further inhibit cooperation and destroy morale. Unmanageable stress increases production of the hormone cortisol, which initiates a cascade of effects that damage the heart and other organs. Cortisol also suppresses the production of oxytocin, and thereby reduces interpersonal trust.[27]

Managers make this a positive circle when they express trust in employees and back it up by fostering workplace autonomy. This increases individual ability to handle high demands and manage stress. A self-aware manager who balances input before making a decision will evaluate the strengths, experience, and development needs of team members before allocating tasks. A manager who works to build transparent relationships with employees will enjoy a level of rapport that makes those conversations flow easily. Endowed with balanced processing, the manager will solicit input from employees as he considers how to design fulfilling, strategically important jobs. What better way can a manager communicate trust than by saying, "Tell me how your job should be defined and let me know what support you need to accomplish it. Your work should give you plenty of autonomy because I trust that you will do the right thing and perform well." Paul Zak says, "Autonomy works because rather than being the innately selfish *homo economicus*...our research shows that human beings are more accurately described as *homo reciprocans*, or reciprocal creatures....People trust those who trust them, and distrust those who distrust them. Leaders must choose which side of the trust/distrust dichotomy they want to be on."[28]

The second benefit of workplace trust shows up on the economic side of the ledger. Trust reduces the cost associated with vigilance and monitoring, and thereby conserves energy and improves productivity. This effect is relevant both in the microeconomic environment of jobs within companies and in the broader macroeconomy. In the latter arena, economists have placed societal levels of trust among the most powerful growth promotion factors. People who trust each other require less-onerous contracts to do business and so are more willing to make investments without burdensome guarantees or expensive protections.

We could well expect this same effect to emerge in the competitive marketplace. Companies with higher endowments of trust should experience better cooperation among individuals, teams, and units; less employee time investment in monitoring events and negotiating for rights; less manager time required to defend decisions; and more rapid acceptance of work requirements. Each of these could contribute to a cost advantage or an edge in innovation or customer responsiveness.

Developing People

Employee development, and the goal setting and performance assessment processes that support it, require dialogue. Managers who amass critiques and data to unload on people at annual review time create an environment in which employees feel scrutinized and untrusted.

Alternatively, continuous discussion of goals and performance reinforce employee belief in interpersonal and informational fairness and build confidence in manager trustworthiness. Relational transparency helps form the basis for this kind of high-trust exchange. Particularly in flexible career models like the lattice-and-ladder approach, trust is critical to ensuring that all parties—individual, manager, and organization—benefit from creative work and development arrangements. A manager who conveys self-awareness and relational consistency gains insight into others and can interpret employee words and actions in the right context. He can differentiate manifestations of individual personality from artifacts of the work environment (the dilemma posed by the actor-observer bias). Conversely, a manager with intellectual honesty, bolstered by balanced processing, will have a counterweight to the illusion of transparency. This provides a way to avoid overestimating how well he understands employees' mental states. When these factors come together—when employees believe that supervisors have acted fairly and in good faith to help them craft personalized development and career advancement paths—their confidence in supervisor fairness and their trust in their managers increase.

Delivering the Deal

We know from our discussion of the deal between individual and enterprise that this exchange incorporates both tangible and intangible elements. The intangible, social elements of the exchange tend to have indefinite terms, long time frames, and unspecified value metrics. In other words, they have their basis in relational contracts. Consequently, trust becomes an important part of the ongoing exchange. Indeed, trust grows stronger over time on a foundation of positive interchanges between employee and organization, facilitated by the manager. Self-awareness enables a manager to understand his own reward motivations and to use those as points of reference for considering the deal with employees. Relational transparency helps ensure that the negotiation between employee and manager, acting as agent for the organization, produces a fair outcome for all parties. Employees can have confidence that a manager with a strong internalized moral perspective won't exploit them.

The tangible, financial elements of the deal tend to have programs and formally defined schemes as their foundation. They rely on transactional contracts, which reduce the need for trust between the exchanging parties. In virtually every workplace, employees engage simultaneously in both social and economic exchanges, which tend to operate relatively independently.

But the two kinds of deals differ not only in the amount of trust they require to maintain, but also the behaviors they produce. The social elements of the deal show stronger correlations than do the economic aspects with emotional commitment to the organization (that is, staying with a company because you share its values and feel a bond with the organization and its people). The economic elements of the deal have a closer association with what social scientists call continuance commitment (staying with a company because it's financially risky or costly to leave).[29] Overall performance, attendance, punctuality, and willingness to invest discretionary effort in the job all connect more closely with social, trust-based exchanges than with the transactional, program-based elements of the deal.

"OBSERVE ALL MEN, THYSELF MOST"

In a study of Customer Service Representatives (CSRs) and managers in a Citibank call center, Chip Heath (then of Duke University, now at Stanford) looked at how managers assess their own motivation and what they believe motivates others around them. Managers, he

(Continued)

Table 9.1: Managers Define Their Own Motives As Intrinsic but Others' Motives As Mainly Extrinsic

1 Motivation Factor	2 Managers' Rankings of Importance to Self	3 Managers' Rankings of Importance to Typical CSR	4 CSRs' Rankings of Importance to Self
Accomplishing something worthwhile	1	7	2
Developing skills	2	10	1
Feeling good about oneself	3	8	7
Learning new things	4	9	4
Job security	5	3	6
Helping customers	6	5	3
Quality of benefits	7	1	5
Amount of pay	8	6	8
Good schedule	9	2	9
Praise from manager	10	4	10

Source: Data from Heath, C., "On the Social Psychology of Agency Relationships: Lay Theories of Motivation Overemphasize Extrinsic Incentives," *Organizational Behavior and Human Decision Processes*, 78(1), April 1999, 52–53.

found, misunderstood by a large margin the motivations of the people who report to them. A summary of his results appears in Table 9.1.

Managers thought their own top four motivators (all heavily intrinsic) fell at the bottom of the motivation list for the typical CSR.

Conversely, the managers said that two of their bottom four motivators came near the top of the CSR list. Actually, as a comparison of columns 2 and 4 shows, manager and CSR self-ratings show remarkable overlap. They share three of the top four motivators as well as the bottom three *in order.*

What should managers do to reduce the likelihood of misinterpreting employees' motivations (a form of the transparency illusion)? Chip Heath has a simple observation. Referring to the managers in his study, he says, "Participants could have improved their predictions if they assumed that others were motivated exactly like they were."[30] In other words, you'll more accurately infer others' motivations if you practice self-awareness by thinking carefully about your own. This idea, of course, is not new. In his *Poor Richard's Almanac*, Ben Franklin gave the advice quoted in the title of this sidebar.

The capacity to understand others by reflecting about ourselves is called empathy. Empathy has its roots in the human trait social psychologists call "theory of mind." A theory of mind enables us to understand others by knowing how we would react if we experienced their circumstances. A self-aware manager who knows what motivates him, and who observes empathetically how those around him react to intrinsic and extrinsic motivators, can construct a reward mix that employees will find energizing.

Energizing Change

Trust acts as a lens through which people interpret the messages they receive from managers. Employee attention to the meaning of those messages becomes sharper when they bring news about change, whether small ("Sorry, your budget request was denied") or large ("It looks like we'll be shutting down this division and starting layoffs soon"). When change becomes imminent or real, people naturally speculate about the implications for them. They develop alternative scenarios, counterfactual assessments of reality that allow them to test the fairness of actual or expected outcomes. One counterfactual category focuses on *would:* would circumstances have been better if they had turned out differently—if the promotion had come through, if the merger hadn't happened, if the cotton fiber division hadn't been closed down? A second counterfactual involves *could:* could the manager have taken a different course—worked harder to get me the promotion, argued against the merger, fought to keep the cotton division going? The third type of counterfactual is *should:* should the manager have acted differently, or were the decisions either rational or out of the manager's control?

This process of counterfactual scenario-building provides a general framework for understanding how people process the circumstances of change. In real life, however, things aren't so neat. The preexisting environment of trust between employee and manager exerts a strong influence on how people interpret change-related explanations. According to researchers Brian Holtz and Crystal Harold of Rutgers University, "The level of trust in one's manager can form a heuristic context to evaluate managerial explanations, and the stronger the conviction, positive or negative, the more likely it is that heuristic processing will dominate the processing of specific messages."[31] In other words, people view the manager's explanations about change through the optics of trust. If a history of transparent, trust-enhancing exchanges exists between employee and manager, people will view explanations about change as sincere and legitimate. If employees believe their managers have remained open to receiving information and considering alternatives, they can have confidence that the outcomes of change are likely to be reasonable and fair, if not always favorable. A trusting social context between employee and manager establishes what Holtz and Harold call "a broad zone of acceptance for managerial decisions."[32] But if a manager has compromised trust through lack of openness, vague connection between individual work events and unit success, or violation of the requirements for fairness, then even logical and otherwise credible explanations will be interpreted by employees as inadequate, insincere, and not legitimate.

SUMMARY: THE FABRIC OF AUTHENTICITY AND TRUST

Employees in today's workforce demand competence and judgment from their managers. But they also want more. They come to work each day with a deeply ingrained ambivalence about the necessity for—not to mention the quality of—the leadership they are about to experience. They want fulfilling work, a chance to learn, a fair deal, and a guide through the uncertainty of a changing landscape. But they also want managers who will care about their well-being and refrain from pretense and game playing. In other words, they want authenticity and trust. The endowment of trust shared by employee and manager is a fragile asset, more easily destroyed than created. Building and preserving it requires effort from both sides.

In Chapter Three, we discussed transformational and transactional leadership. Although authentic leadership overlaps with both to some degree, the differences, especially with transformational leadership, are instructive. Authentic leaders, as we've emphasized, are guided by an inner compass, by their own deep sense of self. Transformational leaders may be just as honest and ethical, but their behavior has an external orientation. Transformational leaders nurture and develop the next generation of people with aspirations to senior leadership. Authentic leaders, in contrast, develop a population of people who share the value of authenticity. Leaders with a transformational style often project charisma, even star appeal. A manager executing his leadership duties authentically, in contrast, will be honest and forthright, though not necessarily charismatic. An authentic manager will project charisma only if that aspect of personal presence forms part of his true character. People acting with authenticity tend to rely more on personal example than on emotional appeal when it comes to inspiring action among followers.[33]

Hence, authentic leadership works best on a personal, one-to-one level, consistent with our definition of the leadership required of first-line supervisors and managers. A manager who demonstrates the highest levels of authenticity will consistently:

- Not just act with honesty and integrity—these are table stakes—but also remain mindful of all facets of her personal brand, understanding how employees experience her leadership style across a range of situations

- Achieve the difficult balance between perceiving and responding to individual employee differences while also considering that employees may react to workplace conditions much as she does

- Not merely perform thorough analysis of data and information, but also go further by seeking out contrasting opinions and challenging points of view

- Reinforce the connections among individual, work unit, and organizational strategy, because underscoring the importance of work builds trust, reduces stress, enhances resilience, and supports well-being

- Follow the fairness requirements scrupulously, even when organizational programs and executive decisions may make the criteria difficult to uphold

Demonstrating authentic and trust-engendering behaviors takes time and energy. The manager who sits isolated in her office may produce much direct output, but only at the cost of a lost opportunity to spend time with employees. People trust people they know, and they know people with whom they interact and share experiences—which happens on the other side of the office door and outside the cubicle walls.

CHAPTER OUTLINE

**Manager Role Structure and Performance Model—
A Summary**

What Makes a Great Manager?
Requisite Variety
Cognitive Fluidity
Ability to Catalyze Action
Ability to Navigate the Organization
Social Intelligence

Can a Good Manager Manage Anything?

Make Versus Buy

Notes for Those Who Want Managers to Succeed
What Executives Can Do
What Human Resources Can Do

10

Fitting the Pieces Together

In the final act of Shakespeare's *The Tempest*, Prospero, magician and exiled Duke of Milan, presents a group of shipwrecked prisoners to his daughter, Miranda, for inspection. The only people she knows are her bitter old father and his deformed slave, Caliban. She is struck by the sight of the men: "O, wonder! How many goodly creatures are there here! How beauteous mankind is! O brave new world that has such people in't!" By "brave" Miranda doesn't mean courageous, but rather stunning and splendid. Her father knows better, having experienced the world beyond their small island. He responds simply, "'Tis new to thee."

As we reflect on the manager job we've constructed here, we confess that it will take a splendid person to carry it off. But we're optimistic that such men and women are plentiful in many companies. Organizations merely need a clear view of the human capital required for a manager to succeed and a practical approach to identifying, obtaining, and developing the necessary knowledge, skills, talents, and behaviors. There is no dearth of manager and leader competency models. We don't propose to create yet another one. Instead, we want to lift our sights and provide a few higher-level thoughts about the attributes that matter most for the manager role we've defined.

Manager Role Structure and Performance Model—A Summary

Before we launch into our discussion of high-level attributes, let's first review what we think managers need to be able do. Figure 10.1 depicts the elements of the manager role architecture and performance model we've defined. It takes the components illustrated in Exhibit 3.1 and shows the connections among them.

At the center sit the five basic job segments and time allocation opportunities available to an individual manager. Those structural components are expressed through the action elements of the performance model: executing tasks, developing employees, delivering the deal, and energizing change. As the graphic shows, strategic requirements inform job structure and task definition. Development of human capital gives individuals and teams the capability to carry out those strategically critical tasks; delivery of an engaging, intrinsically valuable deal reinforces task-execution success. The world doesn't stand still, however, so good managers must maintain momentum by responding to and inspiring change. When managers perform well in all these elements,

---

Figure 10.1: How the Manager Performance Model Works

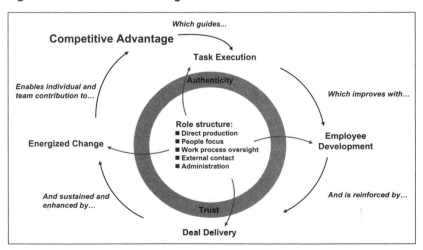

demonstrating authenticity and building trust in the process, engaged employees accomplish their goals. When that happens, organizations win in the marketplace and prosper as a result.

What Makes a Great Manager?

Executing well in this system requires managers to possess a generalized set of cognitive, emotional, and action-oriented characteristics. They must have the intellect to plan work and monitor results, ensuring a consistent focus on what matters to business strategy. They must have sufficient social and emotional insight to structure fulfilling jobs, ensure meaningful learning, understand individual reward needs, and sustain employee engagement. And they must know how to identify and exploit organizational resources to keep their teams executing and moving forward.

It's a daunting list of requirements, but we think not an impossible one, provided managers bring the right human capital to the job. We define the right human capital as a set of broadly scoped elements, each with plenty of room to comprise more precisely specified competencies. We're suggesting the main ingredients for manager success. Competency experts can translate these into a recipe.

We've intentionally left some contributors to manager performance off the list. For one thing, we haven't touched on the technical side of the job. We know from thinking about the S-Zone (Exhibit 4.1) that technical knowledge plays a role in managerial performance. However, we're leaving the definition of "technical competence" to individual organizations and functions. We simply reiterate that outstanding manager performance relies more on other elements than on technical prowess. We also haven't touched on the abilities and attitudes required of everyone in the organization, factors like business acumen, or comfort with diversity. Instead, we've concentrated on the classes of factors specifically required for supervisors and managers to be successful within the performance model and role structure we've defined.

We have constructed the definitions so that they apply to any strategy category and across any organizational function, albeit with varying interpretations and applications. For instance, navigating the organization will take on a specific meaning for a store manager in a retail operation with a widespread network of outlets but a highly centralized corporate training function. It will mean something different for a high-tech engineering manager who works in a small regional office but has a development team scattered across three continents and five time zones. Catalyzing action will take on different forms for an Internet service provider with an evolving business model, a video rental company facing cost pressure from a Web competitor, and a bank trying to recover from a global financial shock. On the one hand, social intelligence will retain its fundamental meaning in any situation requiring interpersonal interaction. On the other hand, we would expect it to feel different for R&D, marketing, and call center managers.

You will also notice that the performance elements do not fall neatly into leadership and management categories. We have suggested that managers will rarely stop in the middle of an activity and ask, "Am I leading or managing at this moment?" Instead, they should be asking, "What can I do at this moment to help the people in our unit perform best at executing this process and producing the results for which we are responsible?" As they answer this question, managers will think about systems, assets, and processes (the substance of managing) and about how people can exercise self-determination in working with these to execute tasks (the essence of leadership). When we speak of navigating the organization, for instance, we intend it to apply to managing (for instance, identifying and acquiring important assets, such as budget funding for a project or information to guide a decision). But we also mean it to encompass leadership (keeping people focused on strategic goals as they move through an organizational matrix, for example). In a similar way, cognitive fluidity enables a manager to see how two systems might be combined to improve efficiency (a management challenge) or to envision how to foster cooperation among three differently talented technicians to develop a novel solution (a leadership situation).

Here then are the summary attributes that we believe contribute most directly to a manager's success at playing the roles we've outlined, across strategies, companies, and functions.

Requisite Variety

This concept comes from systems theory, specifically the cybernetics discipline. It means simply that a flexible system encompassing many options performs better in an uncertain environment than does a system with fewer options. That is, only variety can respond to variety. For managers, this means having the insight to recognize, and the adaptability to respond to, a range of employee attitudes and behavioral styles. The goal is efficient connection and personal rapport. We don't propose that managers become behavioral chameleons; that would violate the precepts of authenticity. We do suggest, however, that a manager must be able to call on a range of behavioral modes to respond to an equally wide array of employee styles. This adjustability enables a manager to have the kinds of conversations required to craft person-specific jobs, create individualized development plans, and deliver customized reward deals. The required stylistic flexibility has a foundation of empathy. Requisite variety subsumes such traditional manager competencies as adaptability and effective communication.

Cognitive Fluidity

Cognitive fluidity goes beyond simple brain power. It denotes the ability to make intellectual connections across topics and domains. We've borrowed the concept from evolutionary psychologists. They use it to describe the growing capacity among early modern humans to connect intellectual domains—for instance, information about their environment, the tool-making materials at hand, and social relationships—to create and pass on new knowledge. In neurobiological terms, cognitive fluidity calls on the brain's executive function to combine observation, forethought, analysis, and problem solving.

Cognitive fluidity as we mean it requires balance. This implies, for instance:

- An ability to focus on near-term operational requirements without losing sight of the future (that is, being adept at using both a microscope and a telescope)

- A knack for seeing the details of an issue without missing the big picture (having both a sharp pencil and a dull pencil)

- A finely tuned judgment about when to assist and when to maintain distance (displaying conscientiousness balanced with a let-it-be confidence)

- A vision for how the future should both resemble and differ from the past (for example, by employing the counterfactual exercises we outlined)

More than just balance, however, cognitive fluidity calls for connectivity and mental agility. A manager strong in this attribute will prove effective, for example, at determining how a redirection of business strategy will affect unit-level work planning and operational requirements; discerning the meaning for organizational structure; and identifying the ripple effects on individual employees and their deals with the organization. The required intellectual plasticity and balanced processing contribute to stimulating and coping with change and underlie managerial authenticity. Cognitive fluidity incorporates such classic manager competencies as problem solving; analyzing and interpreting; comfort with ambiguity; and capacity to incorporate multiple points of view.

Ability to Catalyze Action

The essential paradox of our concept of the manager's job is that managers can perform better from offstage. This means acting as a catalyst, precipitating results without participating as a functional element in the processes used by individuals and teams. The manager-as-catalyst attribute encompasses classic competencies like results focus, bias for action, and goal-orientation. But we mean something more. To perform as a catalyst, a manager must combine relentless attention to what matters with a highly developed ability to get out of the way. This means paying close attention to results, taking subtle corrective actions when necessary, but rarely interfering directly in work processes. Catalytic management calls for a combination of conscientiousness and what psychologists refer to as emotional stability—equanimity, calm, and an ability to trust others and give up direct control. A successful manager-catalyst will be comfortable designing jobs that offer abundant opportunities for employee mastery and autonomy; creating employee deals that contain plenty of potential for intrinsic fulfillment; and chartering self-managing teams that deliver high performance unimpeded by managerial interference.

Ability to Navigate the Organization

Compared with the other categories, this one may seem mundane and prosaic. But don't be fooled. The ability to find and use an organization's tools and resources contributes as much to manager performance as does any other high-level attribute. This is the ultimate example of firm-specific, how-we-do-things-around-here knowledge. It requires cognitive fluidity, which enables the manager to see readily how to connect disparate resources (such as diverse learning programs) into a unified result (a practical development process for a single employee). Social intelligence also comes into play as the manager forms bonds with allies and builds networks of sources. Those bonds and networks may well extend beyond the boundaries of the company as the manager forages widely for useful ideas and assets. Moreover, by introducing employees to the web of contacts created, the manager multiplies the value of the relationships. Successful organization navigators display such classic competencies as business acumen and boundary spanning.

Social Intelligence

You may wonder why emotional intelligence doesn't appear on our list but social intelligence does. In *Emotional Intelligence*, Daniel Goleman divided emotional intelligence into five major components: knowing one's own emotions, managing emotions, self-motivation, recognizing emotions in others, and handling relationships.[1] The characteristic we call social intelligence did not emerge discretely, but rather was embedded in these dimensions. In his later book called *Social Intelligence*, Goleman admits to a revelation: "As I've come to see, simply lumping social intelligence within the emotional sort stunts fresh thinking about the human aptitude for relationship, ignoring what transpires as we interact. This myopia leaves the 'social' part out of intelligence."[2]

We view emotional intelligence as critical for any person working in the society of others, whether playing a leadership or team member role. It is important for success and fulfillment in any interpersonal interaction. Hence, we consider it applicable to every member of an enterprise. But because the manager's role as we've defined it is essentially social—working with people being the definitive aspect of the job—we've identified social intelligence as the most relevant application of the connective elements in Goleman's conception of emotional intelligence.

Goleman includes two components in his definition of social intelligence: awareness (gathering information on others and understanding how the social world functions) and facility (effective interactions using the information gathered).[3] These attributes provide the interpersonal insight and the influence skill needed to navigate within and outside organizational boundaries. Social intelligence encompasses the authenticity that guides managers to honest understanding of their own and others' strengths and weaknesses. It's a key to working with teams from the right distance and creating the networks that provide learning contacts. Humility is essential; a sense of humor doesn't hurt. A socially intelligent manager typically displays extroversion (positive energy and emotions; interest in exploring; tendency to seek stimulation and to enjoy the company of others), and agreeableness (compassion, forgiveness, tolerance, a spirit of cooperation, and motivation to achieve interpersonal intimacy). Both are personality traits commonly associated with transformational, high-authenticity leaders. Empathy provides a foundation for social intelligence by enabling a manager to gather, reflect on, and interpret the interpersonal information required to build bonds with individuals and groups. Traditional competencies like interpersonal skills, persuasiveness, and team-building come under the umbrella of social intelligence.

Can a Good Manager Manage Anything?

By defining this set of fundamental elements, we've tried to create a general definition of what characterizes a strong manager. It follows that, even across organizations with different strategies and across various functions, high-performing managers should be more similar than dissimilar. But let's consider several variations of the question that heads this section. Sometimes, the question takes this form: "Should we move our R&D manager over to product development?" This idea assumes that the R&D manager has amply demonstrated the knowledge, skills, and talents that we've defined here (and the subordinate competencies they embrace). Otherwise, why would he be a manager in the first place, let alone a candidate for transfer and possible promotion? If an individual demonstrates these high-level attributes, then the question of transfer feasibility boils down to an assessment of technical skills and knowledge. How important are these to the manager's credibility and ability to guide, coach, and develop employees? Does the candidate possess them now? If not, how feasible would it be to develop them (see the make-buy discussion in the next section)? Answers to these questions govern the practicality and advisability of cross-unit transfers.

Another variation on the good-manager theme has to do with hiring from outside the organization: "Can we bring in a new sales manager from our main competitor?" In Chapter Three, we made the case that firm-specific human capital is important to achieving strategic advantage and is often a barrier to successful external hiring. It is risky to bring people from the outside into positions where success depends strongly on company-specific knowledge or idiosyncratic applications of technical skills. We would caution that, in many cases, adding a firm-specific inflection to already developed knowledge and skills will prove either too time-consuming for the individual or too expensive for the organization, or both.

We often encounter this question: "Should we move our best technical performer into a manager role?" As we've tried to make clear, we think promotion chiefly for technical reasons is a big mistake. An exception would be made for a candidate who occupies the far upper right-hand corner of the S-Zone (Exhibit 4.1). This person has strong performance ability along both the managerial and technical dimensions. When you have a candidate with these qualifications, close the deal. Conversely, promoting someone from the lower right-hand corner of the grid is a formula for disappointment across the board. Doing this takes a top producer off line (hurting output); creates at best a mediocre manager (decreasing employee engagement and well-being and diminishing unit performance); and puts an individual into an untenable position (talk about a stressful job!).

Make Versus Buy

Perhaps the most fundamental question facing companies seeking to ensure a population of great managers is this: is it better to develop the performance requirements or to obtain them through hiring and selection? Psychologists debate the degree to which personality elements are subject to change, either from affirmative efforts like training or simply from the effects of maturity as people age. On the one hand, exhaustive analysis of personality traits and their manifestations, often through twin studies, suggests that the five foundational personality factors—

extroversion, emotional stability, conscientiousness, agreeableness, and openness to experience—are between 40 and 50 percent heritable.[4] Personality features, like other characteristics of *homo sapiens*, evolved for a reason: they helped our early ancestors survive long enough to reproduce and be attractive enough to the opposite sex to find a mate. Those traits therefore have a deeply ingrained quality that makes individual change difficult. Psychologist Martin Seligman summarizes the situation like this: "Evolution, acting through our genes and our nervous system, has made it simple for us to change in certain ways and almost impossible for us to change in others."[5]

Dr. R. Grant Steen believes that we must separate the part of the personality that remains stable over time from the part that changes under the influence of life events, including learning experiences. The first element he calls *temperament*; he labels the second *character*. He describes the interplay between our genetic programming and our experience this way: "In a crude sense, we cannot do what we are not programmed to do. But equally true, we cannot do what we are programmed to do if the environment does not facilitate so doing. Environment can amplify or blunt the effect of genes, but environment cannot replace or displace genes. After the connections between neurons are made during development, it is up to the organism to use those connections." Steen also points to the work of Donald O. Hebb of McGill University, who taught that "heredity determines the range through which environment can modify the individual."[6]

Which takes us back to our basic question: given what can be changed and what can't, what's the best way for an organization to create a cadre of managers who possess the attributes we've defined? We suggest that the process depicted in Figure 10.2 provides a way to approach the issue.

The thinking begins with the question of feasibility. The behavioral traits that are most deeply embedded in the personality will prove most difficult to train. We would place elements like requisite variety in this category. Developing this in people who demonstrate little flexibility in responding to others' emotional states will prove a sizable challenge,

Figure 10.2: Building Manager Attributes—Make Versus Buy

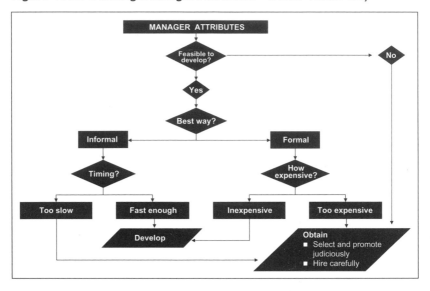

perhaps not impossible with enough time and attention, but difficult nevertheless. In contrast, aspects of catalyzing action (a skill) and navigating the organization (a bundle of knowledge) will more likely respond to training.

Once feasibility has been sorted out, the next question relates to cost and timing. For simplification, we have assumed that formal development programs can be brought on line fairly quickly. An organization can often purchase or design and deliver a training program in relatively short order. We have also assumed that informal learning takes longer to have an effect. On-the-job training and mobility strategies unfold at a pace more measured, less predictable, and more particular to each individual. Conversely, formal training brings a higher price tag than more informal, organic forms of learning.

In any given case, of course, cost and timing advantages and disadvantages may not align so neatly with the formal and informal learning categories. But the point remains that analyzing these factors can help an organization determine whether and how to invest in development approaches. These come down to strategic choices—how much time has the marketplace given us to put great managers in place in a particularly critical function? How much can we afford to spend on building manager capability, given the cost pressures we're feeling? Often, we believe, organizations will conclude that the most sensible approach to populating the company with great managers will chiefly depend on careful assessment and selection among internal candidates. Occasionally, with all the caveats we've suggested, outside hiring might prove feasible. However, this will require the organization to show patience as an individual's preexisting schemas and scripts are rewritten for the new company.

In all this we must remember the thoughts of Stanford's Carol Dweck. She would remind us that executives and learning and development strategists owe it to managers and manager candidates to keep an open mind about the potential to learn. Even Prof. Dweck wouldn't argue that all human traits are infinitely plastic and therefore subject to remolding. She would say, however, that no one, including individuals themselves, can fully understand a person's potential to grow. To those assessing and developing managerial candidates, she would say that they should maintain an optimistic realism about the ability of people to change and grow. They owe it to the organization and to employees to have faith that human capital can evolve and increase. She would admonish them to back up that faith with a thoughtful assessment of how best to create and build an organization's managers.

Notes for Those Who Want Managers to Succeed

Organizations shouldn't expect managers to execute all the elements of the performance model by themselves. Like all employees, they need tangible and intangible resources to meet the demands of their jobs. The executive group and the Human Resources function both play important roles in helping managers effectively perform their task-execution, people-development, deal-delivery, and change-energizing roles. We have some specific thoughts about the support that executives and HR need to provide.

What Executives Can Do

Your job is to lead your organization to the promised land of marketplace advantage. This means looking behind every tree and under every rock for a competitive edge that your company can seize and hold on to. As we've suggested throughout this narrative, we believe your supervisors and managers represent a source of such advantage, latent in most organizations but nevertheless full of potential. Executive leaders can do some specific things to realize this potential:

- Challenge your point of view about your organization's supervisors and managers. Talk about them differently in executive planning sessions. Speak about them frequently when you appear before employees to cite the strengths of the organization. Elevate their profile in the company, making the position a sought-after prize for the successful and truly qualified. Think constantly about how you can take advantage of their contributions and their influence over employee behaviors.

- Make sure your organization's managers have full access to all the detailed strategy information they need to ensure that their units can make the maximum contribution. They can't create a line of sight between jobs and business strategy unless they have this knowledge.

- Do all the things for your managers that you want them to do for their employees. Let them craft their jobs; have autonomy in executing their responsibilities; receive recognition, individually and collectively, privately and publicly, for their success; and increase their self-efficacy and mastery.

- Provide them the same kinds of human capital development opportunities they give their employees, with emphasis on challenging assignments that accelerate their growth. Coach them, guide them, give them access to your network, let them learn from their mistakes— and yours.

- Demonstrate frequently that you care specifically about manager engagement and well-being. They can't enhance employee engagement or attend to people's physical, psychological, and social health if their ability to sustain energy is compromised. Measure and monitor managers' engagement and well-being levels and take action if either deteriorates.

- When difficult change becomes necessary, make the case for change clear to your managers and then let them decide how to take action in their individual units. Adhere to a model of dispersed responsibility for organizational change. Let your managers meet the company's needs by crafting a local response for which you, as executives, can hold them responsible. Avoid hamstringing them by forcing sweeping change that may be insensitive to the circumstances in any single unit and therefore may cripple a manager's ability to deliver the results you need.

- Make your organization the best, and best-known, place to become a high-performing manager, the company that provides the highest rewards, both intrinsic and financial, that such status carries. Think about the advantages you'll gain:

  ○ Competitive superiority (because your managers keep everyone relentlessly focused on doing work that achieves the organization's vision for success)

  ○ Recruiting superiority (because who wouldn't want to come to your company, given its reputation as the place to work with, and become, a great manager)

  ○ Human capital superiority (because your people have better opportunities than your competitors to learn and grow and improve their performance)

○ Workplace superiority (because your people are not only more engaged and more capable than your competitors' employees, but also better able to sustain high productivity and respond to change)

Is there such a word as *quadfecta*? If not, there should be—because these four points make one.

What Human Resources Can Do

HR's first job is advocacy, urging executives to accept that the performance model laid out here produces better economic results for the organization than other manager job concepts. HR professionals must do the economic analysis to prove where on the spectrum between Widget Wizard and People Powermeister an individual manager's job should lie. They must become evangelists for the role structure that makes it possible for managers to fulfill the potential we've identified.

MANAGER SELF-SERVICE

The overall cost of human resource service delivery has become one of the most pressing issues facing Human Resource executives. On the one hand, this concern reflects near-term economic pressure. On the other, it's part of a longer-term story of organizations continuing to try to balance service quality with support cost. One approach HR has taken is to ask managers to perform many of the transactions HR used to do (for example, initiating job requisitions, posting open jobs, viewing employees' employment histories, approving training courses). Tom Keebler, Towers Watson's global practice leader for HR Service Delivery/Technology, confirms the trend: "Undeniably, we're seeing a continuing shift of these kinds of transactions to managers themselves, with the expectation that they will use Web-based tools to do many of the things HR used to handle." The United Kingdom's Chartered Institute of Personnel and Development, Europe's largest professional body dedicated to employee development, has studied the evolution of the manager's role and reached a similar conclusion: "In all our organizations FLMs [front-line managers] were carrying out activities which traditionally had been the bread and butter of the personnel or HR department.... The reasons for this expansion of the role have been much written about—organizational restructuring and the consequent decline of the middle manager, the growth in teamworking, increasing recognition that responsibility for managing people rests with the line rather than with a specialist, and the move toward leaner methods of working. These changes undoubtedly place an increasing workload on the FLM."[7]

But just how much has the shift of HR transactions to the to-do lists of managers added to their administrative burden? Towers Perrin surveyed HR practitioners in 2009 and found that greater use of manager self-service tools for a broad range of HR and pay-related transactions has added somewhat to managers' workloads. Of the 155 respondents to the survey, 43 percent said managers had to do more work following the introduction of manager self-service tools; 41 percent said these tools had reduced manager workload. In contrast, the respondents said, HR personnel across the board had less administrative work after their organizations implemented manager self-service.[8]

What determines the impact of the HR-to-manager task shift? "It depends on how you do it," Keebler says. "Managers in companies that do a good job of introducing these tools fare differently and react differently from managers in other organizations. It mainly comes down to two things: how the Web portal design process was handled and how the company managed the introduction and

(Continued)

process change." The best design protocols, he says, pay attention to how information is organized on the manager portal, to the overall look and feel of the Web site, to the implementation of tools (like single sign-on to ease use), and to rigorous usability testing before release. "Once design is done, change management matters a lot," Keebler says. "The most effective processes feature heavy involvement from managers, plenty of communication throughout the design exercise, and easy-to-use on-line tutorials. Generally, we find that high involvement, such as manager focus groups during the design effort, is considered the most effective tactic." The data suggest, however, that only 18 percent of the respondents' organizations made extensive use of manager involvement approaches.

Here are some of the specific requirements:

- Make sure your managers understand the broad human capital strategy of the firm and how it links with the enterprise business strategy.

- Don't compromise on the required attributes when filling open supervisor and manager positions. Search diligently until you find candidates in the S-Zone. Examine your compensation systems, titling conventions, and cultural norms for prestige. Don't allow these factors to drive your company to promote people into positions where they can do more harm than good to the organization, their employees, and themselves. Waiting for the right candidate, even if the wait is uncomfortably long, is better than putting the wrong person in any supervisor or manager job. Whatever benefit comes from filling a position quickly soon disappears if employee engagement, development, performance, and well-being are sacrificed. Design and implement a sound process for identifying and nurturing people in, or on the edges of, the S-Zone.

- Make it a top priority to do something about the low-performing managers in the organization. Some should go back to being individual contributors—and they would probably be happier if they could. Others simply may not belong in the company. Don't prolong their agony and yours by keeping them in positions that drain their energy and hinder organizational success.

- Consider letting individual contributors have a trial run in their first supervisor position, perhaps overseeing a specific initiative or a modest project. Make it a brief, no-harm-no-foul experience, and then decide whether they can best contribute as managers or as direct output producers (but not both). Let them choose that path with impunity.

- Define manager performance metrics that reflect the full contribution of the role. Don't overemphasize the manager's direct production. Instead, focus chiefly on the unit's production and financial performance, but also monitor the growth of employees' human capital, the state of their engagement, and their levels of perceived well-being. Monitor the links between manager behavior and health care cost. Ensure that metrics are few in number, clearly linked with enterprise strategy, insightful, and suitable for guiding action.

- Structure managers' reward portfolios—the deal they have with the organization—so that they align with these ways of measuring. Don't tilt the pay system toward individual output.

- Prepare managers to play their part in delivering the deal. Don't make them solve mysteries about the components or intention of the organization's reward systems. Give them latitude to apply those systems with judgment and individual sensitivity. Executing this responsibility requires that, at a minimum, HR will:

  ○ Ensure that managers understand both the high-level philosophy and the details of individual reward system components, financial and nonfinancial

- ○ Provide information to managers on the competitive reward environment and the relative market positioning of the organization's reward programs

- ○ Educate managers in how to communicate the intent and the outcomes of reward system events, such as incentive payments

- ○ Train managers rigorously in using the company's performance management system, including both the mechanics of the process and the relational elements of employee coaching and feedback

INVOLVING MANAGERS IN SETTING REWARD STRATEGY

Yes, even in defining the financial elements. One organization we know that did so is salesforce.com. In its ten-year history, sales force.com has grown to about 60,000 customers and 1.5 million subscribers by focusing relentlessly on customer success. Doing so has required that the organization hire and retain the most capable technical, service, and marketing people the employment market has to offer—the same talent that organizations like Google, Oracle, and Yahoo are targeting. Moreover, like all companies in a competitive market, even one focused on product and service differentiation, salesforce.com must carefully manage the cost of its rewards programs. All this requires the organization to sharply focus the elements of its deal on the rewards that yield the highest perceived value to employees for every dollar invested by the company.

To construct its rewards strategy, salesforce.com put together a project team that included senior HR professionals, as well as managers and executives in positions ranging from senior manager to senior vice president. Salesforce.com used a sophisticated survey tool, along with a series of focus groups, to gather information on employees' valuations of a variety of rewards programs. The survey gave the project team insight into how employees value various aspects of the company's compensation, benefits, and learning programs. The project team spent many days reviewing the results and drafting the organization's reward philosophy word by word. They debated over how to structure the rewards portfolio to meet the needs of individuals, hiring managers, organization units, demographic groups, and shareholders. Managers and executives personally led employee focus groups to gather further employee input on reward elements and explain the company's rewards direction. This approach provided employees with information about salesforce.com's intentions, as well as a voice in the final design, and met the criteria for high procedural and informational fairness.[9]

- Make sure your managers have full information about the organization's learning and development opportunities. In particular, help them map the available cross-organization moves, so that they can guide employees in their use and integrate them suitably with other learning strategies. Also ensure that managers' efforts to help employees develop their human capital align with goal setting, performance evaluation, and rewards. HR must own the fully articulated system that managers apply.

- Don't give in to the temptation to shift HR duties to managers without a careful assessment of the workload and time allocation implications. Our performance model places high enough demands on them. Don't make managers' jobs harder by giving them a heavy load of HR administration tasks.

- Help managers themselves develop a growth-supporting perspective. To do this, a workshop conducted by the SMU–University of Toronto team took a group of managers through an exercise with these five elements:

○ Scientific testimony, delivered via an article and a videotape, about how the brain, and hence intelligence, can grow strong much as a muscle does.

○ Exercises in which participants generated responses to the question, "As a manager, what are at least three reasons why it is important to realize that people can develop their abilities? Include implications for both yourself and for the employees you (will) manage."

○ Reflections on their own experience, with the managers considering areas where they had improved and thinking about how they were able to make those changes.

○ Writing an e-mail to a struggling hypothetical protégé about how abilities can be developed; participants were encouraged to include anecdotes about how they had personally dealt with development challenges.

○ Having participants identify three instances when they had observed someone learn to do something they had believed the person could never do, explain why they think the achievement had occurred, and reflect on the implications.

This format focused chiefly on self-persuasion. At the end of the training, managers who had held a fixed-ability philosophy tended to migrate to a more flexible point of view.[10]

• Remember that employee well-being is a whole-system concept that requires close connection between managers and HR. Make it a campaign to work with managers to understand and improve well-being. The potential health care cost savings are dramatic.

• Never put managers in a position where they must compromise the trust they have built with employees. This means always ensuring that they have full information about the organization and its strategy, challenges, and position in the marketplace. It also means giving them freedom to respond to organizational change in ways that preserve their integrity and reinforce their authenticity.

Your relationship with managers should have many facets—ally, trusted adviser, coach—with each party playing these roles for the other as the situation requires. When the relationship works best, manager and HR will act as partners—investment partners, business partners, sparring partners. After all, you have a common goal: to make the enterprise competitively successful through the contributed strengths of the employees who work there. You should need no more powerful bond than that goal, and no greater reason to do all you can to ensure that your manager population becomes a source of sustainable success.

Preface

1. Kark, S., and van Rensburg, B. J., "Ecotones: Marginal or Central Areas of Transition?" *Israel Journal of Ecology & Evolution*, 2006, *52*, 30–31.

2. *The New Employment Deal: How Far, How Fast and How Enduring*, Towers Watson, 2010. In the text, this source will be referred to as the 2010 Towers Watson global workforce study.

3. http://bobsutton.typepad.com/my_weblog/2008/10/management-by-getting-out-of-the-way.html.

Chapter One

1. *Army Leadership: Competent, Confident and Agile*, Headquarters, Department of the Army, 6–22, October 2006, 3–7.

2. Samuelson, R. J., *The Good Life and Its Discontents: The American Dream in the Age of Entitlement—1945–1995*, New York: Times Books, 1995, 48.

3. Drucker, P. F., *The Practice of Management*, New York: Harper & Row, 1954, 4.

4. Ibid., 320.

5. U.S. Department of Commerce, Bureau of Economic Analysis, *Corporate Profits Before Tax by Industry: 1929–2007*, http://data.bls .gov/PDQ/servlet/SurveyOutputServlet?series_id=LNS14000000.

6. Samuelson, 114.

7. Davenport, T. O., *Human Capital: What It Is and Why People Invest It*, San Francisco: Jossey-Bass, 1999, 5.

8. Atwood, J., Coke, E., Cooper, C., and Loria, K., *Has Downsizing Gone Too Far?* University of North Florida, December 1995, 7.

9. U.S. Department of Labor, Bureau of Labor Statistics, Current Population Survey, *Unemployment Rate: January 1992–June 2009*.

10. Davenport, 5.

11. Atwood, 7.

12. U.S. Department of Labor, Bureau of Labor Statistics, Current Population Survey, *Employed Persons by Detailed Occupation and Sex, 2000–2007 Annual Averages*.

13. Throughout the book, we will use the terms "supervisor" and "manager" more or less interchangeably. In all cases, we are referring to the first-line positions at or below the middle of the organizational pyramid.

14. Wikipedia, *Middle Management*, http://en.wikipedia.org./wiki/ Middle_management.

15. Saxon, M., sidebar entitled "Leadership as Core Competency," in "Who Executes? Why CEOs Should Encourage Those in the Middle to Lead the Way," *The Conference Board Review*, Fall 2009, 49.

16. Kaiser, R. B., Hogan, R., and Craig, S. B., "Leadership and the Fate of Organizations," *American Psychologist*, February–March 2008, 107.

17. Gosling, J., and Mintzberg, H., "The Five Minds of a Manager," *Harvard Business Review*, Reprint R0311C, November 2003, 1.

18. Grace Hopper Quotes, http://womenshistory.about.com/od/quotes/a/grace_hopper.htm.

19. Leadership versus Management, www.1000ventures.com/business_guide/crosscuttings/leadership_vs_mgmt.html.

20. Rowe, W. G., "Creating Wealth in Organizations: The Role of Strategic Leadership," *Academy of Management Executive*, 2001, *15*(1), 82.

21. Byrnes, N., and others, "Reuben Mark, Colgate-Palmolive: The Detail Man," www.businessweek.com/print/magazine/content/02_38/b3800006.htm, September 23, 2002, 1.

22. Jones, D., "Even Good CEOs Can Pick the Wrong Direction," http://usatoday.com/money/companies/management/2007–11–06-mistakes_N.htm, 1.

23. Martin, R., "The Age of Customer Capitalism," *Harvard Business Review*, January-February 2010, 61–62.

24. "Employees First: Strategies for Service," http://knowledge.wpcarey.asu.edu/article.cfm?articleid=1620, June 26, 2008, 1.

25. Schultz, H., and Yang, D. J., *Pour Your Heart into It: How Starbucks Built a Company One Cup at a Time*, New York: Hyperion, 1997, 6.

26. Ibid., 245.

27. Buckingham, M., "What Great Managers Do," *Harvard Business Review*, Reprint R0503D, March 2005, 1–2.

28. Vogl, A. J., "Managerial Correctness," *The Conference Board Review*, July/August 2004, 21.

29. See Davenport, *Human Capital*, for a more detailed discussion of the people-as-investors metaphor.

30. *Closing the Engagement Gap: A Roadmap For Driving Superior Business Performance*, 2007, Towers Perrin.

31. Ibid.

32. *The New Employment Deal: How Far, How Fast and How Enduring*, Towers Watson, 2010.

33. Andel, Marie, personal communication with Tom Davenport, March 2010. Used with permission.

34. Welbourne, T., "Employee Engagement: Doing It vs. Measuring," www.eepulse.com/documents/pdfs/HR.com-9–8–03.pdf, September 10, 2003.

Chapter Two

1. Linden, G., "First, Kill All the Managers," http://glinden.blogspot .com/2006/05/first-kill-all-managers.html, May 30, 2006.

2. Turmel, W., "I Don't Want to Be a Manager! View from the Middle," www.management-issues.com/2007/5/14/opinion/i -don't-want-to-be-a-manager.asp, May 14, 2007.

3. "Managers of Tomorrow: Setting a New Standard," *2009 World of Work Topic Report*, Randstad, 2009, 2.

4. Turmel.

5. Randstad, 2.

6. "Are Companies Prepared for the Looming Manager Shortage?" Press release on Randstad, "Managers of Tomorrow: Setting a New Standard," *2009 World of Work Topic Report*, July 23, 2009, 1.

7. U.S. Department of Labor, Bureau of Labor Statistics, Current Population Survey, *Employment Status of the Civilian Noninstitutional Population by Sex and Age, Seasonally Adjusted*, www.bls.gov/cps/ lfcharacteristics.htm#laborforce, and *Civilian Labor Force Level— Bachelor's Degree and Higher 1992–2008*, http://data.bls.gov/PDQ/ servlet/SurveytOutputServlet.

8. *The New Employment Deal: How Far, How Fast and How Enduring*, Towers Watson, 2010.

9. U.S. Department of Labor, Bureau of Labor Statistics, Economic News Release, *Table 1: Median Years of Tenure with Current*

Employer for Employed Wage and Salary Workers by Age and Sex, Selected Years, 1983–2004, 1996–2008, www.bls.gov/ news.release/tenure.t01.htm and www.bls.gov/opub/cwc/tables/ cm20050926ar01t1.htm.

10. Towers Watson.

11. U.S. Department of Labor, Bureau of Labor Statistics, Economic News Release, *Table 1: Median Years of Tenure with Current Employer for Employed Wage and Salary Workers by Age and Sex, Selected Years, 1983–2004, 1996–2008,* www.bls.gov/ news.release/tenure.t01.htm and www.bls.gov/opub/cwc/tables/ cm20050926ar01t1.htm.

12. *Home Broadband Adoption 2009,* Pew Internet & American Life Project, 2009, 3, 14.

13. *Addressing Email Chaos: The Email-Manager™ Solution,* The Radicati Group, Inc., 2008, 4.

14. Walsh, M., "Survey: Social Networks Not So Hot in the Workplace (and No One Cares)," MediaPostNEWS, www.mediapost.com/ publications/?fa=Articles.showArticle&art_aid=109046, July 2, 2009.

15. Facebook, www.facebook.com/press/info.php?statistics.

16. Smith, J., "Fastest Growing Demographic on Facebook: Women over 55," www.insidefacebook.com/2009/02/02/fastest -growing-demographic-on-facebook-women-over-55/, February 2, 2009.

17. Johansmeyer, T., "Size Matters and Twitter's Got It with Tweet Volume," www.bloggingstocks.com/2010/02/13/size-matters-and -twitter-s-got-it-with-tweet-volume/, February 13, 2010.

18. "Social Networking and Reputational Risk in the Workplace," *Deloitte LLP 2009 Ethics & Workplace Survey Results,* Deloitte Development LLC, 2009, 11.

19. Towers Watson.

20. Similar trends have been forecast for Europe. For example, it was predicted that in 2008, two million European jobs in the financial services sector would have been transferred to India. (See Grint, K., *The Sociology of Work*, 3rd Edition, Cambridge: Polity Press, 2005, 339.) In many European countries, a shift from bureaucratic to market-led forms of social exchange has led to an increase in the contractualization and commoditization of work. (See McGovern, P., Hill, S., Mills, C., and White, M., *Market, Class and Employment*, Oxford: Oxford University Press, 2007, 44–45.) Although peaks and troughs in employment have largely paralleled economic trends, concerns about job security have grown dramatically. An analysis of newspaper articles in the United Kingdom between 1986 and 1996 revealed a 100-fold increase in the frequency of news stories on the topic of job insecurity during a period when unemployment actually fell (Grint, 126).

21. U.S. Department of Labor, Bureau of Labor Statistics, Current Population Survey, *Unemployment Rate: January 1990–April 2010*, http://data.bls.gov/PDQ/servlet/SurveyOutputServlet.

22. U.S. Department of Labor, Bureau of Labor Statistics, *Extended Mass Layoffs in 2006, Report 1004*, and Extended Mass Layoffs— First Quarter of 2010, Economic News Release USDL 10–0644, May 12, 2010, www.bls.gov/news.release/mslo.nr0.htm

23. Towers Watson.

24. Saxon, M., sidebar entitled "Leadership as Core Competency," in "Who Executes? Why CEOs Should Encourage Those in the Middle to Lead the Way," *The Conference Board Review*, Fall 2009, 49.

25. Keltner, D., Gruenfeld, D. H., and Anderson, C., "Power, Approach, and Inhibition," *Psychological Review*, 2003, *110*(2), 277.

26. Van Vugt, M., "Evolutionary Origins of Leadership and Followership," *Personality and Social Psychology Review*, 2006, *10*(4), 354.

27. Woodard, B., "First Sergeant: Leadership by Example," www.fairchild.af.mil/news/story.asp?id=123126830, December 5, 2008.

28. Van Vugt, M., Hogan, R., and Kaiser, R. B., "Leadership, Followership, and Evolution: Some Lessons from the Past," *American Psychologist*, 2008, *63*(3), 186.

29. Erdal, D., and Whiten, A., "On Human Egalitarianism: An Evolutionary Product of Machiavellian Status Escalation?" *Current Anthropology*, 1994, *35*(2), 178.

30. Ames, D. R., and Flynn, F. J., "What Breaks a Leader: The Curvilinear Relation Between Assertiveness and Leadership," *Journal of Personality and Social Psychology*, 2007, *92*(2), 308.

31. Ibid., 308.

32. Boehm, C., "Egalitarian Behavior and Reverse Dominance Hierarchy," *Current Anthropology*, 1993, *34*(3), 232–238.

33. Selvin, M., "States Putting Bullying Bosses on Notice: Act Like a Jerk and You Risk a Costly Suit," http://articles.sfgate.com/2007 –08–22/business/17258237_1_working-america-lobbying-arm -bad-boss-worst-boss, August 22, 2007.

34. Bono, J. E., Foldes, H. J., Vinson, G., and Muros, J. P., "Workplace Emotions: The Role of Supervision and Leadership," *Journal of Applied Psychology*, 2007, *92*(5), 1363.

35. Miner, A. G., Glomb, T. M., and Hulin, C., "Experience Sampling Mood and Its Correlates at Work," *Journal of Occupational and Organizational Psychology*, 2005, 178–179.

36. Ibid., 183.

37. Van Vugt, 2008, 189.

Chapter Three

1. Richerson, P. J., and Boyd, R., *Not by Genes Alone: How Culture Transformed Human Evolution*, Chicago: The University of Chicago Press, 2005, 105.

2. For a full discussion of competitive strategy, see for example Porter, M., *Competitive Advantage: Creating and Sustaining Superior Performance*, New York: The Free Press, 1985; Treacy, M., and Wiersema, F., *The Discipline of Market Leaders*, Reading, MA: Addison-Wesley, 1995; and Kaplan, R. S., and Norton, D. P., "Having Trouble with Your Strategy? Then Map It," *Harvard Business Review*, September-October 2000.

3. Hatch, N. W., and Dyer, J. H., "Human Capital and Learning as a Source of Sustainable Competitive Advantage," *Strategic Management Journal*, 2004, 25, 1171–1173.

4. Ibid., 1172.

5. Clark, R., "Inside Intel, It's All Copying—In Setting Up Its New Plants, Chip Maker Clones Older Ones Down to the Paint on the Wall," *The Wall Street Journal Online*, http://pqasb .pqarchiver.com/djreprints/access/224262211.html?FMT=FT &FMTS=ABS:FT&type=current&date=Oct+28%2C+2002& author=By+Don+Clark&pub=Wall+Street+Journal&edition= &startpage=B.1&desc=Inside+Intel%2C+It%27s+All+Copying++— ++In+Setting+Up+Its+New+Plants%2C++Chip+Maker+Clones+ Older+Ones++Down+to+the+Paint+on+the+Wall, October 28, 2002.

6. Edwards, C., "Inside Intel: Paul Otellini's Plan Will Send the Chipmaker into Uncharted Territory. And Founder Andy Grove Applauds the Shift," www.businessweek.com/print/magazine/ content/06_02/b3966001.htm?chan=gl, January 9, 2006.

7. Southwest Airlines Co., *2009 Annual Report to Shareholders*.

8. *Air Travel Consumer Report*, U.S. Department of Transportation, Office of Aviation Enforcement and Proceedings, May 2010, 4–5, 28–29, 38.

9. Gittell, J. H., "Supervisory Span, Relational Coordination and Flight Departure Performance: A Reassessment of Postbureaucracy Theory," *Organization Science*, July–August 2001, *12*(4), 477.

10. Ibid., 478.

11. *Southwest Airlines Fact Sheet*, www.southwest.com/about_swa/ press/factsheet.html.

12. "Something Special about Southwest Airlines," CBSNews.com, www.cbsnews.com/stories/2007/08/30/Sunday/printable3221531 .shtml, September 2, 2007.

13. "Performance Measures: Southwest Airlines Compared to All Low-Cost Carriers," *Research and Innovative Technology Administration (RITA)*, Bureau of Transportation Statistics, www.bts.gov/ programs/airline_information/performance_measures_in_the _airline_industry/, First Quarter 2007.

14. "SAS Fraud Management Wins Technology Innovation of the Year Award," SAS press release, September 23, 2008.

15. SAS Corporate Statistics/Facts & Figures, www.sas.com/presscenter/ bgndr_statistics.html.

16. Florida, R., and Goodnight, J., "Managing for Creativity," *Harvard Business Review*, Reprint R0507L, July–August 2005, 3.

17. Ibid., 6.

18. Ibid.

19. Fishman, C., "Sanity Inc.," www.fastcompany.com/node/36173/ print, December 18, 2007, 2.

20. Wang, J., "Investigating Market Value and Intellectual Capital for S&P 500," *Journal of Intellectual Capital*, 2008, *9*(4), 559–561.

21. Hatch, 1170–1172.

22. Ibid., 1171.

23. Dokko, G., Wilk, S. L., and Rothbard, N. P., "Unpacking Prior Experience: How Career History Affects Job Performance," *Organization Science*, January-February 2009, *20*(4), 51, 54.

24. Ibid., 59.

25. Ibid., 51–52.

26. The task-execution and people-development elements of this model have roots in a rich leadership literature emphasizing a manager's need to balance a focus on tasks with a focus on people. See for example Judge, T. A., Piccolo, R. F., and Ilies, R., "The Forgotten Ones? The Validity of Consideration and Initiating Structure in Leadership Research," *Journal of Applied Psychology*, 2004, *89*(1), 36–51. The addition of energizing change was proposed by Yukl, G., Gordon, A., and Taber, T., in "A Hierarchical Taxonomy of Leadership Behavior: Integrating a Half Century of Behavior Research," *Journal of Leadership and Organizational Studies*, 2002, *9*(1), 15–32.

27. "Jobs at Intel—USA—Compensation and Benefits," www.intel.com/jobs/usa/bencomp/bonus/htm.

28. Sekula, R. D., "Air Superiority: How Colleen Barrett Builds a Culture of Comfort, Friendliness and High-Flying Spirit to Fuel Growth at Southwest Airlines," Smart Business Network, www.sbnonline.com/Local/Article/10596/71/0/Air_superiority.aspx, January 2007.

29. Ibid.

30. Fishman, 4.

31. Ibid., 5.

32. Florida, 3–4.

33. Walumbwa, F. O., and others, "Authentic Leadership: Development and Validation of a Theory-Based Measure," *Journal of Management*, February 2008, *34*(1), 95–97.

34. Davis, J. H., Schoorman, F. D., Mayer, R. C., and Tan, H. H., "The Trusted General Manager and Business Unit Performance: Empirical Evidence of a Competitive Advantage," *Strategic Management Journal*, 2000, *21*, 573.

35. Bass, B. M., Avolio, B. J., Jung, D. I., and Berson, Y., "Predicting Unit Performance by Assessing Transformational and Transactional Leadership," *Journal of Applied Psychology*, 2003, *88*(2), 215.

36. Ibid., 216.

37. The manager effectiveness items in our 2010 global workforce study yield a single coherent manager performance factor with high internal reliability (Cronbach's alpha of 0.97). Subsequent factor analysis allocated items to four sub-components of the overall performance factor. The grouping that resulted aligned closely to the executing tasks, developing people, energizing change, and authenticity and trust elements. Cronbach's alphas in each case were high: 0.91 for executing tasks, 0.88 for developing people, 0.92 for energizing change, and 0.89 for authenticity and trust. We repeated the analysis separately for each of the twenty-two countries. In all cases, the four subcomponents were replicated, indicating that the conceptualization of manager behaviors into these four areas largely transcends country and cultural boundaries. One factor, developing people, had an element we believe aligns more intuitively with deal delivery. So, for ease of discussion, we have separated out delivering the deal as a distinct element of the model.

38. We took a close look at the variations in how employees across twenty-two countries experience the performance of their immediate managers. Using an index of items chosen from those in Table 3.1, we calculated manager effectiveness scores by country. The results are shown in the following table.

Manager Performance Index—Variations by Country

Country	Percentage Agreeing That Immediate Manager Is Effective (%)
India	70
China	67
Malaysia	63
Mexico	61
Singapore	58
Switzerland	57
Ireland	55
U.S.	54
Brazil	54
Australia	54
Russia	53
Canada	52
Hong Kong	51
Germany	49
Netherlands	49
U.K.	48
Belgium	46
South Korea	45
France	44
Italy	43
Spain	42
Japan	33

Source: The New Employment Deal: How Far, How Fast and How Enduring, Towers Watson, 2010.

At a broad level, we can discern a difference between emerging markets and established economies. Additionally, there are some geographic trends. In Europe, for example, employees in northern countries tend to record higher scores than their Mediterranean counterparts. We have found that, across a range of scoring categories, including employee engagement and manager effectiveness, Japanese survey takers tend to give responses at the low end of the scale.

39. Ellinger, A. D., Watkins, K. E., and Bostrom, R. P., "Managers as Facilitators of Learning in Learning Organizations," *Human Resource Development Quarterly*, Summer 1999, *10*(2), 112.

40. Hamel, G., and Breen, B., *The Future of Management*, Boston: Harvard Business School Press, 2007, 60.

41. Sendjaya, S., and Sarros, J. C., "Servant Leadership: Its Origin, Development, and Application in Organizations," *Journal of Leadership and Organization Studies*, 2002, *9*(2), 59.

Chapter Four

1. *The Fallacy of the Player-Coach Model*, The Boston Consulting Group, Inc. 2006.

2. *Redefining the Role of the Manager in the 21ˢᵗ Century Organization*, Towers Perrin, presentation of a Web cast to the Human Capital Institute, November 6, 2008.

3. Turmel, W., "I Don't Want to Be a Manager! View from the Middle," www.management-issues.com/2007/5/14/opinion/i-don't-want-to-be-a-manager.asp, May 14, 2007.

4. Bingham, T., and Galagan, P., "Doing Good While Doing Well," *Training + Development*, June 2008, 33.

5. Cincinnatus was a Roman leader who, after losing a political battle, was forced to retire to his farm. In about 458 BC, the Romans found

themselves at war with the Aequians, who had surrounded the Roman army in the Alban Hills. Cincinnatus was plowing his field when a group of senators informed him he had been appointed dictator for six months so he could defend Rome against its enemy. Cincinnatus took the job and defeated the Aequi. He then gave up the title of dictator sixteen days after it had been granted and returned to his farm. http://ancienthistory.about.com/od/rulersleaderskings/p/Cincinnatus.htm.

6. Towers Perrin, *Redefining the Role of the Manager in the 21ˢᵗ Century Organization*, Webcast.

7. Hysong, S. J., "The Role of Technical Skill in Perceptions of Managerial Performance," *Journal of Management Development*, 2008, *27*(3), 276.

8. Blanthorne, C., Bhamornsiri, S., and Guinn, R., "Are Technical Skills Still Important?" *The CPA Journal*, www.nysscpa.org/cpajournal/2005/305/essentials/p64.htm, March 2005.

9. Laborde, S. A., and Lee, J. A, "Skills Needed for Promotion in the Nursing Profession," *Journal of Nursing Administration*, www.ncbi.nlm.nih.gov/pubmed/11006785, September 2000, 1.

10. Faria, J. R., "An Economic Analysis of the Peter and Dilbert Principles," Working Paper No. 101, School of Finance and Economics, University of Technology, Sydney, 6.

11. Roberts, K., and Biddle, J., "The Transition into Management by Scientists and Engineers: A Misallocation or Efficient Use of Human Resources?" *Human Resource Management*, Winter 1994, *33*(4), 573.

12. Van Vugt, M., Hogan, R., and Kaiser, R. B., "Leadership, Followership, and Evolution: Some Lessons From the Past," *American Psychologist*, April 2008, *63*(3), 190.

13. Anderson, C., John, O. P., Keltner, D., and Kring, A. M., "Who Attains Social Status? Effects of Personality and Physical Attractiveness

in Social Groups," *Journal of Personality and Social Psychology*, 2001, *81*(1), 121.

14. Ibid., 122.

15. Ibid., 125–126.

16. *Organization and Operations Results—U.S. Human Capital Effectiveness Report 2009/2010*, Saratoga, a service offering of PricewaterhouseCoopers, LLP, 5.

17. Gittell, J. H., "Supervisory Span, Relational Coordination and Flight Departure Performance: A Reassessment of Postbureaucracy Theory," *Organization Science*, July–August 2001, *12*(4), 468.

18. Evslin, T., *Fractals of Change: The Flattening of Almost Everything #1: Organizations*, http://blog.tomevslin.com/2005/02/the_flattening_.html.

19. Ibid.

20. Gittell, 473, 475–476.

21. Gittell, 479.

22. Doran, D., and others, *Impact of the Manager's Span of Control on Leadership and Performance*, Canadian Health Services Research Foundation, September 2004, 2, 14–16.

23. Ibid., 24.

24. Ibid., iv, 3.

25. Hechanova-Alampay, R., and Beehr, T. A., "Empowerment, Span of Control, and Safety Performance in Work Teams After Workforce Reduction," *Journal of Occupational Health Psychology*, 2001, *6*(4), 280.

26. Hagel, J., Brown, J. S., and Davison, L., "Talent Is Everything," *The Conference Board Review*, www.tcbreview.com/talent-is-everything.php, May/June 2009, 6.

27. Anderson, C., and Kilduff, G. J., "Why Do Dominant Personalities Attain Influence in Face-to-Face Groups? The Competence-Signaling Effects of Trait Dominance," *Journal of Personality and Social Psychology*, 2009, *96*(2), 496.

28. Dierdorff, E. C., Rubin, R. S., and Morgeson, F. P., "The Milieu of Managerial Work: An Integrative Framework Linking Work Context to Role Requirements," *Journal of Applied Psychology*, 2009, *94*(4), 973–974.

29. Ibid., 983.

30. Cloughley, Brian, personal communication with Tom Davenport, January 2010. Used with permission.

31. Anderson, 2009, 500.

32. Ibid., 501.

Chapter Five

1. Maslow, A. H., "A Theory of Human Motivation," *Psychological Review*, July 1943, *50*(4), 370–396.

2. Hodgkinson, G. P., and others, "Breaking the Frame: An Analysis of Strategic Cognition and Decision Making Under Uncertainty," *Strategic Management Journal*, 1999, *20*, 979.

3. Flyvbjerg, B., *Eliminating Bias through Reference Class Forecasting and Good Governance*, NTNU, Concept Report No. 17, Chapter 6, 92.

4. Ibid., 102–103.

5. Kray, L. J., Galinsky, A. D., and Wong, E. M., "Thinking Within the Box: The Relational Processing Style Elicited by Counterfactual Mind-Sets," *Journal of Personality and Social Psychology*, 2006, *91*(1), 34.

6. Sinickas, A., "Employees Prefer Intranets to Supervisors 2 to 1," *Strategic Communication Management*, *13*(6), October/November 2009, 11.

7. Schwartz, L., "5 Reasons Why Social Networking Websites Increase Productivity in the Workplace," http://blog.convergeinternational .com.au/?p=143, August 24, 2009.

8. See, for example, Wrzesniewski, A., and Dutton, J. E., "Crafting a Job: Revisioning Employees as Active Crafters of Their Work," *Academy of Management Review*, 2001, *26*(2), 179–201; Butler, T., and Waldroop, J., "Job Sculpting: The Art of Retaining Your Best People," *Harvard Business Review*, September-October 1999, 144–152; De Fruyt, F., and Mervielde, I., "RIASEC Types and Big Five Traits as Predictors of Employment Status and Nature of Employment," *Personnel Psychology*, 1999, *52*, 701–727.

9. See Bakker, A. B., Demerouti, E., and Verbeke, W., "Using the Job Demands-Resources Model to Predict Burnout and Performance," *Human Resource Management*, Spring 2004, *43*(1), 83–104; Bakker, A. B., Demerouti, E., and Euwema, M. C., "Job Resources Buffer the Impact of Job Demands on Burnout," *Journal of Occupational Health Psychology*, 2005, *10*(2), 170–180; Bakker, A. B., and Demerouti, E., "The Job-Demands-Resources Model: State of the Art," *Journal of Managerial Psychology*, 2007, *22*(3), 309–328; Bakker, A. B., Hakanen, J. J., Demerouti, E., and Xanthopoulou, D., "Job Resources Boost Work Engagement, Particularly When Job Demands are High," *Journal of Educational Psychology*, 2007, *99*(2), 274–284.

10. Gosling, J., and Mintzberg, H., "The Five Minds of a Manager," *Harvard Business Review*, Reprint R0311C, November 2003, 7.

11. Adapted from Langfred, C. W., and Moye, N. A., "Effects of Task Autonomy on Performance: An Extended Model Considering Motivational, Informational, and Structural Mechanisms," *Journal of Applied Psychology*, 2004, *89*(6), 943.

12. Hall, A. T., and others, "Relationships Between Felt Accountability as a Stressor and Strain Reactions: The Neutralizing Role of Autonomy Across Two Studies," *Journal of Occupational Health Psychology*, 2006, *11*(1), 94–95.

13. Moss, S., Ritossa, D., and Ngu, S., "The Effect of Follower Regulatory Focus and Extraversion on Leadership Behavior: The Role of Emotional Intelligence," *Journal of Individual Differences*, 2006, *27*(2), 93.

14. Grant, A. M., and others, "Impact and the Art of Motivation Maintenance: The Effects of Contact with Beneficiaries on Persistence Behavior," *Organizational Behavior and Human Decision Processes*, 2007, *103*, 58.

15. Bond, F. W., and Flaxman, P. E., "The Ability of Psychological Flexibility and Job Control to Predict Learning, Job Performance, and Mental Health," *Journal of Organizational Behavior*, November 2006, *26*(123), 125.

16. O'Brien, J. M., "Zappos Knows How to Kick It," http://money .cnn.com/2009/01/15/news/companies/Zappos_best_companies _obrien.fortune/index.htm, January 22, 2009.

17. Ibid.

18. http://about.zappos.com/our-unique-culture/zappos-core-values/ deliver-wow-through-service.

19. O'Brien.

20. Wrzesniewski, A., and Dutton, J. E., "Crafting a Job: Revisioning Employees as Active Crafters of Their Work," *Academy of Management Review*, 2001, *26*(2), 191.

21. Ibid., 192.

22. Bakker, A. B., and Demerouti, E., "The Job Demands-Resources Model: State of the Art," *Journal of Managerial Psychology*, 2007, *22*(3), 322.

23. Wrzesniewski, 183.

24. Navin, Peter, personal communication with Tom Davenport, March 2010. Used with permission.

25. Letzring, T. D., "The Good Judge of Personality: Characteristics, Behaviors, and Observer Accuracy," *Journal of Research in Personality*, 2008, *42*, 929.

26. Nicholson, N., "Seven Deadly Syndromes of Management and Organization: The View from Evolutionary Psychology," *Managerial and Decision Economics*, 1998, *19*, 419.

27. Pond, R., "My View: Cisco's Councils and Boards," http://blogs .cisco.com/news/comments/my_view?ciscos_councils_and _boards/, August 26, 2009.

28. Chambers, J., "The World According to Chambers," www .economist.com/PrinterFriendly.cfm?story_id=14303574, August 27, 2009.

29. Nicholson, 419.

30. "Leadership at Cisco, Part 2: A Manager Monday CCrit," http://noccrit.com./steveblog/2009/07/leadership-at-cisco-part-2-a -manager-monday-ccrit/, July 13, 2009.

31. Whitney, L., "Xerox CEO Anne Mulcahy to Retire," http:// news.cnet.com/8301–1001_3–10236443–92.html, May 21, 2009.

32. Bryant, A., "Xerox's New Chief Tries to Redefine Its Culture," www.nytimes.com/2010/02/21/business/21xerox.html, February 21, 2010.

33. Wageman, R., "How Leaders Foster Self-Managing Team Effectiveness: Design Choices Versus Hands-on Coaching," *Organization Science*, September–October 2001, *12*(5), 562–563.

34. Ibid., 565–566.

35. Ibid., 568.

36. Ibid., 567, 570.

37. *2008 Contact Center Operations Report*, International Customer Management Institute, p. 18.

38. Ibid., 19.

39. Hagel, J., *Capturing the Real Value of Offshoring in Asia*, Working Paper, 2004, 6.

40. Ibid., 5–6.

41. Ibid., 6.

Chapter Six

1. Televised speech delivered April 18, 1977.

2. Lakoff, G., and Johnson, M., *Metaphors We Live By*, Chicago: The University of Chicago Press, 1980, 156.

3. *The New Employment Deal: How Far, How Fast and How Enduring*, Towers Watson, 2010.

4. Frasch, K., "Leadership: Ripe for Change," *Human Resources Executive*, September 2002, 61.

5. O'Keeffe, Erin, personal communication with Tom Davenport, May 2009. Used with permission.

6. Davenport, T. O., *Human Capital: What It Is and Why People Invest It*, San Francisco: Jossey-Bass, 1999, 146, 149.

7. Higgins, M. C., and Thomas, D. A., "Constellations and Careers: Toward Understanding the Effects of Multiple Developmental Relationships," *Journal of Organizational Behavior*, 2001, *22*, 240.

8. Ibid., 243.

9. Sparrowe, R. T., and Liden, R. C., "Process and Structure in Leader-Member Exchange," *Academy of Management Review*, 1997, *22*(2), 541.

10. "Cisco Systems Announces New Organizational Structure—Eleven Technology Groups Formed to Replace Line of Business Structure," Cisco Systems press release, http://newsroom.cisco.com/dlls/corp _082301b.html, August 23, 2001.

11. Benko, C., and Weisberg, A., "Implementing a Corporate Career Lattice: The Mass Career Customization Model," *Strategy & Leadership*, 2007, *35*(5), 32. For a discussion of lattice and ladder career issues, see also BizWiseTV episode 14, www.cisco.com/ en/US/solutions/ns340/ns339/ns638/ns915/html_BWTV/bwtv _episode_14.html.

12. Ibid., 32.

13. Ibid., 35.

14. Monaghan, Susan, personal communication with Tom Davenport, April 2010. Used with permission.

15. "The New Face of Recruiting in a Changing Marketplace," Conference Board, People Solutions 2001, November 28, 2001. Used with permission.

16. Ellinger, A. D., Watkins, K. E., and Bostrom, R. P., "Managers as Facilitators of Learning in Learning Organizations," *Human Resource Development Quarterly*, Summer 1999, *10*(2), 115, 120.

17. "Managers of Tomorrow: Setting a New Standard," *2009 World of Work Topic Report*, Randstad, 2009, 3.

18. Gurven, M., Kaplan, H., and Gutierrez, M., "How Long Does It Take to Become Proficient? Implications for the Evolution of Extended Development and Long Life Span," *Journal of Human Evolution*, 2006, *51*, 467.

19. Dweck, C. S., "Can Personality Be Changed? The Role of Beliefs in Personality and Change," paper based on keynote address delivered at the annual conference of the Association for Psychological Science, Washington, DC, 2007, 5.

20. Ibid., 3.

21. Heslin, P. A., Latham, G. P., and VandeWalle, D., "The Effect of Implicit Person Theory on Performance Appraisals," *Journal of Applied Psychology*, 2005, *90*(5), 843.

22. Heslin, P. A., VandeWalle, D., and Latham, G. P., "Keen to Help? Managers' Implicit Person Theories and Their Subsequent Employee Coaching," *Personnel Psychology*, 2006, *59*, 883.

23. Dweck, C. S., *Mindset: The New Psychology of Success*. New York: Ballantine, 2006, *72*, 178, 198.

24. Dweck, 2007, 7.

25. Ibid., 9, 10.

26. Mike, B., and Slocum, J. W., "Slice of Reality: Changing Culture at Pizza Hut and Yum! Brands, Inc.," *Organizational Dynamics*, 2003, *32*(4), 322–324.

27. Ibid., 324–325.

28. Bryant, A., "At Yum Brands, Rewards for Good Work," www .nytimes.com/2009/07/12/business/12corner.html, July 11, 2009.

29. Mike, 327.

30. Yum! Brands, Inc., *Yum! Brands 2009 Annual Customer Mania Report*.

31. *Reward Challenges and Changes—Top Line Results*, Towers Perrin, 2007, 35.

32. Nicholson, N., "Seven Deadly Syndromes of Management and Organization: The View from Evolutionary Psychology," *Managerial and Decision Economics*, 1998, *19*, 415.

33. Baumeister, R. F., Bratslavsky, E., Finkenauer, C., and Vohs, K. D., "Bad Is Stronger Than Good," *Review of General Psychology*, 2001, *5*(4), 323.

34. Ibid., 329.

35. Bono, J. E., Foldes, H. J., Vinson, G., and Muros, J. P., "Workplace Emotions: The Role of Supervision and Leadership," *Journal of Applied Psychology*, 2007, *92*(5), 1358.

36. Ibid., 1364.

37. Bandura, A., *Self-Efficacy: The Exercise of Control*, New York: Freeman, 1997, 3.

38. Ibid., 116–117.

39. Ibid., 125.

40. Ibid., 136.

41. Findley, H. M., Giles, W. F., and Mossholder, K. W., "Performance Appraisal Process and System Facets: Relationships With Contextual Performance," *Journal of Applied Psychology*, 2000, *85*(4), 635.

42. Csikszentmihalyi, M., and Csikszentmihalyi, I. S. (Eds.), *Optimal Experience: Psychological Studies of Flow in Consciousness*, New York: Cambridge University Press, 1988, 30.

43. Chatzkel, J. L., *Knowledge Capital: How Knowledge-Based Enterprises Really Get Built*, Oxford, U.K.: Oxford University Press, 2003, 235.

44. Towers Watson analysis.

45. Monaghan, Susan, personal communication with Tom Davenport, April 2010. Used with permission.

Chapter Seven

1. The *New Employment Deal: How Far, How Fast and How Enduring*, Towers Watson, 2010.

2. Ibid.

3. Csikszentmihalyi, M., *Flow: The Psychology of Optimal Experience*, New York: HarperPerennial, 1990, 16.

4. Shaw, J. D., and others, "Reactions to Merit Pay Increases: A Longitudinal Test of a Signal Sensitivity Perspective," *Journal of Applied Psychology*, 2003, *88*(3), 538.

5. Wayne, S. J., Shore, L. M., Bommer, W. H., and Tetrick, L. E., "The Role of Fair Treatment and Rewards in Perceptions of Organizational Support and Leader-Member Exchange," *Journal of Applied Psychology*, 2002, *87*(3), 590.

6. Eisenberger, R., and others, "Reciprocation of Perceived Organizational Support," *Journal of Applied Psychology*, 2001, *86*(1), 42–43.

7. Eisenberger, R., Huntington, R., Hutchison, S., and Sowa, D., "Perceived Organizational Support," *Journal of Applied Psychology*, 1986, *71*(3), 500, 504.

8. Rousseau, D. M., Ho, V. T., and Greenberg, J., "I-Deals: Idiosyncratic Terms in Employment Relationships," *Academy of Management Review*, 2006, *31*(4), 978.

9. Raja, U., Johns, G., and Ntalianis, F., "The Impact of Personality on Psychological Contracts," *Academy of Management Journal*, *47*(3), 352, 362.

10. Tuna, C., "Theory & Practice: Pay, Your Own Way: Firm Lets Workers Pick Salary—Big Bonus? None at All? In Throwback to '80s, Employees Make Call," http://online.wsj.com/article/SB121538266278030925.html, July 7, 2007.

11. Lai, L., Rousseau, D. M., and Chang, K. T. T., "Idiosyncratic Deals: Coworkers as Interested Third Parties," *Journal of Applied Psychology*, 2009, *94*(2), 552–553.

12. *O.C. Tanner 2008 Global Recognition Study.*

13. Ashby, F. G., Isen, A. M., and Turken, A. U., "A Neuropsychological Theory of Positive Affect and Its Influence on Cognition," *Psychological Bulletin*, 1999, *106*(3), 529, 531, 533–534.

14. Starz, Cynthia, personal communication with Tom Davenport, March 2010. Used with permission.

15. *Reward Challenges and Changes—Top Line Results*, Towers Perrin, 2007.

16. Pfeffer, J., "Sins of Commission," *The Conference Board Review*, July/August 2007, 34.

17. Towers Watson analysis.

18. Pfeffer, 35.

19. DuBois, W.E.B., address on his 90th birthday to his newborn great-grandson, 1958.

Chapter Eight

1. Niebuhr, R., *The Serenity Prayer*, 1943.

2. Bandura, A., *Self-Efficacy: The Exercise of Control*, New York: Freeman, 1997, 459–460.

3. Schraeder, M., Swamidass, P. M., and Morrison, R., "Employee Involvement, Attitudes and Reactions to Technology Changes," *Journal of Leadership and Organizational Studies*, 2006, *12*(3), 93–96.

4. Jimmieson, N. L., Terry, D. J., and Callan, V. J., "A Longitudinal Study of Employee Adaptation to Organizational Change: The Role of Change-Related Information and Change-Related Self-Efficacy," *Journal of Occupational Health Psychology*, 2004, *9*(1), 25.

5. Gosling, J., and Mintzberg, H., "The Five Minds of a Manager," *Harvard Business Review*, Reprint R0311C, November 2003, 8.

6. Reed, J., and Love, S., "Army Developing Master Resiliency Training," www.army.mil/-news/2009/08/05/25494-army-developing-master-resiliency-training/, August 5, 2009.

7. Antonelli, K., "Army Turns to Resilience Training," www.allmilitary.com/board/viewtopic.php?id=26968, December 22, 2009.

8. Luthans, F., Vogelgesang, G. R., and Lester, P. B., "Developing the Psychological Capital of Resiliency," *Human Resource Development Review*, March 2006, *5*(1), 28.

9. Fiveash, K., "HP Imposes Staff Wage Cuts—Mark Hurd Lowers the Floor to Save Workers," www.theregister.co.uk/2009/02/19/hp_pay_cuts/print.html, February 19, 2009.

10. *Cost-Cutting Strategies in the Downturn—A Delicate Balancing Act*, Towers Perrin, May 2009, 3–4.

11. Herold, D. M., Fedor, D. B., and Caldwell, S. D., "Beyond Change Management: A Multilevel Investigation of Contextual and Personal Influences on Employees' Commitment to Change," *Journal of Applied Psychology*, 2007, *92*(4), 943.

12. Wanberg, C. R., and Banas, J. T., "Predictors and Outcomes of Openness to Changes in a Reorganizing Workplace," *Journal of Applied Psychology*, 2000, *85*(1), 134.

13. Richardson, G. E., "The Metatheory of Resilience and Resiliency," *Journal of Clinical Psychology*, 2002, *58*(3), 312.

14. Greenfield, H., "Culture Crash: A Lehman Brothers Insider Reveals Why the Firm's Best Traits Turned Out to Be Its Worst," *The Conference Board Review*, Fall 2009, 63–64.

15. Ibid., 64.

16. This statement, or one like it, has been attributed to Charles Darwin, an attribution many scholars dispute. It has also been traced back to Clarence Darrow, of Scopes monkey trial fame, quoted in *Improving the Quality of Life for the Black Elderly: Challenges and Opportunities: Hearing Before the Select Committee on Aging*, House of Representatives, One Hundredth Congress, first session, September 25, 1987 (1988). We won't try to sort through the attribution tangles. We simply suggest that it expresses a sensible way of thinking about the importance of adaptability.

17. Greenberg, A., "When Google Grows Up," www.forbes.com/2008/01/11/google-carr-computing-tech-enter-cx_ag_0111computing.html, January 11, 2008.

18. Tierney, P., and Farmer, S. M., "The Pygmalion Process and Employee Creativity," *Journal of Management*, 2004, *30*(3), 426.

19. Ibid., 428.

20. Janssen, O., "The Joint Impact of Perceived Influence and Supervisor Supportiveness on Employee Innovative Behaviour," *Journal of Occupational and Organizational Psychology*, December 2005, *78*, 578.

21. Burke, C. S., and others, "Understanding Team Adaptation: A Conceptual Analysis and Model," *Journal of Applied Psychology*, 2006, *91*(6), 1189–1190.

22. Ibid., 1201–1202.

23. Presenteeism means coming to work in spite of illness and performing below typical levels.

24. Osterweil, N., "Heartless Bosses Create Coronary-Prone Workers," *MedPage Today*, www.medpagetoday.com/Cardiology/AcuteCoronarySyndrome/1991?pfc=101&spc=230, October 25, 2005.

25. Ischemic heart disease (ischemia) refers to a condition of reduced blood flow to the heart, usually occurring as a result of coronary atherosclerosis (hardening of the arteries), but possibly resulting from other causes of coronary vascular resistance. The reduced flow of oxygen-rich blood may cause cardiac dysfunction, which can manifest itself as angina, or severe chest pain.

26. Nyberg, A., and others, "Managerial Leadership and Ischaemic Heart Disease Among Employees: The Swedish WOLF Study," *Occupational and Environmental Medicine*, 2009, *66*, 54.

27. Ibid., 53.

28. Loeppke, R., and others, "Health and Productivity as a Business Strategy: A Multiemployer Study," *Journal of Organizational and Environmental Medicine*, April 2009, *51*(4), 411.

29. Ibid., 423.

30. Nissen, Dale, personal communication with Stephen Harding, March 2010. Used with permission.

31. Coy, Geraldine, personal communication with Stephen Harding, March 2010. Used with permission.

Chapter Nine

1. Adams, D., *Dirk Gently's Holistic Detective Agency*, New York: Simon and Schuster, 1987.

2. Colquitt, J. A., Scott, B. A., and LePine, J. A., "Trust, Trustworthiness, and Trust Propensity: A Meta-Analytic Test of Their Unique Relationships With Risk Taking and Job Performance," *Journal of Applied Psychology*, 2007, *92*(4), 910–911.

3. Dirks, K. T., and Ferrin, D. L., "Trust in Leadership: Meta-Analytic Findings and Implications for Research and Practice," *Journal of Applied Psychology*, 2002, *87*(4), 616.

4. Drucker, P. F., *Managing the Non-Profit Organization: Practices and Principles*, New York: HarperCollins, 1990, 19.

5. Walumbwa, F. O., and others, "Authentic Leadership: Development and Validation of a Theory-Based Measure," *Journal of Management*, 2008, *34*(1), 95–96.

6. Avolio, B., and others, "Unlocking the Mask: A Look at the Process by Which Authentic Leaders Impact Follower Attitudes and Behaviors," *The Leadership Quarterly*, 2004, *15*, 806.

7. Zak, P. J., and Nadler, A., *Using Brains to Create Trust: A Manager's Toolbox*, Claremont, CA: Center for Neuroeconomics Studies and Department of Economics, Claremont Graduate University, 2009, 4.

8. *2009 Edelman Trust Barometer*, Edelman, 2009, 12.

9. Dirks, 2002, 614, 619.

10. "11 Facts about Hurricane Katrina," www.dosomething.org/tipsandtools/11-facts-about-hurricane-katrina.

11. Zander, R. S., and Zander, B., *The Art of Possibility*, New York: Penguin, 2000, 89.

12. Dirks, K. T., "Trust in Leadership and Team Performance: Evidence from NCAA Basketball," *Journal of Applied Psychology*, 2000, *85*(6), 1009.

13. Ibid.

14. Baker, P., "How Obama Came to Plan for 'Surge' in Afghanistan," www.nytimes.com/2009/12/06/world/asia/06reconstruct.html, December 6, 2009.

15. Colquitt, J. A., "On the Dimensionality of Organizational Justice: A Construct Validation of a Measure," *Journal of Applied Psychology*, 2001, *86*(3), 389.

16. Choi, J., "Event Justice Perceptions and Employees' Reactions: Perceptions of Social Entity Justice as a Moderator," *Journal of Applied Psychology*, 2008, *93*(3), 525.

17. White, D., "Eliot Spitzer, Attorney General & New York Governor," http://usliberals.about.com/od/stategovernors/p/ElliotSpitzer.htm.

18. Spitzer, E., "Strong Law Enforcement Is Good for the Economy," commentary for *The Wall Street Journal*, www.happinessonline.org/InfectiousGreed/p39.htm, April 5, 2005.

19. Hakim, D., and Rashbaum, W. K., "Spitzer Is Linked to Prostitution Ring," www.nytimes.com/2008/03/10/nyregion/10cnd-spitzer.html, March 10, 2008.

20. Koerwer, V. S., "Featured Interview Sherron Watkins, Former Vice President for Corporate Development of Enron," www.allbusiness.com/educational-services/business-schools-computer/290768–1.html, June 22, 2004.

21. Fowler, T., "Enron's Implosion Was Anything but Sudden," www.chron.com/disp/story.mpl/special/enron/2655409.html, December 20, 2005.

22. Zak, P. J., "Values and Value: Moral Economics," Gruter Institute Project on Values and Free Enterprise, http://papers.ssrn.com/sol3/papers.cfm?abstract_id=927485, 2007, 8.

23. Gardner, W. L., and others, "Can You See the Real Me? A Self-Based Model of Authentic Leader and Follower Development," *The Leadership Quarterly*, 2005, *16*, 352.

24. Koerwer.

25. Zak, P. J., *The Neuroeconomics of Trust*, http://papers.ssrn.com/sol3/papers.cfm?abstract_id=764944, August 2005, 16–17.

26. Zak, P. J., Stanton, A. A., and Ahmadi, S. "Oxytocin Increases Generosity in Humans," PLoS ONE, www.plosone.org/article/info:doi%2F10.1371%2Fjournal.pone.0001128, November 2007, Issue 11, 4.

27. Zak, 2009, 5.

28. Ibid.

29. Shore, L. M., Tetrick, L. E., Lynch, P., and Barksdale, K., "Social and Economic Exchange: Construct Development and Validation," *Journal of Applied Social Psychology*, 2006, *36*(4), 849.

30. Heath, C., "On the Social Psychology of Agency Relationships: Lay Theories of Motivation Overemphasize Extrinsic Incentives," *Organizational Behavior and Human Decision Processes*, April 1999, *78*(1), 58.

31. Holtz, B. C., and Harold, C. M., "When Your Boss Says No! The Effects of Leadership Style and Trust on Employee Reactions to Managerial Explanations," *Journal of Occupational and Organizational Psychology*, 2008, *81*, 781.

32. Ibid., 793.

33. Walumbwa, 104.

Chapter Ten

1. Goleman, D., *Emotional Intelligence*, New York: Bantam Books, 1995, 43.

3. Goleman, D., *Social Intelligence*, New York: Bantam Books, 2006, 83.

3. Goleman, *Social Intelligence*, 84.

4. See for example Bouchard, T. J., and McGue, M., "Genetic and Environmental Influences on Human Psychological Differences," *Journal of Neurobiology*, 2003, *54*, 23, and Steen, R. G., *DNA & Destiny: Nature & Nurture in Human Behavior*, New York: Plenum Press, 1996, 171.

Psychologists commonly study five specific personality traits:

Conscientiousness: Orderliness, self-control, dutifulness, attention to detail, and discipline in the pursuit of goals. A by-product is the ability to delay gratification and pursue planned-for rather than spontaneous objectives.

Agreeableness: Compassion, a spirit of cooperation, forgiveness, tolerance, and motivation to achieve interpersonal intimacy.

Openness to experience: Pursuit of intellectual novelty and complexity, tendency to make associations between disparate domains. Openness may be manifested in unusual ideas, curiosity, and appreciation for art.

Extroversion: Positive energy and emotions, interest in exploring, tendency to seek stimulation and enjoy the company of others.

Neuroticism: Anxiety, depression, anger, guilt, and heightened risk aversion. Neuroticism is often expressed positively in its opposite form, *emotional stability*—equanimity, calm, freedom from persistent negative feelings. Freedom from negative impulses does not mean that emotionally stable people feel strong positive emotions, however. That trait tends to be captured by extroversion.

5. Seligman, M. E. P., *What You Can Change ... and What You Can't*, New York: Fawcett, 1993, 6.

6. Steen, 18–19.

7. *Bringing Policies to Life: The Vital Role of Front Line Managers in People Management*, Chartered Institute of Personnel and Development, 2003, 6.

8. *Evolving Priorities and the Future of HR Service Delivery*, Towers Perrin, 2009, 10.

9. O'Keeffe, Erin, personal communication with Tom Davenport, May 2009. Used with permission.

10. Heslin, P. A., Latham, G. P., and VandeWalle, D., "The Effect of Implicit Person Theory on Performance Appraisals," *Journal of Applied Psychology*, 2005, *90*(5), 851–852.

THE AUTHORS

Tom Davenport and Stephen Harding are both senior practitioners with Towers Watson, a global professional services company that helps organizations improve performance through effective human capital, risk, and financial management. Tom, who works out of the San Francisco office, concentrates chiefly on assisting clients in equipping and engaging their people to meet business and financial goals. In addition to numerous articles and book chapters, he is the author of *Human Capital: What It Is and Why People Invest It* (Jossey-Bass, 1999). Stephen, from the London office, specializes in employee engagement research. He is the author, with Dave Phillips, of *Contrasting Values in Western Europe* (Macmillan, 1986) and has also published and spoken regularly on how organizations can best engage their employees.

Tom earned a BA, magna cum laude, Phi Beta Kappa, from the University of California, Los Angeles. He also earned an MBA from the Haas School of Business at the University of California, Berkeley, as well as a master's degree in journalism from the University of California, Berkeley.

Stephen has a BA, Honours, from the University of Swansea in Wales and a PhD in psychology from the University of Sussex, England. He is a chartered psychologist and associate fellow of the British Psychological Society.

INDEX